IBIZA CHRONICLES

TREASURE, TRAGEDY, AND REDEMPTION ON THE HASHISH TRAIL

IBIZA CHRONICLES

TREASURE, TRAGEDY, AND REDEMPTION ON THE HASHISH TRAIL

JESSE LEE KINCAID

KINCAID PUBLISHER
MARIN COUNTY
CALIFORNIA
UNITED STATES

IBIZA CHRONICLES

TREASURE, TRAGEDY, AND REDEMPTION ON THE HASHISH TRAIL

The Hippie Trail
by Richard Gregory

Max the Dog
By Michael Malone

ISBN 978-0-9899757-0-4
1. Travel 2. Formentera, Ibiza, Spain, Europe,
India, Afghanistan 3. Music
4. Hashish 5. Prison

jesseleekincaid.com

From heart to heart love spins a line
So delicate the thread and fine
Life's storm may rage below above
Yet can't break the line of love

Cosmic Tony, Barcelona

Contents

Prologue

The journeys in foreign lands described herein began for me with a first psychedelic experience that opened a trail extending further than could have been imagined, leading to a quest that achieved the highest heights, and descended to the lowest depths when risky behavior became a trap, the trail ended, and time set us free.

The writing of this book was facilitated by memory of these events, some researched facts, and interviews with the persons chronicled within. The names of selected individuals have been changed to preserve anonymity. There are no fictional occurrances or characters. Though not all of the truth, the story is true. Everything described actually happened.

Part 1

One

Quest

Two Tabs

Effervescent thought dreams bubbled on a fluid surface, sailing briefly, then burst in an explosive aerial ballet that plunged to submerge in liquid depths like a phantom submarine, a silent sentinel. Fragmented images flashed as my mind swirled, separated, and reunited. Leaves danced on the ghostgust breeze. The green lawn undulated. Plucked strings resonated a musical anchor in the jumble tumble ocean. My tripping brother gave me two psilocybin tablets for my first psychedelic experience.

"Take them together," he advised.

A head appeared in the doorway of the adjacent house.

"Hey, man, what's happening? Trippy sound."

"The psilocybin's come on."

"Wow. Cool. Come in."

Interaction was a reprieve.

We walked through a kitchen into a large room where upholstered chairs and a couch faced a fireplace. He lit a flame on candles and ignited incense.

"We'll have some tea."

The psychedelic rush had transited to a rainbow-edged mist. We sipped sweet mint tea. He played his guitar and sang. My sitar followed his melody.

Coming down from Tangier town
I spied a child something wild
Turned my head up to the sky
And asked it why no reply
Beggar's hand was tried on me
But never found never found

The Scene

The Sixties was the cultural decade beginning in 1963 and ending in 1974, noted for a complex of inter-related cultural and political trends across the globe. The decade was one of counterculture and revolution in social norms about clothing, music, drugs, dress, formalities, and schooling. The period was also labeled the Swinging Sixties because of the fall or relaxation of social taboos particularly relating to racism and sexism that occurred during this time. Rigid cultures, unable to contain the demands for greater individual freedom, broke free of the social constraints of the previous age. The period was marked by excess, flamboyance, and decay of social order with extreme deviation from the norm.

LSD, marijuana, and free love were on minds and magazine covers along with The Beatles, Rolling Stones, and San Francisco and Hollywood bands popularizing the changing direction. A generation with fresh perception awakened from conformity into a new age dawn. Rock music, getting high, long hair, tie-dye clothing, and bell-bottoms, even nudity became fashionable. Still, police needed no warrant to stop longhairs and search them and their vehicles. Arrest for marijuana could, and often did, result in prison terms.

Immigrants

Twenty years ago my father, mother, brother, grandmother, and grandfather arrived with me at the western end of the North American continent. My grandparents and father were immigrants from Croatia. They came to America, arriving at Ellis Island, in New York. They found employment in the garment district sweatshops, before moving to Detroit to labor in the automobile factories.

In 1949 we migrated from the east coast to Adelanto, a desert town near Los Angeles. My grandparents worked for a Croatian family operating a chicken ranch. Grandmother removed feathers. Grandfather extracted intestines. My father sold chickens in a one refrigerator poultry store before chucking chickens altogether. We left the desert and joined the ten million others in Los Angeles. Most of these were immigrants, too, moving west.

At age twenty-five, my classical guitar scholarship, the result of a passing interest in that art, was directing me to Beethoven, Brahms, and Bach when my interest was in The Beatles, The Rolling Stones, and songwriting. My band had some success performing in the Sunset Strip scene and recording but with no hit record we disbanded. My parents were long divorced; my marriage to a Hollywood actress was over. My income derived from songwriting royalties. Searching still, even the sitar music that had become my major study, switching from guitar, was too obscure to keep me engaged. Times were changing, people were strange, behavior was unpredictable, and familiar patterns were dissolving.

Being on my own was traumatic.

We children of European voyagers who reached the end of the road in the concrete expanse of Los Angeles were without traditions that had characterized our parent's culture, and we had yet to acquire our own. Ours would be born of new world necessity.

Skip, A Rascal

My tea-making, guitar-playing neighbor called himself Skip, a variation of his given name Stanley. He and his wife, Kate, were newly released from a Swedish prison.

"We got busted bringing hash from Morocco into Sweden. We did four months, and then we came home. We're going back. You could come with us."

They talked about a place where windmills stand near Roman watchtowers that face toward the blue-watered Mediterranean Sea. There people experienced good vibes and free love for little money on a Spanish island called Formentera.

"There are only six cars on the whole island. People live in windmills and bake their own bread," Skip related.

An adopted son, Skip was tall, lanky, curly haired, and of undetermined ethnicity. He was cool, charismatic, and fond of spinning fantasy tales while adopting a rascal's air.

We played music, smoked hash, ingested LSD, and composed a few songs. Occasionally, neighborhood acquaintances gathered to take acid and tune in to music albums. Dubious characters frequented their house with legal problems caused by illegal substances. Flower Power masked Skip's use of opiates, a secret endeavor.

We sat around high, listening to the Beatles. What did it mean? Was there a message playing the record backward? Was Paul dead? The Beatles were separating and becoming individuals. In like fashion, my family was coming apart and my school participation was evaporating. In their wake lurked an unfamiliar newness and confusion, fueled by marijuana, hashish, and LSD.

In spite of our having minimal cash and no realistic employment opportunity, Skip projected a vision of us thriving in Spain where we would be welcomed as mystic performers on a magic island. The lure of travel, combined with increasing consumption of pot and acid, begun to exert a transitional effect on me leading to the ultimate abandonment of formal studies in favor of going forward on an open road. Being chained to a desk in a classroom wasn't living and the conjuring of new horizons proved an irresistible temptation. My stoned tribal companions were leading me to the crossroads, where looking for myself was to get me lost in a faraway land, and, ultimately, in trouble with legal authority. But, before the fire of hell, the healing hands of heaven.

A Fresh Start

On a chilled overcast December morning at the conclusion of the tumultuous Sixties decade, we ventured forth with me at the wheel of my 1948 Chrysler New Yorker, previously owned by a little old lady from Pasadena. With my girlfriend Sharon beside me and Skip and Kate in the rear seat we departed Los Angeles forever, never again to reside in that urban sprawl.

From Hollywood, we drove to Highway 40 east, cruising the Dwight D. Eisenhower System of Interstate and Defense Highways with doublewide roads spanning sea-to-sea. We rolled forth under the vivid blue bowl of the western sky, in anticipation of what lay ahead beyond the continent and the distant ocean. The concrete world where our parents ended their journey was falling behind as the mystique of an exotic shore loomed ahead.

Florida Woman

Sharon was spotted in Hollywood, wiggling down the sidewalk wearing blue jean cutoffs, a tie-dyed tank top sans brassiere, and sandals. A rabbit fur bag was slung over her shoulder, brushed by long, reddish-brown curls that rolled and flowed down her breast.

"Want a ride?"

"Sure. Nice car." The big Chrysler with its straight-eight engine, hydramatic transmission, and dark green woolen seat covers was luxurious. We drove to my Silver Lake cottage for a chicken Renoir dinner, then to her place in Laurel Canyon.

"This apartment isn't mine," she stated. "It belongs to a friend. She's a prostitute. She's on vacation. You want to sleep over?"

Sharon was raised down south in a Florida town where her father was the chief of police. There had been family problems back home. Her fingertips were red and raw from biting the nails. Sometimes she sucked her thumb. Our relationship was physical, and the lack of common ground would later be problematic. For now,

Sharon was on the road to the Empire State and beyond.

We sped across the golden desert through Albuquerque, the city in New Mexico straddling the Rio Grande River, and Amarillo in the Texas panhandle, past Oklahoma City in the Great Plains, switching to Interstate 44 over the rolling hills of Missouri, forded the wide Mississippi River at St. Louis. Beyond Indianapolis, home of the largest single day sporting event in the United States, the Indianapolis 500 car race, lay Ohio's green pastures of plenty and the populous cities of Dayton and Columbus. We negotiated Pennsylvania's snow-storming turnpike eastward to a tree-lined road in New Jersey that fed across the river into Manhattan. Stopping only to eat, we crossed the nation in two and a half days.

Our destination was the Bronx where Sharon's grandmother lived in an apartment. In order to score wedding gift money to pay for her trip Sharon had planted the story that we were newlyweds. We visited aunts and uncles where the ersatz husband was presented, as briefly were his companions, and envelopes of cash were entrusted to the imposter bride.

With marital obligations concluded we bought plane tickets. A corner gas station mechanic paid seventy-five dollars to buy the Chrysler in a rush sale. He drove us back to grandmother's apartment, pleased with his purchase. Tomorrow we would manifest destiny, from a Los Angeles high to a fantasy island in the Mediterranean Sea.

Chilling In Copenhagen

Icelandic Air flew us for one hundred dollars each from the Promised Land to the Old Country. My father made the ocean liner crossing to America in ten days. By air we covered the same distance in seven hours. From Frankfurt, we boarded the train to the island of Zealand, and Copenhagen, the Harbor of Merchants. Winter here spelt an ever-shrouded sky, lightened at ten, darkened at four. Stores closed for Christmas holidays. My companions went to a friend's apartment, too small for Sharon and me. We booked into a youth hostel but were not united in that still chill of Danish winter. Relationship shock was beginning.

New Year's Eve Acid Trip

We commemorated New Year's Eve, 1969 at the apartment of Skip's friend, smoking hashish the European way, mixed with strong dizzying tobacco in conical pipes called chillums. We dropped acid to increase the intensity of our Seventies launch and sallied forth into snow flurries en route to a party. At midnight a cacophony erupted, lights flashed, sirens sounded, church bells pealed, and a fireworks rocket sprayed sparks flying by my head, disorienting me as LSD coursed through my system. We followed the leader and entered a building to climb flights of stairs.

The guide knocked on a door that opened to our rambling and stoned group. Sedate people reclined on couches in conversation; heads topped with pointy paper hats fastened with rubber band chinstraps. They coldly regarded us. We were too high and incoherent and soon departed, spiraling down to the cold sidewalk on a Nordic New Year street.

When we became separated from the group, a hotel provided shelter for Sharon and me, but our untested relationship was straining. We quarreled and in the morning Sharon departed, appearing two days later having moved in with a Danish bass player. They had me in for tea while Sharon explained that she was no longer with us and preferred to stay in Copenhagen.

To Sunny Spain

Returning to Frankfurt Skip bought a low cost Volkswagen van for our nascent explorations. After twenty years in classrooms, pushing pens and reading about life, the open roads of Europe spread before me. Adventure beckoned at the beginning of the highway. We were awash with expectation like a wave crashing in an ocean of possibility.

Germany was cloaked in a blanket of ghostly snow on a grey-misted and somnambulant landscape of black trees silhouetted against a sunless sky. We sped along the autobahn past Mannheim and Karlsruhe and before we were prepared we encountered the border of France. Skip passed a chunk of hash to Kate who hurriedly chewed and swallowed the mass, just as French customs began a search of the car, our luggage, and us, looking for exactly what Kate just devoured, but they found nothing. Having negotiated the first border crossing with our passports stamped, we entered the land of bread, fries and kisses.

After dinner at a country inn we slept in the van by the road. Kate vomited all night from her hashish ingestion that saved us from arrest.

We munched baguettes with Camembert cheese while progressing through the rustic and warming countryside. In Lyon a theater marquee displayed *More*, filmed on location in Ibiza, our destination, with music by Pink Floyd. The film depicted a descent into drug-fueled hedonism, heroin, and death, but the whitewashed farmhouses and Ibiza's cyan sea were compelling. In Montpellier a Roman aqueduct still carried water to the stone bathhouse where we washed away road grime. We journeyed on through Béziers, on a hill above the river Orb, and Narbonne, inhabited during the Iron Age by Celtic tribes in what was then called Gaul, toward Perpignan, the medieval town where James I, the Conqueror, king of Aragon and count of Barcelona founded the Kingdom of Majorca in the thirteenth century. We had our first glimpse of the Mediterranean Sea.

Spanish frontier police were indifferent, stamping our passports without incident. We entered Barcelona in a twilight glow and parked at the ferry terminal at Port Vell. We walked up the Ramblas, a tree-lined promenade from the port to Plaça de Cataluña. Vendors displayed their wares, flowers, newspapers, souvenirs, and songbirds. In a narrow cobblestone alley by Plaza Real's square, drunken sailors caroused beneath glowing neon colors with gaudily painted, brightly attired fat whores.

We slept in the van at the docks, near the statue of Christopher Columbus stone gazing toward the Mediterranean. Rather than wait three days for the next ferry to the fabled islands, we motored down the coast to

Valencia for an earlier crossing. Citrus groves flanked the highway. The bouquet of ripe fruit seduced us into walking through the trees to pluck plump ripe oranges. In Valencia we bought two-dollar fourth-class tickets for the boat and slept on the beach. The next evening our van was driven on the ferry and we boarded the ship for the ninety-mile crossing to Ibiza.

The humid heat below forced us from our cabin bunks out on to the cool deck where guitarists, hand clappers, and singers were laying down the duende soul of flamenco. Glimmering constellations sparkled above. We slept on reclining deckchairs. The ship parted the wine dark sea on its course to the eastern isle.

Ibiza

In Egypt during the period of The Old Kingdom in 3000 BC *Bes* was a deity worshipped as a protector of households, mothers and children, and since he drove off evil and killed snakes, Bes symbolized life's good things, including music, dance, and sexual pleasure. Egyptian dancers, musicians, and servant girls tattooed Bes on their thighs.

Among many Egyptian gods exported to other countries, Bes was popular with the Phoenicians, the ancient maritime trading culture on the eastern Mediterranean from 3200 BC to 300 BC, famed as traders in purple from their precious purple dye used for royal clothing and obtained from the predatory Murex sea snail. Phoenicians traveled the Mediterranean waters in galleys, man-powered sailing vessels propelled by rowing. They spread their innovative written alphabet from which all modern phonetic alphabets are derived.

In 650 BC the Phoenicians founded a colony on the island known today as Ibiza. Impressed with the lack of venomous snakes on the island they thought it to be the land of Bes. Romans later called it Ebusus.

The Greeks liked the island's dense coverage of Aleppo pines for shipbuilding. The island became a trading post along the Mediterranean's main commercial sea routes. In Roman times, Ibiza's governors negotiated a favorable treaty and federal status within the growing empire. Eventually Ibiza became a quiet imperial outpost.

After Rome fell, Vandals, Byzantines and Moors conquered Ibiza in succession. In 1108 the neighboring island Formentera was raided by a crusading Norwegian king on his way to Jerusalem. The islands were conquered in 1235 by James II of Aragon, and as a vital frontier post were given self-government. In 1715 Philip V of Spain abolished this autonomy. In 1977, democracy was reinstated and led to Ibiza, Formentera, Majorca, Menorca, and forty-six smaller islands being designated the Balearic Autonomous Community.

In the predawn darkness we stood on deck as our ship entered port. Above we could see the silhouette of the fortified acropolis. The steep slopes provide a vantage point over the sheltered bay and flat farmlands.

We disembarked and waited for the van to be hoisted from the deck and deposited dockside. With a two-hour wait before we continued on to Formentera, we entered a quayside café. Workers tossed back shots of cognac with morning coffee and smoked cigarettes of black tobacco. They wore dark work shirts and trousers, topped with berets. Their animated conversation was punctuated by drained shot glasses slammed to the bar.

We drank hot sweet coffee and ate omelets as the eastern sky lightened to blue, then gold. Beams of sunlight stabbed through clouds of cigarette smoke.

We walked from the docks up the hill in the old town. Making our way past walls built in the time of the Roman Empire, past houses washed white and gleaming against the bluest of blue sky, past black-clad women sweeping doorways, washing clothes, and talking in high pitched voice, we climbed on the path through a tunnel in a wall to the top of the old town cliff. There with the sea stretching all around we saw Vedra, the island where the beautiful but dangerous Sirens lived in Greek mythology. Passing there brave Odysseus surrendered to sensuous temptation and heard their song as he was tightly lashed to his ship's mast to resist their fatal call while his crew had their ears filled with wax to not hear the Sirens and thus avoid being lured by their enchanting music to shipwreck on the rocky coast of their island.

A small lazy cloud hovered above Vedra's twin-peaked zenith. Sheer cliffs made a precarious landing for those who would come ashore. Wild goats are the rocky island's only inhabitants. We looked south and had our first glimpse of Formentera lying low on the horizon, a shining stretch of white, a luminescent jewel in Mediterranean blue.

The Joven Dolores, a weathered, paint-flecked, aging vessel that had for many a year borne the responsibility of providing ferry service between the two islands, now with some well-earned implied silent pride bore the irony of being an old woman with a young girl's name, *joven* being Spanish for young. We paid twenty-five pesetas each and boarded. The boat's crane lifted our Volkswagen on to the one space on deck and we left port.

Beyond the harbor, ocean swell caused the round-bottomed craft to pitch and roll instigating passenger discomfort, while the nonchalant crew ate sandwiches, drank coffee with cognac, and conversed in raised voice in order to be heard over the engine's roar, the splashing sea, and the whistling wind.

We passed fishing boats on their way out to sea, their nets gathered and suspended above deck. The Joven plied the waters until Formentera became large in our sight as we left the open sea and entered Marina La Savina. Sunlight sparkled on rippling water as winter seemed seduced, disguised by the soothing caress of a warm breeze.

Island Of Stone

A crane lifted our Volkswagen from the deck and deposited it on the island. Whitewashed buildings gleamed in radiant sunlight. With anticipation, we observed blue water, small puffs of white clouds above, and red earth beyond. The only sound was lapping water.

A two-lane asphalt road rose toward one of the island's two towns. Stone walls divided fields and property. Constructed without mortar, their longevity is due to the local mason's precision in shaping and arranging. Stones covered the island. White farmhouses with blue doors faced south.

San Francisco Javier was a street of small stores, terracotta tiled roofs, a post office, and a church. Only a few people were on the streets of the town. Beyond, the paved road gave way to a rocky earthen track flanked by orchards of olive, almond, and fig trees, and clusters of pine. We passed a giant fig tree called *Na Blanca*, its

numerous limbs extending far, supported by a hundred crutch-like posts.

"This," said Skip, "is one of the largest fig trees in the world. It's in The Guinness Book of World Records."

The van bounced on the rocky road, dipping in and rising from potholes while shaking us like popping corn.

California Dreamers

While slowing on the rutted road, two longhaired American-looking young men gave us a wave from the patio of their roadside house. We stopped. They approached and glimpsed the guitar and sitar through the window. Michael and Bob were from California. They were enthusiastic with the arrival of musicians, and promised to visit. We were going only to the next house.

Now the road became smooth, done with ruts and

rocks, sloping toward the sea and the last house on the west side of the island. As we approached we saw two agave plants, their stalks rising above the low roofline.

The road ended. Beyond were pine thickets and further a band of slate sea in the distance. The bowl of blue sky met the water out on the horizon. Skip killed the engine. All was still.

Beginning

We heard only an unbroken silence, then the sound of a beaded curtain rattling as it was drawn aside. A blonde-haired woman peered through, smiled, and walked toward us. She wore a white cotton skirt, a matching blouse, and rope-soled canvas shoes with laces wrapped around her ankles.

"Skip and Kate. You made it. Wow, it's been a while. We got your letter."

Eyeing me, she introduced herself.

"Hi, my name's Carol. Where have you been? Arthur's gone to town. Come on in."

We stooped, parting the doorway curtain that deterred flies, and passed beneath the low lintel. Doors remained open during the day, for light. Thick walls held only one small barred window to admit some light but withhold unwanted intruders. The interior was dim. Stout wooden front doors with iron bolts secured entrance to the stone fortress.

Entering the central room we saw an adjacent kitchen. A door opposite led to a storeroom and a ladder climbed above to a loft for sleeping. Carol produced some bread, cheese, and figs as we sprawled on mats and cushions, stretching the road out of ourselves.

Hashish From The Rif Mountains

Skip asked the inevitable question.
"Is there anything to smoke?"
"We have some pollen. It hasn't been pressed yet, but it's fresh and really strong"
Carol produced a cloth bag containing a pound of green pollen gathered from flowering Cannabis. It would later be pressed into one-ounce balls of what Arthur would reference as the best hashish in the world that he harvested himself in the Rif Mountain town of Ketama, in northern Morocco. Carol handed over a little *sebsi* pipe. Skip loaded some pollen in, held a flame to it, and we inhaled an aromatic flowery smoke. With the first hit a tether connecting me to an outworn state of existence was cut and a new journey began as we sailed over the edge of expectancy into deep colorful but uncharted multi-hued tranquility. The effect was more pronounced than smoking marijuana and not a little unsettling to have reached our destination and be under the influence of powerful Cannabis in a remote stone farmhouse on an island far from familiarity. Silence resonated, minds levitated, spirits elevated, and we got situated.
The beaded curtain rattled. Skip's friend had returned with a bulging esparto basket dangling from his shoulder from a shopping walk to town. Arthur was tall, with closely cropped, fair hair. Blue eyes peered over spectacles. He had a steady gaze, a British accent, and friendly intelligence.
The remainder of the day passed in conversation,

unloading the van, arranging sleeping places, and more pipe sessions. As darkness gathered, our hosts lit candles and kerosene lamps. Electricity had yet to reach here or anywhere else outside town. We cooked brown rice and vegetables on the fireplace and on a small gas stove. After dinner, further blasted by the hashish, we gathered our instruments and gave way to music.

Jellaba Man And The Buckskin Kid

The two Californians we met up the road arrived, smiling as they entered, hearing the music and smelling the herb. Michael was wearing a long black and white striped *jellaba*, a hooded Arabic cloak. Bob was sporting a Western fringed buckskin jacket. The two exchanged greetings, settled in to sit cross-legged on the cushions, took a few tokes on the pipe, and joined in playing hand drums from Arthur's small collection, while he played a drum of his own making, embellished with an Om painted on its head.

To kick things into higher gear, Arthur produced a one-gallon double-spouted water jar he'd converted into a hookah. One spout was for drawing the smoke; the other held a bowl and stem attached with a tight seal that went down into the water at the bottom, to cool the heat. He heaped a good quantity of hash into the bowl and passed it to Michael, who began drawing on the spout while Arthur held fire to the bowl. Michael inhaled, bubbling the jug. He held it in, nodding with smiling contentment, then exhaled abruptly in a fit of coughing, to much merriment. The water pipe was passed round while we took turns hitting on it. A strong inhalation was required to properly force the smoke through the water resulting in a large amount of power blasted hashish entering the lungs.

We played guitars, pumped beats on drums, and sang favorite songs. Cocooned in the island dwelling and stimulated by the high quality herb our music led us to a unification of our spirits in spontaneous interaction.

That night we celebrated our journey from the modern to the ancient. We walked outside and gazed at the glistening stars in the inky black night. A canopy of diamonds sparkled in silent radiance. We wiped the dust from the mirror and saw the universe as it had never before been seen, immense, glowing, eternal, and untouched by the corrupting hands of urbanization and industry.

Island Life

Farmhouses were stone dwellings with three or four rooms, stone floors and one fireplace, without plumbing or electricity, constructed decades if not centuries previously. Furnishings were the most basic, consisting of wooden beds, a few cabinets, chairs, and tables. Young Formenterans were moving away from the subsistence farming life for employment in hotels, restaurants, and discotheques. With a decrease of indigenous population once occupied but now empty houses were being rented to *extranjeros*, foreigners, among them European, American, and Australian. Thirty dollars bought a month's rent or an ounce of hashish. Sixty bought both.

The first thing of purchase for an extranjero was invariably an Ibiza basket. Made from woven esparto grass, the basket's rope handles allow it to hang comfortably from the shoulder when carrying small articles such as might be obtained on a walking trip to town.

Young foreigners often wore locally produced white cotton pants and blouses and Moroccan shirts with embroidery and multiple buttons made of fabric that fastened into loops, with the addition of bright colored vests, tie-dyed shirts, and Spanish rope-soled canvas shoes with string laces. Formentera farmers wore somber black. Women dressed in flowing skirts and blouses, often with an embroidered shawl over the shoulder, tied in front. Wide brim straw hats reduced the sun. Men favored berets, but preferred straw for fieldwork.

Spiritually minded and adventurous international island residents were journeying overland to India, a distance of five thousand miles, crossing Europe, Turkey,

Iraq, Iran, and Afghanistan. In addition to being a source for matters of a sacred nature, those environs were the major hashish producing countries on the planet. Some travelers to the lands of Eastern enlightenment devised methods of sequestering hashish in their vehicles bound for Europe. Spain was not overly diligent in enforcing strict prohibition, preferring to facilitate a free flow of tourist income.

Alternatives

An alternate approach with unprocessed foods prevailed. Instead of the unconscious ingestion of comfort foods high in fat and sugar, we converted over to basic brown rice, vegetables, and bread baked with whole wheat instead of processed white flour, along with herbal teas. We avoided meat, sweetened carbonated drink, candy, chips, and the usual fast urban junk food. Every farmhouse had an attached outdoor stone oven where we could bake bread by building a fire with pine branches and brushwood until the walls were hot, then raking red-glowing embers to the sides and inserting prepared dough on a long-handled peel. With one oven being large enough for numerous items we encouraged acquaintances to bake with us.

Offering tools, skills, and intellectual endeavors for the back-to-the-land movements of the Sixties counterculture, the Whole Earth Catalog was a publication found in households on the island. Our host Arthur immersed himself in self-reliant study and technique. He was an avid learner, sharing his knowledge with those who expressed interest. His influence was felt in myriad ways. He demonstrated how to make yogurt by heating milk to kill bacteria and denature the milk proteins so that they set together rather than form curds, then adding a yogurt culture from the previous batch. The liquid was poured into bottles, and placed in sunlight for the day, to maintain temperature and allow fermentation into yogurt.

Arthur introduced me to the writings of Gurdjieff, an influential spiritual teacher and writer who brought to the West a tradition of development and personal awakening, using the diverse impressions of ordinary life to reveal the underlying hidden reality. Arthur possessed an open mind continuously searching for ways to expand capacity and potential. His enthusiasm was infectious, and his British reasoning effortlessly mature.

"Leave a place better than it was when you found it," Arthur said.

On the first full moon night after our arrival, Arthur invited friends for a music party. With a blazing bonfire in front of his house, musicians were outside playing when a flatbed truck arrived, turned round, and backed to the edge of the music circle. A drummer was hitting the beat with his drum kit on the bed of the truck. Mindblower.

The Hash Contest

Arthur's green Moroccan hashish was strong but Afghani was reputed to be superior. An enthusiast with some quantity of that Afghani suggested a contest. The Moroccan Marauder versus the Afghan Avenger.

We put forth a determined test of the two titans by

inhaling these potent varieties through Arthur's water jug pipe, both rendering us too stoned to determine a clear winner, but we were smoking the finest psychedelicized Cannabis on the planet, far beyond the weak and coarse stems and seeds brown Mexican marijuana for ten dollars a lid back home.

Return of the Florida Woman

When Sharon's Copenhagen liaison had run its course she reverted to the original plan of going to Spain. Arriving on the island she made inquiries in town, and appeared late in the day at Arthur's door. Her presence was awkward but as night was approaching, we could not turn her out. Sharon explained that she hoped to reunite, but it was not to be. The cleansing fire of change precluded return to the previous entanglement of slim reason. Finding me unwilling to reconcile, she fell to repetitious begging, into evening and through the night. Awake on her pallet upstairs Sharon whimpered loud and long, disrupting and exasperating the household.

"Pleeeeeeeeasssse, pleeeeeeease pleeeeeeeassseee, puhleeeeeeeaase," Sharon moaned in her isolated rack. Interspersed with pleading were periods of crying, alternated with thumb sucking for comfort. With dawn's gracious relief we escorted the dejected reject to town, where Sharon became acquainted with English Annie and secured a room in her house.

English Annie and Sharon were to visit Bob when he later rented a house on La Mola, the remote higher part of the island. The women arrived on an afternoon and stayed into evening, smoking hash and engaging in sensual physicality, until Sharon demurred.

"This is getting weird," she said, departing for the field, to slumber beneath a carob tree under the silvery moon and rhinestone stars. In the morning a passing farmer lingered for an eyeful of the girl, clad only in lower underwear. For a people whose culture hadn't changed in centuries, Formenterans tolerated well the behavior of foreigners fueling the tourist economy. Specially the naked chicks.

Rental House

A month after our arrival Arthur learned that an adjacent vacant farmhouse situated on rocky terrain devoid of vegetation was available. He communicated with the owner who agreed to rent it for thirty dollars a month.

There wasn't much in the place. Skip and Kate commandeered the main bedroom with a black and pink checkerboard marble floor that lent a colorful touch and a window that faced the sea. The second locked bedroom was used for the owner's stored belongings. The former winemaking room was mine. A few boards on top of the rectangular wine trough with foam over that served as my bed five feet above the floor. A small circular table was hung from the ceiling, swaying each time anything was placed on it or removed. The house had an *entrada*, or main room, and a small kitchen with a fireplace. There were no appliances, and no electricity or running water, but there was a well. The place was stone basic but we had an independent residence for our alternative existence.

Acid Day

Having reached the destination we were done with the road. Skip sold his Volkswagen and used the proceeds to buy a half-kilo of Arthur's hashish to sell for living money. To escape intrusive police detection, the hash was stashed in one of the rock walls along the house's perimeter.

Hollywood songwriting royalties provided my source of revenue, a treasure in small measure, but sufficient income to survive in the inexpensive Spanish economy.

At the kitchen fireplace with gathered wood from the nearby pine forest we prepared our simple oatmeal or

pancakes in the morning, and rice and vegetables for
lunch and dinner. We smoked hash throughout the day.
Fridays were declared acid day and for a few weeks we
took Lysergic Acid Diethylamide to trip around our end
of the island. We did some jaunts through the pine groves
to the nearby cliffs where an abandoned Roman
watchtower stood mute sentinel to the sea. On cloudless
days the silhouette of the mainland appeared in the
distance. The island's silence, its stark landscape, and the
aqua sea before us with expansive cerulean sky,
intensified the acid's effect. Vivid color and intense light,

red earth, green trees, and an absence of ambient noise created a marked contrast to the smoggy, heavily trafficked, industrial-sounding Los Angeles cityscape.

Heavy Hip Mama

Arthur and Carol were our neighbors at about a thousand yards on one side, and five hundred yards the other way were The Buckskin Kid and the Djellaba Man, Bob and Michael.

The two friends attended the same high school at the time of the San Francisco psychedelic explosion. They smoked reefer, dropped acid, and rocked out at The Fillmore Auditorium and The Avalon Ballroom.

The Haight Ashbury scene enthralled Michael in the beginning but a couple of years later he was disenchanted. Maybe he was getting older or the spirit of the Summer of Love was becoming polluted. Negative events like The Rolling Stones' infamous concert at Altamont Speedway where a man was stabbed to death, and the Black Panthers' police confrontations, began to sour the rush of love and music.

First John, then Robert Kennedy was assassinated. Martin Luther King's murder shook him. With Muhammad Ali, Jane Fonda and so many public people against the Vietnam War, yet nothing happening to end it, Michael felt like he was in caught in a whirlpool. All that amazing, inspiring music, such positive energy, but mixed up confusion and so much going wrong.

It didn't help that Michael's brand new Triumph Bonneville motorcycle got stolen from Golden Gate Park at the Human Be-In while he was there with friends when

The Grateful Dead and Jefferson Airplane were playing in Speedway Meadows. After the concert the bike wasn't where he had parked it. Part of the innocence of that era ended for him then.

With insurance money from his stolen motorcycle Michael decided to leave the United States for Europe. When he shared his plans with Bob the two agreed to meet in Amsterdam. Michael flew to Luxembourg on inexpensive Icelandic Airlines. He and Bob met and traveled together for a time. Bob went to France to surf in Biarritz and Michael tripped around the continent on his own, flush with freedom and feeling the old world ambience. He had escaped the turmoil of the turbulent sixties. His friend Eric, who bought a farmhouse in Ibiza with Jim, a mutual acquaintance, wrote to say that he would soon be coming back from Morocco, bound for Ibiza.

Michael went to Spain, taking the boat to Ibiza and, subsequently, took the ferry to Formentera for a visit. Finding the island to his liking, Michael located a vacant farmhouse on the unpopulous western side. Rental was a mere twenty-five dollars a month. To supplement expenses he rented spare bedrooms to acquaintances on their travels in Europe.

Michael was usually to be found dressed in his Levis and red checkered shirts in the *entrada*, the front room, singing and playing his nylon string guitar with no great skill, but with pleasure. His repertoire included *Goodnight Irene*, and *Keep Your Hands Off Her* with the refrain, *She's a heavy hipped mama with great big legs*, that he intoned with much mirth. Michael toked on his hash pipe, dropped acid to enhance the mood, and listened to Dead tapes on his portable cassette player.

We sometimes congregated at Michael's house for company, conversation, and guitar playing. His favorite comic effect was to lie on his back, lift his legs up over his head, strike a match, put the match right by his butt, and expel gas that ignited in a brief but bright explosive flurry. He would pull this stunt in the company of both Formentera and Ibiza farmers, if he knew them well, and it never failed to amuse them. They eventually took to calling him El Bruto.

In addition to his enthusiasm for surfing Bob cultivated an interest in Buddhism, inspired in some measure by Alan Watts, a British practitioner in California. Bob attended Watts' lectures and studied the teachings. The quest was to guide him to India, Nepal, and Ceylon, where he would become a Buddhist monk.

Grey Daze

Winter became cold and overcast, with a chill sea wind blowing and biting ceaselessly across the flat island. We were confined in the stone walls of the old rockbound house. The monotonous diet of oatmeal, pancakes, brown rice, vegetables, cheese, and yogurt had little variation. Warmth was by the kitchen fire, but the house was cold. Relief was either the fireplace or slathered with blankets in bed.

Novelty transited to routine. Uneasiness replaced excitement. There was no schedule and no employment. Playing music together was forgotten. Then they started with opium.

One night we went across the island to visit an acquaintance of Skip's. With no road signs, wrong turns were common, causing us to pass the same rock wall more than once. At our destination LSD was consumed. Later in the evening, Skip and his fellow stoners subdued the acid with opium. Too rolling stoned to return home we slept there. Our frazzled host walked by me at dawn with his butt poking out from his sleeping shirt. These people seemed overly stoned and stupefied. Glamour had faded.

The Road

It is one thing to have friends and another to live with them. The pleasure of my housemates' company was diminishing. Things might be better without sharing quarters with people who now seemed directionless. Independence beckoned.

Departing from the house on Formentera, on a bright and brimming clear expectant day in early spring, as the sun rose high in a sapphire sky, with only a basket over my shoulder and a gleam in my eye, there was no way to know that the next four years were to be ones of untethered wandering. To the Moorish castle Alhambra in Spain's Sierra Nevada mountains, to the grey-shrouded, green mountains of Andalucía, to Gibraltar, on the southern end of Spain at the juncture of the Atlantic Ocean and the Mediterranean Sea, to the snowy peaks of the Atlas Mountains, and Marrakech, The Rose City in Morocco, where refined elements have a roughness to them, yet what is rough has its own refinement. To London, where rain fell every day in summer and thieves made off with my few possessions, to Amsterdam, where busking with my guitar in the street landed me in a jail cell, to Paris, Venice, California, Colorado, driving the length and breadth of Europe again, then the Middle East, moving on trains, busses, hitchhiking, walking, working for film companies, sailing on ships crossing the Mediterranean from west to east and back again, making music with drummers, guitar players, and international singers of songs.

The connections of my youth to people and place were severed. There were good times, bad times, lost times, found times, cultural interaction, and worldly experience. You have to live it to sing about it.

Two

Treasure

The Old Country

The train from Italy stopped in the small city of Sisak, located at the juncture of the Kupa, Sava, and Odra rivers, thirty-five miles south of Zagreb, the capitol of Croatia.

Townsfolk directed me to walk out and across the outlying open fields toward the Kupa River. Vurot, a village with a population of fifty, was a cluster of unpainted, aging, wooden houses that lay in sight across the water. My father was born and lived here until he emigrated to America at age ten. He still visited on occasion. The family was used to some of us arriving from time to time.

"Juro. Juro, Juuuuroooooohhhh."

A woman walking her cow heard my calling and summoned my cousin. He waved his arms, then signaled that he would fetch the boat and cross for me. This wasn't my first time. The family hosted me seven years previously, during a six-week Eurailpass student excursion. They coincided my first arrival from America with Branka's wedding to Miro, an affair that required a tent being erected in a field for over a hundred attendees to eat pig and calf and drink alcohol and stay up all night singing.

On the wedding day a horse drawn wagon rolled into the village carrying the expectant groom, family members, and a trio of musicians playing cacophonous folk melodies on clarinet, accordion, and guitar. Their wagon made a celebratory entrance before the house in the dirt yard where the groom approached the door to request the presence of his bride from her family. Instead of her appearance, a man was ushered forth in white wedding dress with garish red lipstick below his mustache to momentarily trick the groom and amuse the assembly. After extensive merriment the bride came forth.

Juro crossed the river, gathered me in, and rowed to the opposite side where he secured the boat. We walked up the embankment to a green field marked by wooden fencing, and onto a dirt path leading past the pig enclosure, then past the barn where their horse and cow were penned. The powerful smell of accumulated animal excrement hit my nostrils. Before us was the old three-room house containing a storeroom, a kitchen, and a shared bedroom where Juro and his wife along with his father and mother all slept.

My hair was long. My beard was full, with a large handlebar mustache. The innocent student look of a few years ago was gone. My Sixties-enhanced urban refugee appearance would either alarm or amuse these peasant folk whose men were shorthaired and clean-shaven.

Plowing Knee Deep in Loose Earth

The family welcomed me with work, more than enough to eat, and the kitchen couch for sleeping

We woke in the black before dawn. Teta's rough purring voice repeated,

"*Dobar dan, kava, kava.*"

Good morning, coffee, coffee.

Juro woke, dressed, and went to the barn to harness the horse. Stefo, the old man, sat on the side of his bed, wrapping handkerchiefs around his feet that he used in place of socks. He pulled his boots on.

Leading the horse, we walked on a path beside the river to a field edged with trees. A plow rested in one corner and our steed was hitched to it, with a halter around its neck and guidelines streaming back for the plowman.

On command, the horse surged forward. Juro guided the plow straight and deep, creating furrows of freshly dug earth. With four muscled legs, the horse was a fast walker. Juro passed the reins to me. We were no match in speed or strength. Intense exertion was required to keep pace. With every step our feet sank deeply into the freshly turned earth. Lifting each foot free from the clods increased the effort.

In little time we were pouring sweat. Sunrise brought summer heat that intensified as morning wore on. To refresh ourselves we drank from a bottle of water mixed with wine. The alcohol kick so early in the day made me dizzy. By midmorning, soaked from the effort, grimy with dirt, and throbbing, we returned to the house for eggs fried in pig fat, with bacon, white bread, cold goose, and steaming coffee, with grounds floating in the cup. Our hunger quenched, we returned to the field to plough the earth to plant the corn that would feed the pigs that the people consume.

The villagers were overweight with heart problems. They were better off not laboring to grow corn to feed pigs to eat fat that congested their arteries. All the alcohol they consume couldn't help either.

Drunken Cow Herding

The midday meal in Europe is styled like American dinner. Meat, potatoes, freshly picked cucumbers, tomatoes, and beer. The combination of exhaustion, heat, heavy food, and alcohol, lured me to lie on the kitchen couch after lunch. Invariably, before sleep had time to refresh me, Teta woke me, crooning,

"*Krava, krava.*"

Cow, cow.

As the newcomer and least farm-skilled of the family, my job was to walk the family cow out to pasture and supervise her grazing. Cow herding was a job for children and old people. Waking and staying awake in the heat of a mid-afternoon pasture was the first challenge.

Keeping the grazing bovine from the garden, where she was tempted to lay waste to the vegetable plot, was the next goal. The family's land was not of one piece. Parcels were scattered. An unplanted pasture might be next to a vineyard or unfenced garden, requiring supervision of grazing animals.

Occasionally old Bessie made a break for it, leaving me behind, but she always stopped to feed, allowing me to catch and redirect her. My eventual request to have her hobbled was received with amusement and good-natured ribbing in my direction.

Village Dance

The family introduced me to a musician, a distant cousin. Vlado's family lived on their farm in Selo, a nearby village on the highway between Sisak and Zagreb, an hour away by car. Saturday night Vlado and his band had a performance at the community hall. They wanted me, the big American rock star, to play.

Saturday afternoon Juro walked with me through field and forest to Selo where introductions to the family were made. He departed leaving me to stay the night. At the appointed time Vlado took me, along with some of his acquaintances, including a red-headed country girl casting optimistic looks in my direction, to the crowded hall where drinks were offered to me at the bar with much raucous insistence that they be consumed. Drinking alcohol is a significant part of the social structure of Croatians. They drank shot glasses of vinac, a blend of wine and cognac. Vlado insisted. The band eagerly looked on, waiting with eager anticipation for me to down the shot. Bam. Applause. Another. The band stared, waiting. Slam. Another shot. Immediate yelling, applause, and approval. Another. There was no apparent end point at which convention is satisfied and we can move on. No, this is Saturday night and we drink.

Intoxication hit me in surging waves. There was no way to stand. Forget playing. Things were rolling now. Let me lie down.

"*Spava, spava.*"

Sleep, sleep.

Vlado and the band, along with the red-haired farm girl still eyeing me in preparation for Saturday night partying, led me back to the house and up the stairs. They dropped me in a bed, turned out the light, and departed.

Not for long. They returned, bursting in to the bedroom to help me rise and get back to the hall where they guided me up on a dangerously high stage, simultaneously thrusting an electric guitar into my arms. Go Johnny, go. The band rocked, the room rolled. Yet, my fingers found the positions. Drunk or straight, *Roll Over Beethoven* came crashing through. Amplifiers screamed out a warning and the big diesel steamed forward. Satisfaction for a thrashing throng of young twisting gyrators, and old folks, too. Conquered their brew and showed the power of American electric guitar slinging. America very good. Redhead girl good. Dobro.

Bikini Beach

A journeyer in a foreign land eventually longs for the company of one's compatriots and familiar language. Michael responded to my letter with an invitation to stay with him in Ibiza, where he had moved from Formentera. Departing the farm, a train carried me from Zagreb to Barcelona, and the ferry took me to Ibiza. Summer visitor's season was underway. Michael was working in San Antonio, a taxi-ride from the port in Ibiza town, at a beach kiosk. He rented sun-shading umbrellas and chairs and sold cold drinks. Europeans sunned themselves and swam before the evening's bar hopping and dancing. Michael greeted me and introduced his acquaintances, Anna, a Swedish woman, and her fifteen-year-old friend Ursula, from Denmark. Warm sand by the blue bay dissolved my diminishing travel vibrations.

Bikini-clad bodies were everywhere, a stark contrast to the sweat-stained T-shirts and shabby work clothes in the farming village that had sheltered me for the last two months. Young Ursula got permission from her mother to accompany us for an overnight stay at Michael's country house. Danish people didn't seem uptight.

First Night On Ibiza

The descending fire of the orange sun was extinguished in the horizon of turquoise sea signaling the approach of evening. Tanned northern European beachgoers gathered their belongings and dispersed to their hotels. After washing away sand and salt, attention would turn to dressing, drinking, dining, and disco dancing.

We helped Michael gather and stack lounge chairs and umbrellas inside the kiosk. He closed the door, set the lock, and we were done. We loaded into his Camioneta sedan for the four kilometer drive to the farmland of Santa Ines valley where Michael lived in a house on the lower part of a hill overlooking the Valley Of The Moon. No road reached the place. He kept his car down the hill at the house he purchased for his father. The crusty geezer retired from the Merchant Marine and followed his son's trail from California to Spain where he lived his golden years in tranquil isolation.

Greetings were exchanged with the old salt who was appreciative of the opportunity for eyes to linger on female form. We proceeded afoot. Michael guided the damsels and me through the pine trees, climbing the hill to view the valley below.

We shared the dinner preparation of brown rice, vegetables, and salad, with a little wine, then fell to at a small wooden table in the combination kitchen and main room. We finished with a few tokes of hashish from a Moroccan soapstone pipe.

Outside we watched as the silver moon rose soundlessly into purple sky. Uncountable numbers of stars radiated far from the distracting light of cities. We saw them as they were in ancient time, before civilization obscured their natural brilliance with fluorescent falseness. Warm wisps of air wafted through the pines, gently stirring the boughs. Serenity was punctuated only by an occasional distant dog barking somewhere in that quiet green valley beneath an eternal night sky. Ursula took my hand and led me indoors to a bedroom.

Stripping off her clothing, the young woman stood before me, naked, the fine golden hair radiant on her tanned skin. Her youthful innocence belied a passion and freedom in her sexuality. Her pink tongue, red lips, blonde hair, and sky blue eyes were a rainbow by candle glow. Ursula's touch initiated a trembling rush, a sensuous sensation that had been forgotten in the years drifting on the lost highway.

Dormie Angel

Summer days were hot but cooler evenings possessed a mystic calm on this remote part of the island. After dinner one night, Michael caught my eye as he produced a small plastic container. He put it to his ear and shook it, making a rattling sound. With an expectant smile he leered at me and extracted a few round white pills.

"Take two," he said.

The drug produced a tingling sensation along with a floating feeling, creating a relaxation of inhibition. They were Dormadinas, like Quaaludes, and available in Spanish pharmacies without prescription.

The medication was described on its packaging as hypnoticos, an aid to sleep, sold over the counter in a blue plastic container with a white sliding top holding twelve pills. People who liked them bought them by the carton of ten containers. While high, the moment of doubt and inhibition one might experience when confronted by sexual opportunity was washed away by an urge to surrender to the first sloppy, gushy impulse. Michael liked to share. He was The Dormie Angel.

Pressing Activity

Olive trees grew on Michael's property that provided a few bottles of oil. When ripe, we spread cloths on the ground below the tree limbs to catch the black spheres as they fell. Poles were rattled up into the limbs to loosen the stems from the boughs.

Once harvested, we carried the olives in sacks to a neighboring farmhouse where a farmer operated an old olive press. The device had wooden parts with two horizontal stone wheels face to face. The olives were placed in between the wheels. The top wheel was raised and lowered by a large, well-worn wooden screw running through its center. The wheel's turning motion was initiated by hand and that revolution combined with the weight of the press crushed the olives. Oil drained down a channel into a receptacle where the liquid was collected, then bottled. A bottle of oil was given to the press operator in return for his service.

House On The Hill

On the arid island there are no rivers or lakes and no source of ground water. There is only rain runoff that is channeled and gathered from roofs and patios that catch the liquid and send it to an underground cistern. Water can be shipped from the mainland and trucked in when a supply is depleted. Every house has a bucket on a rope above a cistern to haul water. Water conservation is diligently practiced.

While fetching water at the well, a blond-haired man strode toward the house from the pine forest and called out hello. Michael told me that Jim, his Californian neighbor, lived at the top of the hill in a large farmhouse, and since the man walked from that direction this must be him. Jim heard about my music background and being a guitar player himself, he was interested.

We talked with Michael a while until Jim invited me up. We walked through the pine forest a short distance until we came to his house. We walked onto the roof of a low corral, like a deck on the side, from which we viewed the valley below.

Spread before us was a chessboard of green and brown two miles in diameter, with tracts in various stages of planting. Farmers tended almond orchards, fig and olive trees, some crops, and vegetable gardens. This valley was *La Corona*, The Crown, referring to the shape like the sun's circumference. Jim called it The Valley of the Moon.

"If you want, you can stay here. There's no payment. It'll be better for you than Michael's little place. You can show me some guitar things once in a while."

New Residence

Unlike most of the one-story houses on the islands, Jim's massive three hundred year old Moorish farmhouse was an anomaly, having two levels.

The stone walls were three feet thick. Like most on the islands, the structure faced the southeast, taking advantage of the maximum of direct sunlight. Two ten feet tall, blue painted dense wooden doors with large interior iron bolts for locking were the portals to the *entrada*, the large entrance room. Two wings of bedrooms were on each side and a storeroom was situated below the north side bedroom. The farmhouse was painted white, both in and out. Dark wooden beams were visible supporting the roof. The floors were pink stone. The house once had a secret room where smugglers could stash their booty.

The south wing contained a downstairs bedroom converted from a former storeroom. Jim's friend Ron was there. Above this room was Jim's bedroom. Just before his door a small room was used as a closet that also led onto an open deck above the porch, an ideal sleeping place in summer, and a panoramic vantage point from which one had the expansive view of the valley looking east where morning light burst radiant and golden and the night moon bathed the valley in a ghostly silver glow. A beauty and quiet that few people will experience in their lifetime was evident daily. The valley's silence was so marked that the sound of a motorcycle entering from the opposite end two miles away was audible in the otherwise still realm.

Two north wing bedrooms were accessed by a short stairway. The room designated for me had both north and east-facing small, barred windows. To enter, one stooped slightly to clear the low doorframe. A bed was on the floor to the left. To the right, the east, a small window let in morning sunlight. A few shelves provided a resting place for books.

From the entrada, a high-ceilinged sky-lit kitchen included a butane powered stove, a sink, and substantial wood counters. Built-in cushioned benches were on either side of a corner fireplace. Adjacent to the kitchen was a sky-lit bathroom. Both of these rooms had been remodeled, adding sinks that could hold water from a storage tank on the roof. A hydraulic hand pump on the side of the house enabled water to be channeled up from the cistern to the tank. The toilet in the bathroom was not used. Instead, outside the house, two long, smoothed tree branches were suspended from a corral's walls a foot and a half off the ground that made a seat underneath which a bucket was placed for excrement. Another adjacent bucket was filled with dirt to cover the waste.

When the bucket filled, the contents were dumped into a compost heap. After a few months, the breakdown of the waste along with vegetable remains mixed with soil produced a fertilizer that was used on the land, returning to earth its harvest.

The corral we first stood on had been used for animals when the farmhouse previously was in Ibicencan hands. They may have kept goats or pigs. Foreigners kept no animals, being removed from farm occupation.

The old structure had been unoccupied for some time and had fallen into disrepair when Jim purchased it for eleven thousand dollars and subsequently began renovation. He lived on an inheritance. His family went back in the history of the United States and included a Secretary of State who was his namesake.

Three On A Motorcycle

Jim's had one houseguest, another American, from Marin County, across the Golden Gate Bridge from San Francisco. Ron had shoulder length hair and full beard. Outside he often wore his straw hat with a pointed crown that gave him the look of Gandalf the Wizard. Farmers described being startled by Ron's wide-eyed wild appearance in their headlights on dirt roads riding his motorcycle returning from a night's revelry. Ron was a sweet person but he often became confrontational under the influence of alcohol, which could be every night. He loved to go into town and carouse, bar hopping and raising hell.

As a youth, Ron and his brother, Joaquin, were known as a mischievous and formidable duo that pulled pranks and when occasion required were the fighting toughs in their neighborhood. What got Ron into trouble was his inability to back down. When challenged, he wouldn't yield.

The garden in front of the house produced tomatoes, lettuce, green peppers, garlic, carrots, fava beans, cauliflowers, onions, and the occasional marijuana plant. The earth was not rich but, with care, vegetables were grown in it adequate for our needs. Here we could look out over the valley as we tended to the horticultural aspects of country life, with aromas of a fresh breeze and newly turned earth.

We were weeding there on a morning when we heard an engine roaring up the road and into the front yard. Ron and two brightly clad women were precariously balanced on his motorcycle. They wobbled slowly to a stop. Ron grinned at us with a knowing and conquering look, then gave forth with an introduction.

"This is Annie and this is Frannie."

"Hi. Wow. Three on a bike. That's amazing."

"Yeah, we rode like this all the way from San Antonio."

"My leg is burned," Frannie said, extending her right leg. The inside of her calf was bright red.

"She burned it on the exhaust pipe," Ron said with a laugh.

"Ron, take her up to the kitchen where we can treat her," Jim suggested. They turned to go up as Jim gave me that look, tongue hanging out, eyes opened wide, head nodding up and down, that meant,

"Chicks!"

The women were British and spoke in thick Cockney accents. While Jim administered first aid to Frannie's burnt calf, we learned that they were secretaries on holiday. They had been out in San Antonio and were charmed by Ron's persuasive requests to visit the country.

"Maybe we'll go over to Michael's," Ron informed us. That was his way of getting them out of the house to a more convenient place for what, presumably, would be the sexual part of their visit. Michael, single man that he was, might enjoy their presence. They walked, rather than trying to recreate their motorcycle balancing act.

Annie

We sat in the kitchen with a visitor in the evening. Our conversation reached speculation as to what Michael and Ron might be doing with Annie and Frannie. Michael was noted for his diligence in trying to get laid by any means. He had a doglike persistence that sometimes resulted in success, despite, or due to, his persistent manner, unlike we sophisticates who were dogs as well but considered ourselves to be more discriminating dogs with a higher pedigree.

Emboldened by the effect of Dormidinas, Jim suggested that my initiative might result in the attainment of Annie's favors, which motivated my attempt of the deed, causing me to set forth toward Michael's house with the goal in mind.

The walk followed a narrow footpath through a pine grove. Below the path was a cave. Occasionally we might walk down to it just to look at its entrance. Above the cave and just off the path a small tent was pitched to provide a sleepover spot. Past the pines Michael's house came into view. He sat at the kitchen table talking with Frannie. Ron was gone to town. Annie lay on the cushioned bench beside the fireplace, festooned in her Scheherazade style harem garments radiating eye enticing color and shine. Wordlessly she took my offered hand and rose, to be led back along the path into the pine grove. We reached the tent, entered, quickly went to it, then retraced our steps back to Michael's house. Annie returned to recline by the fireplace, smiling at my departure. Returning to Jim's place my return was greeted with surprise.

"Back already? Nobody there?"

"We did it."

"What? You did it? With Annie? Your tea didn't have time to get cold. How could you have done it so fast?"

"It was easy. No preliminaries."

"Unbelievable. You fucked her? You dog!"

Hold Him Down And Throw Him Overboard

Ron disappeared. He went to town one night and

didn't return. Three weeks later a small grey sedan with two Guardia Civil drove into the yard. Ron was with them, clean-shaven and sporting a buzz cut, transformed from wild mountain man to scrawny dork. White skin around his ears and neck contrasted starkly with his tan.

"The cops busted me for being drunk and getting into a fight with the Guardia Civil," he recounted.

"They took me to the jail in Majorca and cut off all my hair. They're expelling me from the country. The Guardia brought me here to get my stuff. You want to buy my bike?" he queried of me.

A few minutes later, packed, and fifty dollars richer, Ron was escorted away and off the island. He never returned.

The Montesa motorcycle was black with a red tank. Jim revealed the bike's backstory with incredulous humor in telling of Ron's audacity. Ron saw the bike in town, couldn't resist temptation and stole it. He brought the machine to the house and buried it near the garden. Eventually he and Jim unearthed it and he motored around the island without documentation. None was presented to me on my purchase and no authority found reason to examine my ownership.

Two Stoners On A Motorcycle

Jim and Michael had taken numerous Dormadinas and consumed a few bottles of wine when they decided to head into San Antonio for some late night partying. They reasoned that riding together on Jim's motorcycle would be their best approach. Michael was at the controls but soon realized that he was too stoned to steer while driving through *Sem Moradas*, The Curves.

"Hey, Jim, this is too hard to handle. You better drive."

Jim climbed off the rear and mounted up. He gunned it forward, but Michael hadn't gotten on yet. Just as Jim asked,

"Michael, are you on?"
he plowed the bike into the side of a hill. Michael was laughing from his spot in the road where he had watched his friend dump it. The dudes were done. They abandoned their attempt and returned to quarters to surrender to sleep. Being drunk and stoned doesn't work for two on a motorcycle.

Take One, Take Half

Frequent houseguests contributed to a varied home atmosphere. Americans and Europeans visited while touring Europe or traveling to and from, the East. Mary and Nina, two young and attractive acquaintances of Jim's family, arrived for a stay on their way to India. A night in the kitchen became notable for my persistent but failed attempt to talk Nina into taking Dormadinas. This strategy was invoked with some amusement in the company of those present.

"Nina, take two. They really make you feel great."

"Feeling great happens without pills, you know."

"Yeah, but it's an experience beyond just feeling great. They make you feel loose."

"Is that how you feel now? Because you might be too loose."

"Yeah, possibly. Well, why don't you try one?"

"It's not a good idea."

"Why don't you take half? A half of a Dormadina. That can't hurt you."

"No, drugs really aren't my thing."

"Just half, Nina. Then you'll have the feeling but not too much."

On it went. Nina passed on the Dormadinas. Despite my attempt to storm the castle walls the women went on to India with their chastity intact.

Electric Field Charger

Shawn was an American bound for Morocco to surf who visited that summer. He instructed me in yoga, a routine that became my morning practice on waking. The exercises, with colorful names like The Cobra, The Electric Field Charger, and The Lion, involved stretching positions that limbered and invigorated one's body. The

routine was beneficial when waking at sunrise on the upstairs balcony overlooking the valley. Shawn's yoga was to serve me well when my quarters later became less expansive. The memory of those mornings imbued with the golden promise of the day was to serve as a beacon of light in a subsequent confining fog.

Jamming With The Europeans

Among the Europeans living on Ibiza was a genteel couple emanating a hip Eurocentric awareness. Dylan was British, tall, intelligent, gracious, and communicative. His speech carried a gentle Welsh lilt. Astrid was bright, slim, blond, and blue-eyed, with a compelling soft German accent. Their friends were a mélange of Europeans. The French displayed an exotic and sensual nature, less burdened by conservative social behavior than had been my experience.

Dylan and Astrid owned one home on Formentera and another close to Ibiza town that had access to electric lines for their music studio. With an invitation for us to join them on a mid-autumn afternoon, we mounted our motorcycles and rode out on the dirt road leading to the highway. A couple of miles before the old town a steep driveway led up to their enclave on the hill. The music room was equipped with a drum set, an electric bass, guitars, amplifiers, a couple of microphones wired into a sound system, along with shakers, tambourines, maracas, and hand drums. For the island this was a high tech arrangement and the first time in years that some of us had the opportunity to go electric.

The standard mode consisted of space jams, long

on rhythm. Ibiza's proximity to Egyptian radio broadcasts exposed us to Arabic music and Oum Kulsoum, the great Egyptian singer. Some of that music percolated through British sounds of the time and we likewise incorporated strains of Arabic scales. My participation lent a cohesive direction to the mostly untrained assemblage. We noticed Astrid's increasingly burning gaze being focused in my direction.

Returning to Santa Ines my motorcycle pierced the dark night like an electric arrow on deserted country roads under glistening starglow. Back in the City of Angels ten million people were funneled onto freeway ramps, backed up bumper to humping bumper. We had not known of this island in the Mediterranean Sea or of this enhanced existence. No indication was present that we would not go on like this forever.

An American Event

As summer's long light-filled embrace acquiesced to autumn's cool grasp a healthy balance had resurrected an inner calm and confidence within me. The Thanksgiving feast approached, an American dining motif enjoyed by Europeans with American acquaintances. Jim negotiated a turkey at a nearby farm. Responsibility for making two apple and two pumpkin pies fell to me. Baking and turkey roasting were done in the stone oven outside the kitchen door. Astrid and Dylan would impart continental chic to our guest list.

The feast was prepared. Guests arrived. Astrid turned up alone in her jeep.

"Dylan's not with her. You know what that

means," Jim commented. Before dinner we passed the hash pipe and swallowed Dormadinas that tingled the fingertips. We made our way to the kitchen table where Jim's remarks slurred to a halt mid-scoop as the spoon in his hand embedded in a load of stuffing. With his arm extended he nodded out. The mixture of ground bread and spices did not reach his plate. To our amusement he remained in that position for some time. Astrid's eyes flashed when her gaze met mine.

Up in my room we strummed a couple chords and sang from the heart until late at night. Astrid was the last to leave.

"She likes you," Jim said.

Made You A Pie

A December moon rose to cast silver light on the island. Michael and Anne, Jim's British lover, went with me to San Antonio where an Ibiza band, *Mi Generacion*, was playing in a basement club. We were leaving when Astrid swept down and walked right into us.

"I hoped I'd find you here," Astrid burst out.

"I went to the house to see you but Jim told me you came to San Antonio to hear music. I didn't know where, so I looked for you and now I found you. I made you a pie and left it at the house. Jim ate some and said it was delicious. Why don't you come back to my house? I made two pies and have the other at home."

"Two pies? Cool. Let's go."

Michael and Anne exchanged knowing looks with me as we left. We mounted our motorcycles. Astrid led the way in her orange Volkswagen jeep along the quiet rural route and the curving ascent to her house on the hill.

Astrid lit candles. We sat in the kitchen taking bites of apple pie.

"Why don't you sleep over?" Astrid suggested.

"Dylan has gone to the mainland and left me all alone. Michael, you and Anne can sleep in the guest room."

Astrid fixed her gaze on me.

"You can sleep with me."

Michael and Anne made their way to their room to settle in as best they could, while Astrid put out the house candles. Taking one that was still lit, she led me to her bedroom carrying an orange that she placed on her bedside table then lit more candles and incense.

Astrid stripped away her clothing. Mine was removed quickly. Fine golden hair glimmered on her arms. The hair on her head was so blond it was white. Her toenails were painted a bright red. Astrid was smiling as she peeled the orange.

She plucked a segment of the fruit and placed it in my mouth. Her lips followed. Her mouth engaged mine as she sucked some of the juice. We reached for each other and trembled at our first contact, an embrace with an electric jolt. The distance of cold night melted in her warmth. Our bodies, slim and muscled, pressed together rhythmically. Her mouth was open and wet against mine. In our urgency Astrid raked her fingernails across and into my back, digging in, painfully, but only stimulating me further.

bloom of flower amidst thorn
a flowing stream in arid desert born

At dawn, in a twist of Mediterranean meteorology, white snowflakes fluttered to earth, falling like miniature frozen flower petals released from the benevolent heavens. We observed the unexpected rare snowfall with wonder and a pleasurable afterglow in the joining of body and soul. We lay about, until hunger drove us up and into town. We drank café con leche, ate omelets, and conversed, lingering long until we parted late afternoon.

Back at the house, the liaison was the topic of conversation. My scratched back was displayed like a trophy. Although Astrid was another man's wife affairs of the heart enrich and are not likely extinguished at their beginning. The grill just got smoking so we're not taking the barbecue off until it's burnt. The scratches did hurt, though. Pleasantly.

Winter's Change Covers The Range

Morning mist laid a frosty mantle over the countryside below, lingering, loathe to depart. Dark clouds veiled the island, issuing forth a stinging rain. Cold, biting wind thundered in from the surrounding stormy sea and raced across the land, chilling the stone farmhouse. An air of melancholy loneliness hovered like a never-lifting fog.

We lacked insulating clothing. For added warmth a sweater of Ibiza wool over layers of cotton shirts helped. Staying warm in the house required being by the kitchen fireplace or getting under covers in bed to read by candlelight.

Jim had weekly lessons in town with his flamenco teacher and he was learning my American fingerpicking patterns Reverend Gary Davis style. Gary developed an intricate contrapuntal gospel and ragtime guitar style in the Piedmont region of South Carolina. He recorded for the American Recording Company during the 1930s then left the south and migrated to New York to become a Harlem street singer and preacher. Gary was rediscovered during the folk era of the early Sixties. We met at the Ash Grove, a music venue in Los Angeles. Gary was blind. Day and night were one and the same. While staying with me we often stayed up all night as he showed me his guitar technique.

Jim often recounted stories of traveling in India and trekking in the foothills of the Himalayas. The East was the foremost pilgrimage site of the hip culture. Nearly everyone around me had traveled to the East. That experience had thus far eluded me but seemed relevant as a future possibility.

The Port

Ibiza town's port accommodated nautical arrivals, dockings, and departures. In contrast to our country solitude being in town provided some opportunity for social interaction and people gazing. The farmhouse was on the northern end of the island, near the small pueblo of Santa Ines, consisting of a church, two bars, and a small grocery store. Town was twenty kilometers of a winding road away. We usually rode our motorcycles but occasionally hopped the twice-daily bus. We could shop in the markets, eat in a bodega, and experience as much of an urban environment as was available.

Michael confided that on occasion when he was in

town he would go to the dock when the last boat for Barcelona had departed in an attempt to offer stranded women who had missed the boat a place to stay the night, a ploy that occasionally produced results.

One of the treats in the old town was the *lecheria*, the milk store, where an ancient woman clad in black layers and straw hat would croak,

"Que quiere usted?"

We ordered a couple of yogurts for three cents each. The woman had long grey chin hairs, a source of continual fascination for me.

Songwriting royalties, in the form of money orders, arrived for me from America and were cashed in the bank. Bars were places to drink coffee or beer and order some of the little *tapas*, dishes of squid, liver, or meatballs, that are popular in Spain, for two cents a plate.

The open-air market in the town center sold vegetables, the one health food store had brown rice, and the spice store had sesame seeds. *Principe* cookies, with a chocolate outer layer, were a popular sweet item for hoarding at home. Enough groceries to fill a basket could be balanced back to the house on a motorcycle. Though not strictly vegetarians, junk food was not a part of our diet. Brown rice and vegetables were staples. Ground sesame seeds added flavor. We had cheese on occasion and salad from the garden. We kept chickens for eggs and an occasional dinner.

Full Moon Lover

Music events were still happening at Astrid's house but it felt inappropriate for me to attend now due to concern of confrontation by her husband. There were no telephones in the countryside. We hadn't spoken or seen each other since our first night together. When the January full moon arrived so did Astrid. She and Dylan were involved in extramarital relationships. He was with a young woman he fancied while Astrid sought some measure of comfort with me. Retaining a state of monogamy for married couples was an increasing challenge with so much sexual freedom in this sensuous, open, and exploratory time.

Astrid stayed with me during the few days of the full moon, surrendering to the newly discovered passion between us. Then she, like moonlight, waned and departed, returning to her house in Formentera, leaving in the aftermath of her presence a warmth that sustained me in the chill of Northern Hemisphere's less direct sunlight.

Matanza

Chickens were kept in an enclosure behind the house for eggs and occasional dinner. Killing them was a skill acquired by necessity. My technique was to swallow a couple of Dormadinas half an hour ahead of the moment, then proceed to the coop to select a bird. Once captured and held by the legs, one could step on the bird's neck, and pull its head off. The fowl was suspended upside down from a clothesline to bleed dry, then stripped of feathers and gutted.

The birds provided the only source of meat apart from the occasional tapas in bars, or *sobresada*, sausage made from pork and spice. Each farmhouse made their own sobresada, requiring a pig, a *matadero*, butcher, and a crew for a day of labor for the *matanza*, the killing and processing of the edible parts of the pig. It was time for our house to do our matanza.

Vicente de Plana, a farmer who was to serve as our matadero, arrived in high spirits on the designated morning with two other farmers and their wives to facilitate the labor. To inaugurate the procedure the Ibicencans drank shots of cognac before declaring themselves ready for the task. The pig had been carted to the house and was brought to the yard with squealing resistance. The farmers held it firmly. With one smooth and practiced gesture Vicente plunged his long knife into one side of the animal's throat, pulled across to the other side, and withdrew the blade. The mortally wounded creature bled out the same way as a chicken, but with more blood.

The deceased pig's wiry hairs were burned away with a blowtorch, and the body scrubbed clean and dismembered. Vicente and his cohorts fueled their spirits with shots of cognac during the arduous procedure. Trying to keep up with their intake was the undoing of the less experienced.

All the raw meat excluding a piece to roast was ground together with peppery red spices then stuffed into previously prepared sausage casing of pig intestines. The process occupied the bulk of the morning and continued into afternoon. For storage the uncooked sobresada is suspended from the wooden beams of kitchen ceilings beside bunches of garlic. Insulated from contact with air by the sausage casing, the meat keeps for long periods until cooked. The matadero's payment was a portion of sobresada.

At labor's end we dined on the roast along with

potatoes, salad, and red wine. Jim's girlfriend, Anne, garnered curious attention when she refused to join everyone at the table but sat removed from the group and ate with her fingers from a frying pan on the floor while slurring her speech from the influence of Dormadinas. Apart from overdoing the Ds, which we all did on occasion, Anne was a kind soul who said a prayer for each clove of garlic she planted in the garden.

Comet Kahoutek

An advantage of residing on an island is the enhanced view of celestial events in the night sky. We enthusiastically anticipated the scheduled arrival of Comet Kahoutek in January, touted as the comet of the century, predicted to be visible even in daylight, but the expected view of a fireball filling the daytime sky fizzled. The comet's faint light and fuzzy tail appeared low on the southern horizon for only two nights then was gone, not to reappear for another 75,000 years.

Farmers and Hippie Chicks or We Just Want To Look

Local attitude to the influx of longhaired youth was tolerant, but the black-garbed islanders found the sight of colorfully costumed visitors and scantily clad young women to be an eyeful.

Farm people rarely visited the house, so we were surprised one morning by the unexpected appearance at the kitchen door of Lucas, Miguel, and a physically big but mentally deficient man called El Bruto. The three farmers smelled of alcohol. Their presence claimed the pretense of a social call but it was obvious from their nervous manner and roving eyes that the underlying motivation of the visit was to check out our lightly clad and usually braless girlfriends. Like the Three Stooges, the trio stumbled into the kitchen, embarrassed and out of their element, yet determined to see their voyeuristic mission through to its conclusion.

An attempt was made at cordial conversation but their intention was increasingly clear. After a time, having accomplished their goal and seen our diaphanously attired young women, the rustics took their leave to return to rural affairs and their wives, clad head to toe in folds of dark cloth. Hippie chicks caught their eye and wouldn't let go. We couldn't blame them as we had a similar reaction.

The Band

On a frosty winter morning we lingered before a blazing hearth fire, savoring eggs, potatoes with chopped onions, and spicy sausage, all fried with olive oil in a black cast iron pan. We drank cup after cup of steaming hot sweetened coffee. The door between the entrada and the kitchen, closed to retain heat, gave a piercing squeal caused by the weight of the heavy wooden door moving on old iron hinges. Michael's face appeared in the doorway. We hadn't seen him for a month as he was on a visit to California.

Michael raised his eyebrows and lowered them a few times. Having captured our attention he swept forward and made his entrance.

"Michael, you're back," Jim exclaimed.

"Yeah. Hey, check this out."

His right hand gripped the handle of a black rectangular guitar case. He hoisted the case up and onto the table then laid it flat. Accompanying his moves with further facial gesticulation he slid open the latches and lifted the top. On a bed of crushed orange velvet lay a white Fender Telecaster.

"It's for you," Michael exclaimed, looking in my direction.

"That's not all, there's more."

He returned to the main room and reappeared with another matching but larger case that he placed on the table beside the Telecaster. Inside, on the same crushed orange velvet, lay a companion white Fender bass guitar.

"Whoa, Michael, far out, " Jim said.

"What are you going to do with this?"

"We're going to make a band," Michael said.

"He's too good of a musician not to have a good instrument," he said, glancing at me.

"The guitars are from Music City in San Francisco, and a set of drums and amplifiers for the guitar and bass will be arriving from a music store in Barcelona. And, to power it, we're getting a generator. The drums are for me, and you can be the bass player, Jim."

"But Michael," Jim pointed out, "you don't know how to play drums."

"That's OK," Michael affirmed.

"We can learn. We have our teacher right here."

Music School

As the equipment arrived it was arranged in the entrada. A Cry Baby wah-wah pedal and a Fuzz Tone stomp box were included for the guitar. Drums were positioned and amplifiers were plugged into an electrical junction box, ready to be powered by the Honda gasoline generator on the porch.

When all was ready Michael gave a tug on the starter cord. The generator fired into action. The lights on the amplifiers glowed red. It worked. We were twanging, beating, slapping, and shredding for the rest of the day. But there was a problem. These cats couldn't play. After the initial surge of new enthusiasm the making of music was elusive. Michael had never coordinated a drum set and Jim had no real interest in becoming a rock and roller.

During our fledgling attempts at band creation Ron's brother Joaquin arrived on the island with his Peugeot van that he had driven from Europe to Afghanistan and back. Joaquin had guitar experience and became intrigued enough to try playing bass. He liked the process and developed a determination to be a part of the group. With his van we had the capability to transport ourselves. Performances were still around the corner but in our sights.

Michael got into the physicality of drumming. Stanley and his girlfriend Carolyn were acquaintances who lived on Formentera. They were enthused when they arrived to visit. Stanley broke out his harmonica collection and began blowing some blues.

With a need to amplify our voices Stanley and Carolyn went on a shopping trip to Barcelona and returned with two microphones and a sound system that was strong enough to project the vocals and harmonica over the band's volume. His investment secured his place in the band.

The lads had to learn to play their instruments and the songs. My job was to chart the material, then sing and drive the group with rhythm guitar and sparkly solos. The one concession the house had to appliances was a battery powered record player and a small collection of albums from which we began lifting material. *The Thrill Is Gone*, by B.B. King, *Feel So Bad*, by Little Milton, *Nadine* and *Maybelline*, by Chuck Berry, *Satisfaction*, *Get Back*, and *Oye Como Va?* were some of the songs. The work proceeded on a daily basis, both individually and together. We developed, improved, and prepared to take our show on the road, or in this case, down the road

La Luna

The moon was rising, round, orange, and glowing from a bed of purple twilight. Astrid's jeep pulled to a stop under the carob tree in front of the house. Smiling, she caught my gaze, walked up, and kissed me. Astrid had a svelte build, Nordic facial features with high cheekbones, blonde hair and tan skin. With a personality suggesting sly collusion mixed with an attitude of good humor Astrid projected an aura of self-realization and liberation. She conversed easily with a gentle sibilance in her German accent that lent a characteristically compelling and engaging quality to her English. We had two or three days and nights of the full moon to share our developing bond intensified by the bright silver light before my lunar lover departed and returned to her houses, her child, and her husband.

Mixing Spoon

Jim's farmhouse was a magnet for friends from America and Europe, a type of caravanserai where acquaintances passed to experience the island and exchange stories about where they had been and would be bound.

My former traveling companion Skip appeared at the house. He was the worse for his world wanderings, having fallen steadily over the precipice into an addict's life. With him he brought bottles of Ipecopan, an over the counter cough syrup containing a small amount of opium. To experience the effect of the opium by injection, his preferred method of ingestion, the sweet, thick, sticky liquid had to be reduced by boiling down from a bottle full to a teaspoon. Cooking was accomplished in a large soup ladle Skip carried for this purpose. His debilitated state left him little reserve of intellect to conduct stimulating social discourse. After a short disoriented visit he departed, not to be seen again for some years, when his condition was not dissimilar. We noticed he left behind his blackened mixing spoon which we washed and when used for soup scooping reminded us of the sad state to which people fall who surrender to odious activity.

Un Petit Corral Pour Moi

It was not uncommon for wayward wanderers with withered means to request hospitality. A notoriously undesirable destitute French ragamuffin and his wife turned up to plead for even the meager accommodation of an unused animal corral. The unwashed man clothed in tattered raiment repeatedly requested,
"Un petit corral pour moi."
Their skewed logic stressed that an animal enclosure would be little inconvenience since they wanted not a place in the house but only outside in a corral, implying that their argument was reasonable and might be more readily granted. They were flatly refused. Eventually the disheartened couple departed. For some time after Jim would intone with exaggerated French accent,
"Un petit corral pour moi,"
eliciting derisive laughter among us. Some travelers fell into a vagabond lifestyle devoid of work and wage,

becoming impoverished and stranded in foreign lands.
"A little corral for me."

Astrid's Daughter

Our planet orbited its solar center and began a return to a position of enhanced daylight in the Northern Hemisphere. Spring blossoms released from winter's chill grasp burst from branches on the omnipresent almond trees to blanket the countryside with their characteristic white flowers from which is derived Ibiza's epithet, *La Isla Blanca*, The White Island.

The moon's waxing reached fullness. Astrid returned, and for the first time brought Uli, her tow-headed daughter of four years. A child was a new experience. Our nocturnal intimacy was restrained to avoid disturbing the girl sleeping in the little bed we arranged for her. Astrid's growing presence made separation increasingly difficult for me, but, as always, after the full moon passed so did Astrid, this time along with her petite princess.

A Music Box

When the tilt of Earth's axis became perpendicular to the sun's rays at the Vernal Equinox, the impending tourist season approached. Among the visitors that year, my mother came to Ibiza on her first trip to Europe. Five years had passed since our last meeting and Mom was pleased to reunite and to experience the house and the island.

Astrid arranged a driving tour of the island. On a narrow road her car slowed to a stop behind a farmer inching along on his horse-drawn cart. We felt a rear impact as our vehicle lifted and surged forward from a car that slammed into us while quickly braking in an unsuccessful attempt to avoid a collision. The chain reaction pushed our car almost into the cart ahead but stopped before impact. The farmer didn't even notice or turn around, but continued at a slow pace. The hit dented Astrid's rear bumper, but no injuries were sustained.

After Ibiza, Mom was going on to Paris. We traveled together by boat to Alicante, on the mainland, and took a bus through the mountains to Granada in Andalusia. We checked into the luxurious Washington Irving Hotel next to the Alhambra palace, a major tourist attraction with the country's most significant Islamic architecture.

Pharmacies in Ibiza had stopped selling Dormadinas, due to their overuse, but in Granada, away from the freak culture of Ibiza, the pills were still available. Mom was enlisted to buy small quantities from various pharmacies until we accumulated a supply.

The town's souvenir shops sell black lacquered music boxes that play the song *Granada* when opened. Acquiring one of these, the Dormadinas were dumped in and on my return to Ibiza were presented to Jim. He was amused and pleased with the aesthetically inebriating gift. Everyone was hungry for the hypnotics.

Ruff &The Ryders

Our nascent group of intrepid musicians pressed

on with determination to become a functioning band. We kept to a daily rehearsal schedule but our full force electric assault was disrupting the tranquility of the house. Michael made inquiries and was able to obtain rehearsal space in the basement of the pueblo's bar where a generator provided electricity for a few hours each night.

We were starting to sound like something. Michael's boom, chick, boom-boom, chick drumming was getting steadier and he could insert fills to break the repetition of the pattern. With steady determination and practice Joaquin transferred his guitar knowledge to the bass. Stanley laid some wailing harmonica in there. Once we transferred our rehearsals to the bar local kids crowded in to cheer us on. We became the talk of the pueblo. The locals dubbed me *El Musico*, and referred to me by that term in conversation. We named ourselves Ruff & The Ryders. We were rough but ready to ride.

According to civic code, in order for us to be employed we were required to have at least one Spanish citizen in the ensemble. Michael recruited a young Ibicencan singer/guitarist for this purpose. Damian was sufficiently skilled to provide an alternate vocal and guitar counterpoint to my front position. We became a quintet. Fulfilling the citizenship work requirement, we began a search in San Antonio where hotels catered to the spring and summer tourist season. Before we could catch our shadow we auditioned successfully and began booking weekend shows.

European visitors came to the island for the warm climate and relief from their desk chains back home. During the day they basked on the white sand beaches by the blue water in anticipation of nighttime boogaloo abandon on the dance floor, fueled by weed, wine, and pharmaceutical products. We were on a similar wavelength, minus the alcohol, except we didn't have to go back to our chains in two weeks.

We carted amplifiers, guitars, speakers and ourselves in the van, headed down the dirt road to the paved one, passed the hash pipe around, got to the hotel to load in, passed the pipe again, and performed for dancing guests. More than a few women were sufficiently moved to desire further contact after hours back in our tranquil country quarters away from town. We were a working band and, as a bonus, a chick magnet.

By the height of the summer season, the band was performing in hotels, clubs, parties, and community events. Michael McKuen, a singer and fiery guitar player, arrived on the island with a vintage tweed Fender amplifier and a weathered Fender Stratocaster, through which he channeled the sound and spirit of Jimi Hendrix. Assembling musicians for his band, Mike recruited me to play bass. Rehearsals at his house usually included a bevy of bare breasted blonde women passing hash pipes and inspiring us with their feminine presence.

High And Low

Going from milkshakes to marijuana, boozing in bars never was a part of my behavior. We were hash heads, a quick hit and split. Hashish was used as a stimulating sacrament that enhanced the improvisatory aspect of creating music and didn't impair motor skills. On one occasion the band dined at a restaurant in San Antonio prior to a show. Wine was ordered with encouragement for me to drink. By show time the effect rendered me sloppy, imprecise, and incapable of singing and playing properly. The band carried on and we made it through the night but alcohol and performance are a negative combustible mixture. The first rule of a working musician is never drink on the job even if it's offered.

Between Seduction And The Altar

In my mind, Astrid was the woman for me. The growing possibilities of a relationship to a married woman were questionable from the start, but obscured by the magnetic romanticism of our full moon encounters.

> *the silent pale light*
> *of earth's silver satellite*
> *seduced our vision*
> *when she arrived*
> *on her moonlit mission*

A larger issue intruded. Astrid was used to a high quality of life, with a husband, a child, two houses and steady income. Beyond the thrill of a full moon pleasurable encounter would this woman consider a long-term relationship with an under financed performer? The question took shape in my mind as my attachment grew. But the answer never came. And that was the answer.

Morning

Warm days and long light inspired me to relinquish the confinement of my room for the east-facing balcony overlooking the valley. Dawn's golden hue imbued my eyes with light as the glimmering orb of the sun inched upward and radiance claimed nocturnal shadows. Shawn's waking yoga exercises were followed by breakfast of granola, homemade yogurt, peaches, and lemon juice. Lemons contain vitamin C that requires calcium found in yogurt to be absorbed, while yogurt is cultured and doesn't curdle in combination with lemon juice, as does milk.

Jim departed that summer to travel through France, leaving the house in my care. His realistic insight might have altered the course of subsequent events had he been available for counsel.

Free Love

The sexual revolution of the Sixties released inhibition and allowed new expression while the advent of birth control pills freed women from fear of unwanted

pregnancy. If places were to be categorized as centers of making love, not war, Ibiza was at the head of the line. Warm climate, naked swimming, no electricity, and no distracting television contributed to an environment in which amusement, conversation, entertainment, and pleasure was focused on our interaction. We didn't watch events on a screen. We were events.

Lisa

As summer arrived travelers visited with increasing frequency. Lisa was a young attractive American college student with long brown flowing locks and ears decorated with silver hoop earrings. With the band in full swing the magnetism of cruising in with us was compelling after some days in the quiet country. Lisa joined us in our nocturnal entertainments.

At the conclusion of a night of dancing in town Lisa sat talking with me in the kitchen by candlelight. Our eyes locked and speech drifted away until in silence we rose together and proceeded leisurely up the stairway to my room, kissing and feeling the thrill of contact. We surrendered to the rush of pleasure, savoring the sensation of bare skin once our clothing had fallen away.

Although the initial physical contact was pleasurable our connection was short lived. My relationship with Astrid chilled the affair. Lisa took up residence on another part of the island.

Porsche

Porsche arrived from Germany on vacation from her employment as a secretary. Her sister was an Ibiza resident of Jim's acquaintance. He invited Porsche to stay in one of the bedrooms before his departure for France. A buxom redheaded young woman, Porsche captured our attention on a day designated to work in Michael's garden. Porsche dressed for the occasion in a bikini. While Porsche got some rays we got an eyeful of female pulchritude, engendering a conversation regarding with whom Porsche might sleep. Michael suggested that he be the recipient of her attention. My part was to claim that,

"If anyone should have her it should be me." This chauvinist diatribe occurred within Porsche's

hearing but seemed to amuse rather than offend.

Porsche, too, accompanied us to town for another of our evenings of merriment. Back at the house at night, we were alone and engaged in conversation until the moment arrived.

"You can sleep in your room or you can sleep with me."

With that compelling logic we proceeded upstairs together. We removed our clothing and Porsche went from a standing position to slowly lowering herself on my body, which was kneeling and upright, as was my erect penis, which slipped into her vagina like the oft described warm knife cutting through butter.

Our relations continued for a time until Astrid arrived on her full moon mission and dulled Porsche's enthusiasm. Astrid learned of my dalliances but only smiled knowingly and expressed no concern about the situation.

Far from being angry or jealous, my liaisons with other women had the effect of pleasing Astrid. The ability to attract women appeared to gain respect for me. Although it was never specifically articulated, Astrid implied that she too had other lovers, women as well as men.

Carolyn Returns To America

Stanley's girlfriend Carolyn was a decade or so younger than the rest of us and less sagacious in matters of a discreet nature. After being in Formentera for some years and having made hashish runs to the East, Carolyn attempted to bring contraband into the United States on a flight to Alaska, where she previously resided. The plan was thwarted when her stash was discovered at customs. During interrogation, and in fear of a prison sentence, Carolyn likely revealed information regarding activities of her island acquaintances. Some of our visitors had been active on the Hashish Trail between Europe and the East. Police in Ibiza were increasingly inquisitive about the proliferating influx of longhaired foreigners who lived without apparent means of support. We were to learn some of these facts when cops dropped her name during a search of the house later that summer.

Carolyn was arrested, tried, convicted of possession of illegal substances, and sentenced to a term at the federal prison at Terminal Island, Los Angeles.

With Stanley's squeeze gone and his involvement in the band requiring more time in Ibiza, he abandoned his long residence on the neighboring island for a small rental farmhouse a kilometer from us where he was to reside for a few months before leaving Ibiza altogether for India and Nepal.

Father Arrives And Police Visit

Mother was born in 1917, in Detroit, Michigan. Her parents, Samuel and Nettie, were from Galicia, in Poland. That region is known for producing Klezmer musicians. Mom was on the way to becoming a professional singer in her youth. She even had her own radio show, but her father stopped her budding career when she was seventeen. He cut her short just when she blossomed. Not many people support music as a career choice.

My father was born in 1915, in Vurot, a Croatian village. A soldier raped his mother when she was fifteen. That union produced my father. Nanny, our name for my grandmother, came to America when Dad was five, leaving him in her brother's care in the village. Because Nanny wasn't married, the villagers mocked and taunted the young boy, calling him *fachuk*, bastard, in Croatian. He took to urinating on their porches in revenge. In a metaphoric way this behavior describes my father's edgy character. He was sarcastic much of the time. My grandmother sent for him to come to America when he was thirteen. Dad made the voyage alone on a passenger liner, passing Lady Liberty in New York Harbor. He disembarked at Ellis Island.

In 1939, with war clouds gathering in Europe, my father went to Spain to fight in the Spanish Civil War. He joined the Abraham Lincoln Brigade, a group of American volunteers who were part of the resistance to the military revolution led by General Francisco Franco against the democratically elected government of Spain. Franco was supported by the kill creep Hitler, leader of the Nazi Party and Chancellor of Germany, and by Mussolini, leader of the National Fascist Party and Prime Minister of Italy. My father survived the war and returned to the United States, where he met and married my mother in my birthplace, Detroit, Michigan.

In 1949 we moved to Los Angeles. After another decade together my parents divorced. Dad remarried and had two more sons. He commuted an hour each way to and from Anaheim, in primarily Republican Orange County, to his job as a designer for the Kwikset Lock Company, ironically placing him, a leftist leaning man, in a company and climate of conservative and politically right wing employees.

Intrigued by reports of my island life, my father came to Ibiza on his way to visit an acquaintance in Switzerland. He planned to complete his sojourn by visiting his former Croatian village.

Michael volunteered to drive me to the airport to meet my father. Ten minutes after our return to the house, a contingent of police arrived. Spanish authorities didn't require a warrant to go through a residence. The leader of the group, an older man with grey hair, asked me,

"Do you know an American woman named Carolyn?"

"Yes."

He extended his arms, making a sign of wrists crossed. Handcuffs. He studied my reaction.

"She's very young."

"Yes, she's young," he concluded. The cops searched the house in a cursory fashion, seemingly content to observe the interior and its inhabitants. They thanked me and departed. Although cordial, their presence was alarming and the first time police had visited.

Obviously, Carolyn had given up some information. No criminal activity was taking place, beyond hash smoking, and nothing incriminating was found during their search.

Could these cops know that Dad was a veteran of their Civil War in the 1930's and fought against Franco, the present head of state? Were they seeking retribution? Did they think he was a drug courier? The synchronicity of the police arrival just as my father landed was not to be overlooked. We were in their crosshairs, a fact that we would have been wise to consider more carefully in light of events to come.

A day later a neat little pyramid of green hashish in Jim's room caught my eye, out in the open on a table next to the bed. Jim must have prepared it to smoke and forgotten about it. Although the room had been searched the hashish had gone unnoticed by the police. Or had it?

Naked Swim

Dad could be abrasive and alcohol exacerbated that behavior. While my father was with us he drank port wine constantly and wisecracked his way through his visit. We took him to Ibiza town, San Antonio, and to our swimming place, *Cala Aubarca*, accompanied by Astrid, Porsche, and two other women.

On occasion we rode our motorcycles through the quiet valley to Cala Aubarca, a wide inlet by the sea with no beach but sheer rock formations that plunged down in a straight wall thirty feet to the bottom of the clear water bay.

Accessing this isolated spot required a six hundred foot climb down that was repeated in reverse at the end of the day, a trek that discouraged tourists. In spite of the old man's presence in his modest swimming trunks, we all stripped naked to swim in the gentle waters of the sheltered summer sea. Dad was blown away by our abandon, as this was his first encounter with nudity. His most repeated comment while with us was,

"They're not going to believe this."

When asked how he liked the island Dad replied, "It's a nice place to live but I wouldn't want to be buried here."

After a few days in our company my father departed for Zurich, Switzerland, followed by a reuniting with his family in his Croatian village. We weren't to communicate for another two years.

Tolerance

My knowledge of female sexuality did not extend to any method on what was necessary for a woman to achieve orgasm. Beyond body-to-body contact and male penetration and fulfillment the reality of vaginal finger stimulation and simultaneous clitoral tongue movement was still unknown to me.

As summer reached her blazing zenith Astrid arrived. While conversing during a quiet moment she described being brought to orgasm by her massage therapist. This confession probably was intended to be a subtle suggestion for me to consider my method to achieve that result. No woman, including Astrid, had informed me that my pleasure might not also be hers. Ours wasn't the only sexual relation for Astrid and other women were a part of my experience. The cocoon surrounding our full moon encounters had built-in lines of weakness that could tear easily from inside. We were young and attractive in a moment of social awakening. Abandonment of old restrictive behavior had given way to an increase of social sexual permissiveness. Tolerance was a necessarily acquired skill.

Himalayas

Three hundred million years ago, *Pangea* was one supercontinent, consisting of the entire landmass of Earth. *Panthalassa* was the single surrounding vast global ocean. Two hundred million years ago, Pangea began to separate into component continents that we know in their current configurations of North and South America, Europe, Africa, India, Asia, Australia, and Antarctica.

The Himalayan Mountain Range formed as a result of a continental collision that began 70 million years ago, when the north-moving Indo-Australian Plate collided with the Eurasian Plate. The Himalayas were produced in the fold between the two plates and are among the youngest mountain ranges on the planet.

The Himalayas lie at the north of the Indian subcontinent and includes the Karakoram, the mountain range spanning the borders between Pakistan, India, and China; the Hindu Kush, that stretches between central Afghanistan and northern Pakistan; and other ranges that extend out from the Pamir Knot, the mountain range that spans Tajikistan, Kyrgyzstan, Afghanistan, Pakistan, and China.

The Himalayan mountain system is the world's highest, and home to the world's highest peaks, including Mount Everest and K2. Aconcagua in the Andes rises 22,841 feet and is the highest peak outside Asia, but the Himalayan system includes over 100 mountains exceeding 23,600 feet.

Some of the world's major river systems arise in the Himalayas, and their combined drainage basin is home to three billion people, half of Earth's population, in eighteen countries. The Himalayas have profoundly shaped the cultures of South Asia. Their peaks are sacred in Hinduism, Buddhism, and Sikhism.

In the foothills of the Himalayan Range, in Afghanistan, Pakistan, Kashmir, and Nepal, lie the planet's major Cannabis growing fields that have produced hashish and opium consumed by people on Earth for thousands of years.

Hashish

Hashish is a sticky, dark-colored resin made from the flower of the female Cannabis indica plant. Cannabis leaves and flowers contain chemicals known as cannabinoids, substances that create the high. Both marijuana and hashish are obtained from the Cannabis plant. Hashish has much more of the chemical THC, (delta 9 tetra hydro cannabinol), than marijuana.

Hashish is produced by rubbing palms and fingers of the hands on Cannabis buds for hours to accumulate resin that is scraped off the hand, then gathered and pressed. Hashish is most often ingested by smoking in a pipe. It can also be eaten. When people use hashish sensations come about. One can feel happy, relaxed, silly, and maybe cloudy. The term high means the effects produce mental stimulation. Being stoned renders a relaxed and observational state. A high can create a stimulation leading to exaggerated imagination and over analysis on simple subjects.

Hashish is stronger than marijuana, and large amounts might induce seeing imaginary colors, patterns, and visions, not actually present. Hallucinations can occur. One can become strange, or scared, as if something bad is going to happen. This state is paranoia.

Hashish and marijuana are not addictive like heroin and cocaine. Hash can be used recreationally and ceased with no reaction but repetition and habit do engender psychological dependence.

Indica grows wild everywhere on the Indian sub-continent. Varieties of the herb are cultivated. Hashish production is a social tradition throughout regions of the Himalayas.

The earliest recorded use of Cannabis dates back 5000 years. Uses are recreation, religious, spiritual rite, and medicinal. Pipes unearthed from William Shakespeare's garden contain Cannabis.

The Hippie Trail

For many centuries in the modern era the Himalayas and the route to them were unknown to Europeans until Marco Polo's thirteenth century travels to Asia. Practical overland travel from Europe to the Himalayas started in the twentieth century when in the 1950s expeditions began to travel east from England in Land Rovers to climb the world's highest peaks and to do scientific studies and surveys of the mountains. These travelers often published stories of their grand journeys, which encouraged others to follow. In addition to the scientific and mountaineering aspects, the exotic places and cultures of the east fascinated Europeans and others who read about them. Air travel was just beginning, but for those seeking adventure, the prospect of an epic overland journey by motorcar was increasingly attractive and affordable. The first established bus service to ply the overland route was The Indiaman British Bus Company in 1957, followed by Swagman Tours which became Asian Greyhound. More bus companies increased transportation to the region in the 1960s.

Western young people began traveling the route in 1967, when Eastern mysticism was gaining interest. The Beatles came to India in 1968, inspiring increasing numbers of young people to hit the road from Europe. Their ranks included Europeans, Americans, Canadians, and traditional backpacking Australians and New Zealanders. They looked for spiritual enlightenment, escape from conventional lifestyle, sought chances for profit in trade, and some just wanted to see the world.

The route went from London, through Europe, to Istanbul, Iran, Afghanistan, Pakistan, Kashmir, India, and Nepal. Because so many young people in the sixties had long hair, the route was often referenced as The Hippie Trail, although longhaired westerners didn't really refer to themselves as hippies. That was more of a media term. They were *freaks*. Because it led to the major hashish producing countries of Afghanistan, Pakistan, and Nepal, the route also came to be called The Hashish Trail.

Taking advantage of the newfound interest in travel east, a booking agency in Amsterdam called The Magic Bus arranged places on independent bus companies. In addition to bus travel, people drove in cars, vans, minibuses, and motorbikes on the five thousand mile journey each way, on rough roads, through scorching deserts and high mountain passes. Some rode the railway to where it ended in Istanbul. From there cheap buses hopped from city to city. Western drivers also gathered passengers from the city's famous Pudding Shop, where rides in independent vehicles could often be arranged. Low-cost rail travel resumed in Pakistan and India. Some even hitchhiked, particularly on the way home, when they ran out of money on their travels.

The Hashish Trail started at Istanbul, the point at which all roads from Europe converged. From here the direct route led straight across Turkey, though some headed south for Lebanon, for centuries the main hashish producer of the Middle East. From Turkey the route continued across Iran, a secular country run by the Shah, and on to Afghanistan, where foreigners were made welcome and where many of the population were hashish smokers themselves. After Afghanistan some would head north toward Chitral in Pakistan, while most continued on to India, where blazing hot summer often motivated travelers up to the cooler regions of Kashmir, and in Northern India Manila was another popular center of marijuana cultivation. In winter most westerners went south for the beaches of Goa, where hashish was available, and in the summer there was also mountainous Nepal, where there were many hashish and opium shops operating legally.

Visas, where required, could be obtained easily at the borders or towns en route. British passport holders did not require a visa to stay in India long-term. In Kathmandu, Nepal, many hashish and opium shops were located on *Jochen Tole*, commonly called Freak Street, including the famous Eden Hashish Center whose advertising slogan was *Let Us Take Higher*. The center operated legally and offered, from apothecary jars on its shelves, varieties of hashish, including Nepalese Temple Balls and Afghani Flying Saucers. *Tolas*, a unit of mass equivalent to 10 grams of sticky black opium, were likewise on sale to provide a soporific slide into the netherworld. For musical ambiance the center's portable low fidelity cassette machine played music by western groups such as Pink Floyd and The Rolling Stones.

In every major stop along the way there were hotels, restaurants and cafes that catered almost exclusively to the pot-smoking westerners, who networked with each other as they wandered east and west.

This influx of longhaired western youth initially was a curiosity to the locals, who were unaccustomed to tourists of any sort. But hospitality was extended, and extra income derived from the process.

The hipsters tended to spend more time interacting with the local population than traditional sightseeing tourists. They had no interest in luxury accommodation, even if they could afford it, which few could, and some would go native after a fashion, particularly in India. Of course, they were still tourists really, although of a different sort, and hedonism was the primary aim.

There were casualties. Staying healthy could be difficult, particularly in wild and unrefined Afghanistan. There was culture shock. Some became severely ill, or ran out of money, and had to be flown home. Others wound up in jail, not a pleasant experience anywhere and particularly tough in a third world country. Some stayed on and found ways to live in India. Most survived, and in telling their stories on their return, inspired others to follow in their footsteps.

Smuggling Scheme

Hashish smoking had been part of our daily routine since we came to the Balearic Islands. On Formentera and Ibiza we were acquainted with people who had earned income by carrying hashish from Afghanistan to Europe packed into suitcases, traveling by air. They were runners, couriers, paid to carry the dope. Stanley made the run numerous times. Some made the trip overland in vans with larger hidden quantities.

There was a man from the islands who went to Pakistan to arrange deals. For an air courier, a two-week trip could bring two thousand dollars, enough to survive on the islands for a year. The organizer made ten times that.

In the absence of gainful employment for foreigners of long residence on Ibiza, many succumbed to the temptation to earn easy money, although with risk, by becoming involved in hashish smuggling. People around me had been doing these runs successfully for years, reinforcing the impression that smuggling dope was a normal activity.

Michael had previously succeeded in one of these ventures from which he derived enough income to enable the purchase of a house for his father. He was in contact with the man in Pakistan.

After nearly five years of travel on an almost nonexistent budget my finances had ground to a near halt. Songwriting royalties had ceased arriving. My Hollywood connections were severed. Expenses were only ten dollars a week for food and motorcycle gas but there was no upward ability. Living in Jim's house rent-free could not go on indefinitely. As summer ended so did our seasonal band work.

When my concerns and vulnerability weighed on me Michael suggested a solution. Fly to Afghanistan and transport twenty pounds of Afghani hashish packed in two suitcases to Copenhagen, a favored European sale site. Michael would organize and finance the operation and earn twenty thousand dollars from the deal. He would pay me two thousand dollars. By engaging me to do the job, Michael planned to minimize his risk while maximizing his gain.

Hungry for income, removed from rational thought process, too long on the trail, with depleting resources, the concept was born of desperation. The dangerous plan, thinly cloaked as adventure, percolated through my thinking and in the absence of a clear alternative we struck the bargain. Going down to the crossroads. A long risk for a fast gain.

Still, numerous doubts and fears wavered my determination. Michael's girlfriend, Janet, was irate at the prospect of my declining the trip that was to bring her and Michael income.

"You've lived for free, off of other people, and you need to be responsible for yourself," she chastised.

Janet had recently made the same hashish run. My misgivings were raised in discussions with acquaintances. They all encouraged me to take the shot. Apparently the flip side of paradise was mass psychosis.

Be My Baby

In September, Astrid arrived for our usual full

moon rendezvous. My attachment to her had grown, so much so that a day after her departure her presence was missed to the point of inspiring me to go to Formentera to ask her to chuck her life and be with me. Her husband was away visiting his lover.

My motorcycle carried me to the port, where the ferry was boarded that deposited me on Formentera.

My arrival surprised Astrid but she was having none of my plan. Instead she invited her girlfriend to share our bed. Reality crept into my dreamy perception of our relationship. Astrid wasn't giving up her marriage, her houses, and her standard of living for me, with empty pockets and no residence of my own, stout heart not withstanding. She didn't take my presumptuousness seriously and, as my alternate plan was in the making, our potential future was put on hold pending the outcome of my risky choice.

Mouse In A Bottle

The juncture of the autumnal equinox brought a shortening of the long waves of luminescent summer light and marked both a diminishing of island visitors and an end to the band's working season. A conclusion had begun, with impending change and a need for individualism, indicating to me that my course had reached a transitional phase.

Stanley departed on a trip to the mainland. He left the key to his house and minimal care of the place in my hands. Astrid joined me there on what was to be our final full moon together.

The little farmhouse had none of the grace and

grandeur of the house on the hill. Lacking a panoramic high view, the place rested in a low valley surrounded by scruffy hills, creating a quality of being below rather than above. As any cat knows, the more vulnerable position below is less preferable.

The undistinguished and inexpensive rental house had an interior that reeked of emptiness and anonymity, lacking the care that had been lavished on the elegant, majestic, and renovated farmhouse that had been my residence.

The thought of the impending journey weighed heavily on my mind like an elephant standing on an egg. My inquiry to Astrid,

"Is this the right thing for me to be doing?"
while hoping for a last minute note of caution, a common sense prohibition, a reprieve from a risky and unfamiliar gamble, was met with only acceptance and vague encouragement.

"Well, see how it goes, and hope for the best."

In an unfamiliar bed in a darkened room, lit inadequately by a few less than lustrous candles, we lay in our last lover's embrace and noticed on the bedside table an empty Coca-Cola bottle that a small mouse had somehow entered and in which that creature was now dead and entombed, encased in a glass sarcophagus that once held twelve ounces of effervescent sweetened beverage with the secret formula known only to its famous manufacturer.

The observation suggested a disconcerting glimmer of what can happen when the plan goes astray and a seeker desirous of achievement becomes a trapped and transformed victim, never more to roam, succumbing to captivity and eventual starvation.

In the light of morning Astrid was gone, leaving me to the unavoidable inevitability of my decision. Departure was fast approaching. No more wiggle room remained that might release me from this bizarre commitment. My freedom began to slip away even as the island still held me in her final embrace before flight would lift me beyond her tranquil clasp to a risky unknown. The same exploratory momentum that brought me today was in resurrected motion revolving toward tomorrow.

The End

In October a barber removed my decade-long locks, causing my neck and shoulders to feel an unfamiliar chilled nakedness. Michael drove me to the airport on my motorcycle and handed me two thousand dollars for expenses and to pay the man at the other end. He reviewed the plan. The cheery innocence he displayed when greeting me a year ago was replaced by a nervous and worried countenance. Then he started the motorcycle, revved the engine, eased the transmission into first gear, released the clutch, and with a roar and a rumble was gone from my vision. Ahead lay Barcelona and wild, primitive, unconquered Afghanistan.

Three

Tragedy

Passport

Barcelona, the capital of the autonomous region of Catalonia and the largest metropolis on the Mediterranean Sea, was named after the Carthaginian general Hamical Barca who founded the city in the third century BC. Barca's well known son Hannibal, one of the greatest military strategists in history, marched an army that included elephants from Spain over the Pyrenees and the Alps into Italy, which he conquered and occupied for fifteen years before his voluntary exile to Bithynia in Asia Minor, eventual betrayal to Rome, and suicide by poisoning.

Barcelona and Los Angeles share similar geographic features. Both cities are massive bowls by the sea ringed by mountains. On hot days the heat and carbon monoxide of automobile and factory exhaust blankets the metropolis with foul smelling pollution. The cities become giant pressure cookers that swelter its residents without relief. So it was on my arrival, as waves of heat seemed to shimmer in the sultry air.

In order to cross borders carrying contraband past government officials a new passport was needed from the American Consulate to replace the old photo with giveaway long hair.

Smuggler attire required conservative clothing. A lightweight grey suit along with shirt, shoes, and a belt comprised my new, sedate costume.

At a travel agency my ten-day air itinerary was

arranged. Barcelona to Rome, an Alitalia flight to Kabul, Afghanistan, followed by a flight from Karachi, Pakistan back to Rome, and a transfer to Barcelona. In between flights road and rail would include a taxi from Kabul through the Khyber Pass to Peshawar, Pakistan, and a train from Peshawar to Karachi. Once arrived in Barcelona the schedule included a train to Copenhagen and delivery of the suitcases.

The agent looked at me quizzically.

"We got one. Definitely a drug smuggler. Get ready to bust him."

But nothing. The agent took my money and gave me the tickets without incident.

Kabul

After a one-day stopover in Rome, two Dormadinas got me slightly numb, masking my nervousness on the plane. Kabul is a landlocked city thousands of years old on the ancient trade route of The Silk Road. Numerous empires have controlled this enclave that the ancient Rigveda texts of Hinduism refer to as the ideal city, a vision of paradise set in the mountains, but to a newly arriving twentieth century eye the paradise part was not apparent.

Viewed from above, Afghanistan appeared a vast emptiness between towering peaks. Kabul's small, funky airport was a departure from the architectural expanses of the urbane metropolis. After clearing customs, a taxi took me to the Intercontinental Hotel, on a hill overlooking the city. From the hotel to the bazaar by the river was a distance of two miles. With my taxi through the Khyber

Pass the following day there was time enough to walk. Afghani men were dressed in loose white cotton trousers with flowing shirts and dark vests. Women were swathed head to foot in burkas. Many of the people are big, and looked fierce. A turbaned merchant sold me yards of cotton cloth in a variety of colors and floral patterns intended to pad my contraband suitcases.

A performance at the hotel of Arabic music with pop rock instrumentation concluded my brief sojourn in Afghanistan. Two thousand years ago Aristotle's student Alexander the Great conquered the entire Persian Empire on his quest to reach the ends of the world, taking the road to the plains of India where tomorrow we would drive at dawn to Pakistan.

Torkham Khyber

In the morning my taxi arrived helmed by a talkative English-speaking driver. We departed Kabul for our journey through *Torkham Khyber*, the Khyber Pass, a thirty-three mile passage through the Hindu Kush Mountains that connects the northern frontier of Pakistan with Afghanistan. Khyber has long been a trade route and a strategic military location between central and south Asia.

On a flat stretch of empty highway we overtook a European bicyclist.

"He is going from France to India. Yesterday he was thirty miles back," the driver relayed.

Massive stone forts with only one entrance and no windows stand along the route. Men were armed with rifles and bulleted gun belts worn over their shoulders.

Old American automobiles were filled inside and out, with people sitting on the fenders, the hood, and the roofs of cars. Even a donkey stood atop a passing taxi.

Two soldiers with rifles guarded a bedraggled prisoner in rags at the Pakistan border. Shackled at his feet, the wild-eyed fearful man held the corner of his turban cloth in his teeth. He was being led at the end of a chain. Was he suffering the fate of smugglers?

Apprehension, rising anxiety, and fear of potential harmful consequence intruded on me.

Peshawar Hotel

We descended into the obscure greyness of Peshawar, the oldest living city in Pakistan, near the Afghan border. This ancient abode had been controlled by Buddhist Kushans of central Asia, annexed by the Arab Empire, settled by Mughals when Columbus sailed to the New World, administered by Durranis, who founded the modern state of Afghanistan, annexed by the Sikhs, who destroyed the mosques and gardens, and controlled for one hundred years by the British. Peshawar became part of newly created Pakistan in 1947. At first view the city seemed populated with poor bedraggled looking colorless forms in a gathering twilight gloom, made yet darker by the smoke of charcoal braziers being fired up to break the daytime fast of Ramadan.

My destination was The Khyber Hotel, a three-story structure on a busy street jammed with old automobiles, men in baggy pants, and garishly decorated three-wheeled vehicles that serve as taxis. We arrived and the driver accepted the fare. He departed, leaving me on my own to navigate this uncharted environ.

The hotel's entrance led to a center courtyard. A stairway ascended two more levels. In the second floor office a tall rotund man with a flowing grey mustache and grey beard stubble stood behind a counter. He was dressed in a white shirt that plunged below his knees, a black vest, and loose trousers of the same material as the shirt, with a black skull cap perched on the back of his head.

"Hello. Ahmet is expecting me."

"Welcome, welcome.'"

A shorter man in a similar costume sat behind the counter at a small table drinking from a glass containing green leaves.

"You are to be wanting a room."

"Yes. A room will be good."

"This is Omar."

Omar's brown eyes gazed in my direction. His pomaded hair glistened and a dark mustache enhanced gleaming white teeth.

"I am here to help you. Anything you need, come to me. Food, drink, money changing, come to me."

"OK."

"You are American?"

"Yes."

"Very good, I'll take you to your room, and we see Ahmet."

He escorted me down the stairs to the ground floor where we entered a narrow, dark cubicle with a small bed. A thin grey mattress with black stripes was rolled and resting on rope lattice attached to a wooden frame. White sheets, a blanket, and a pillow lay beside the mattress.

"Nice?"

"It's all right."

"It is for you. We see Ahmet now," he said, then turned and led the way back up the stairs to the third floor. At a corner room Omar knocked on a door that opened, revealing a dark-skinned man with long black hair and beard.

"The American."

"Oh, from Ibiza. I'm Ahmet. This is my wife, Francesca."

Sitting on the bed, a pregnant European woman with bright red hair smiled.

"Do you want to smoke something?"

"No, thank you."

After a few preliminary words, Ahmet got right to the affair at hand.

"Two suitcases are being prepared for you. Ten pounds of Afghani hash are in each one, hidden in the top. When you go through customs open and close the suitcases yourself. If customs does it, they'll feel the weight and you'll be busted. A taxi driver will come for you. He'll take you to get the stuff, then to the train station for Karachi. Buy your ticket ahead of time. You have the money?"

Ahmet accepted the cash.

"We're going to dinner. Come with us."

Ahmet, Francesca, Omar, and a couple of their acquaintances gathered down on the street with me. Ahmet engaged two of the little golf cart taxis. We clambered aboard and were driven to a crowded restaurant where we dined on lamb, rice, and bread, among a mostly male clientele. Women were black shapes covered head to foot. Ahmet's wife didn't cover her head. Noticeably pregnant, she had problems with her flaming red, long hair. Peshawar merchants abused her rudely.

"Whore, fuck off," they shouted. The woman answered in kind with insults of her own at these misogynist maltreaters of females. We were in *Ramadan*, the ninth month of the Moslem calendar when people abstain from food and drink during the day for the entire month. Beginning at evening they can eat and drink until sunrise. At sundown grey smoke clouded the streets as fasters stoked the cooking fires. During the day, hungry and dry, people became irritable and short tempered as their tension increased.

Moslem justice can be administered spontaneously. An angry crowd beat a man discovered to have been drinking during the daytime fast. On one of our trips in a golf cart taxi a German acquaintance of Ahmet's became involved in a dispute with the driver. The enraged German took hold of the taxi and attempted to overturn it but was restrained by onlookers. Tempers flared readily and consequences could be violent. Arguments readily erupted.

Residents of the hotel included a number of Europeans who suffered the ennui and debilitating effects of opium addiction. They were ensnared in the squalid condition their addiction engendered, dependent on the easy supply of the drug at the opium store across the street, where bricks of the black tar resin were legally sold. These lost travelers lay about the hotel, stoned and malnourished, with yellowed teeth and wan countenance, chain-smoking hash and tobacco while displaying a fashion style of dilapidated ragamuffin patchwork,

Omar was quick in acquiring commodities of

necessity, from fresh pomegranate juice to money changing. We attended a Pakistani film depicting a love story but devoid of kissing or touching between the male and female protagonists. Physical intimacy in cinema was forbidden. Instead, the black and white movie was replete with fighting, brutal killing; heads bashed in with rocks, and repetitive gory bloodletting. That was permitted. The hero was required to conquer insurmountable obstacles in the form of evil gun holding and sword toting forces to achieve the love of his maiden while leaving a bloody swath in his wake.

Omar eyed and commented on my grey sweater with buttons of silver American dimes fashioned during my time as a silversmith making jewelry of Native American design. The item of decorative clothing was presented to him in gratitude for his facilitations during my stay at the Khyber Hotel.

On the last morning before departure, a boy, maybe fourteen, appeared at the door of my room.

"Are you American? Please, I want to see you naked."

"Ain't happening, dude, and you need to leave, now."

"Please, I want to see you naked."

"Get out of here, you idiot."

Judging from this entreaty, young men in these environs appeared desperate and willing to indulge in homosexual behavior in the apparent absence of potential with the local black swathed females. The obnoxious kid was quickly dispatched.

Later in the day Ahmet came down to my dank quarters to inform me that the moment had arrived.

"Tonight the driver will be here to take you to the

house where the cases will be ready, then to the train station. Remember. You open the cases at customs."

The Run Begins

Nightfall arrived and with it my driver. We departed the hotel in his three-wheeler taxi and drove through the shadowy town to a residence where we entered a high-ceilinged workshop. A group of mustached men welcomed me. One led me to a workbench where two blue suitcases rested. He instructed me to open a case. Raising the top felt noticeably heavier than one would expect from a usually light and practically weightless part of a suitcase. Ten pounds of Afghani hashish was sealed into the case top, behind the lining. When the case was fully extended the top dropped like a rock and resounded with a thud. The smell of glue was noticeable. My few articles of clothing along with the fabric purchased in Kabul's bazaar were put in the suitcases, and they were closed in readiness.

"At customs, open and close the suitcases yourself. You understand? Now we eat. Please sit with us."

We gathered on a rug and sat cross-legged in a circle around a cloth on which was placed a large communal bowl containing rice and lamb. Stacks of flat, round breads were beside the bowl. With the bread we scooped the rice and lamb. An incongruous orange surfboard caught my eye, propped upright in a corner, far from any ocean with waves. Once we had dined, my driver rose, indicating our time for departure. He hoisted a suitcase in each hand and we walked from the house to the taxi. We made our way again through quiet streets to the Peshawar station where the train to Karachi was ready for departure. The driver carried the suitcases onboard to my reserved sleeping compartment where two Pakistani men were already sitting ready for the journey.

"Salaam," he said, then, with a last conspiratorial glance, he turned and was gone.

A few minutes passed and an official entered the compartment.

"Good evening, sir. May you present your passport?" He looked directly at me. His eyes studied the document, then looked back at me. He returned the passport. Seeing my suitcases resting on the floor, he lifted first one, then the other. Bouncing them in his hand he smiled and nodded knowingly. My heart rate increased as the fear mounted.

He did no more and returned the cases to the floor.

"Thanking you sir, good-bye." he exclaimed, then turned and left the compartment.

The train could not leave fast enough for my taste, but the whistle sounded, we felt a jolt, and were underway for the overnight run to Pakistan's main seaport and most populous city, Karachi.

"You are American?"

A crisp British accent emanated from one of my Pakistani companions.

"It is very good what your President Nixon has done in foreign policy."

The enthusiasm for Nixon's achievements was tempered by my expression of disdain for the president's war administration in Vietnam and Cambodia. Night deepened, our train swayed gently and shook occasionally, rocking us toward slumber's refuge.

Karachi

We woke to torrid morning heat on our approach to Karachi, stopping at a station where a work elephant was being led amidst tropical greenery. Food peddlers eagerly shouted their wares for passengers to purchase. A bedraggled man on the platform in police custody was struck hard by one of his escorts, causing his head to shake from the impact. Running afoul of the law here had painful consequence.

Karachi, on the Arabian Sea coastline, is, after Shanghai, the second largest city in the world and the largest in a Muslim country. A thermometer at the train station registered 105 degrees. Outside the bus en route to the airport hotel eight human beasts of burden dressed only in white loincloths sweated profusely as they pulled a massive cart the size of the Budweiser wagon, loaded and stacked with wares, a job for horses, being done by mere men.

Two solitary days passed ensconced in my room, only leaving to go to the hotel restaurant while in wait for my flight that would take me from Pakistan to Europe and through customs with twenty pounds of illegal contraband that, if discovered, would doom my free flowing adventurous course. This unfamiliar caper was underway. There was no escape now. My mood was uptight, fear chilled my spirit, and a sense of entrapment weighed heavily.

At the airport my suitcases were overweight, requiring additional payment, but they weren't opened for inspection. Ahmet had neglected to give me a key to lock the cases. That minimal caution would have been prudent. Baggage handlers attached numbered claim tags and the airline agent gave me luggage identification tags to write my name and my address, although this would link my name with the suitcases. Reasoning that my name would be identified in any event with the baggage numbers assigned to my ticket, this step was completed. Two Dormadinas before boarding tranquilized my jittery countenance, taking some edge from the escalating fear. Smuggling was my official business.

The Alitalia jet landed in Rome, still clothed in predawn darkness. My luggage was checked through to Barcelona so there would be no customs inspection here, only a wait in the modern terminal before my connecting flight.

Lost Luggage

The last two numbing Dormadinas were downed in preparation for arrival in Barcelona, stoned and bringing in the keys. The jet bumped, thumped, touched down, and taxied to a stop on the tarmac where a rolling stairway was maneuvered to the fuselage. Passengers descended to enter the terminal for customs inspection. In spite of the spacy effect of the pills my fear rolled and tumbled in waves. The moment of discovery hovered before me. Just walk straight, be cool, and open the suitcases myself.

An attractive woman was just ahead of me who might divert the attention of customs long enough for me to pass by unnoticed behind her, but the official was indifferent to the Afghanistan and Pakistan visas in my passport, stamping me through without incident.

One more customs station remained that required retrieving luggage and opening it for an inspection of contents. My first suitcase dropped from the conveyor to the luggage carousel. One more to go. Moments progressed into anxious minutes as the second suitcase failed to materialize. The carousel was deactivated. Almost everyone else had gone through customs. A baggage handler indicated there was no more luggage from that flight. One suitcase was missing.

The unexpected lack of the other case threw my already strained mind into confusion but there was nothing to be done except proceed through customs with the one suitcase.

The blue uniformed inspector asked me to open my suitcase.

"Open the cases yourself."

The suitcase was unlatched. My hand cushioned the weight of the heavy top. The case was laid flat with incidental cloth and clothing inside exposed. The examiner felt amidst the contents. He looked directly in my eyes and held my gaze.

"Bien. Passe."

The inspector waved me through into Spain, with ten pounds of the prime number one Afghani hashish undetected and safe. But where was the other case? Fingers of fear tightened their grip.

The flight's final destination was Amsterdam. The suitcase could be on the plane or back in Rome. The police could be on to me and were holding back one case, allowing me to enter the country but surveil my movement. Confusion plagued me while my still stoned mind grappled with indecision.

Our plan included proceeding on the train to

Copenhagen. Customs inspections at European borders were alleged to be less stringent. But half the product was missing. An experienced professional would've stashed the suitcase in a locker and left the country as fast as possible, walking away from a mission gone awry. Instead, my first thought was to report the missing luggage at the Alitalia counter, then return to Ibiza.

"We apologize, sir. We have your name and address and we'll contact you when we find your luggage."

Copenhagen would have to wait. The next plane available carried me to Ibiza airport and a taxi brought me to Michael's house. He was shocked to see me, more so when the story unfolded and the suitcase of hashish was presented to him. He had not expected to be directly involved and in possession. Instead of having the profit in hand from a successful enterprise, Michael had ten pounds of illegal substance and we faced the uncertainty of not knowing the whereabouts of the lost contraband.

The mood had changed. When Jim had returned from his summer in France, Michael revealed the details of the dope run. Jim was angry, disappointed, and fearful. He had left the care of his house with me with this negative result. He felt if he had been there he could have reasoned with me and prevented this lamentable situation. Now it was too late, and making matters worse, my actions were endangering him.

Michael buried the entire suitcase unopened in the corner of his chicken coop then gave his opinion.

"You have to go back for the other suitcase when it's found. It's too valuable to abandon. You have to finish the deal, man."

Two days of crippling mental agony consumed me

as we waited for a response from the airline until a telegram arrived stating that the suitcase was located and could be delivered to the house or retrieved in Barcelona. Neither Jim nor Michael wanted the case sent to them where they might be implicated.

Michael reasoned,

"What you do is find a hotel with a bar across the street. You tell them what time and have them deliver the bag to your hotel. You watch from the bar. If it's the cops, you split."

Is There Anything You Want To Tell Me?

Michael drove me to the airport and quickly departed. In an ominous portent a cameraman filmed passengers boarding my plane.

At the Barcelona airport Michael's plan of watching the delivery of the suitcase to a hotel from a bar was impulsively eliminated by walking straight to baggage claim with my last shred of optimism beneath mounting anxiety.

The Alitalia counter was quiet with one man standing behind it.

"This telegram came to me saying that my luggage has been found.'

"Do you have a claim form? This is you? Just a moment, sir."

He returned with another man.

"Is this your claim form?"

"Yes, it's mine."

Movement overcame my body, sweeping me from standing still to rapid acceleration, though it was not my will that moved me but plainclothes police and armed Guardia Civil who materialized, surrounded me, squeezed my arms in a viselike grip, and propelled me forward as my diminished reservoir of confidence collapsed. The phalanx of police pushed me through a door and into a small room. The second suitcase lay open on a table, raped and violated, its lustrous light blue lining shredded, ripped and ragged. Thick slabs of chocolate green Afghani hashish broken-edged and jagged lay strewn within.

"Sit down."

A man in a light grey suit stood before me. He sat down in a chair opposite me, very close, face-to-face, knee-to-knee, *mano a mano*. His straight black hair was neatly parted on his left side, cut close above the ears and on his neck, where his white skin was visible under the short stubble. His face was round, fat and pale. He leaned in, putting his face close to mine, and smiled. Beads of sweat were gathered on his upper lip.

"Is there anything you want to tell me?"

Truth.

"There's another suitcase."

"Where?"

"In Michael's chicken coop."

He regarded me a moment. From a desk behind him he retrieved a sheet of paper and a pen and passed them to me.

"Make me a map."

A house, a path, an animal enclosure, the buried treasure, x marks the spot. The drawing was passed back. The unctuous cop reached toward me, put his right hand on my left thigh, just above the knee, and squeezed. He leaned in close.

"We're going to my house. You're not going to like my house. It's not a very nice place. We're going to talk."

A big man with a mustache, in brown trousers, brown shirt, and a short, brown leather jacket, was watching. He looked different than the cop in the suit.

"Who do you work for?"

"Happened to be here to help," he responded. He was American.

The Spanish cop and the American exchanged a few words. The American went to the door and called in two men dressed in dark suits. They handcuffed my wrists in front. They asked me to stand then draped my jacket over my hands. The two men and the American took hold of my arms and led me out of the terminal into a waiting sedan curbside. One of the men carried the suitcase, stripped of hashish. They put me in the back seat and put my suitcase in on the seat beside me.

One of the men slid behind the wheel and the American got in beside him. The car pulled away from the airport and made its way through the city. The American admitted to being an agent with the United States Drug Enforcement Agency. The lights of Barcelona glimmered in the sad industrial night.

Secret Police

The sedan turned into a driveway and stopped in a courtyard. The driver led me into a building, through an office, and down a corridor to a cell. A stone bench was against a wall and a latrine was opposite. Iron bars separated the room from the corridor. My handcuffs were removed. The driver opened a door in the bars and motioned for me to enter, placing the suitcase inside after me. The door was slammed shut with a metallic clang. An armed guard sat on a wooden chair opposite my cell. They had me trapped and confined, locked in cold stone and iron. What lay ahead could not be pleasant. Mangled fears tumbled like stones awash in a dark sea surf.

A plate of chicken, potatoes, and green beans, was brought in and passed to me through a port in the bars. The guard brought a blanket and pillow for me to sleep on the stone bench.

The sound of chewing woke me. A rat was consuming what was left of my dinner on the bench next to my head. The guard was eyeing me and holding his carbine.

"Senor, there's a rat here. Can you take the plate?"

He took the food. The rat scurried away through the shadows and down the latrine hole.

Michael's Arrest

Twelve hours after my bust, at four in the morning, Ibiza cops pounded on Michael's door, rousing him from sleep. He rose from his bed and opened the door.

Facing Michael was a large policeman, along with the same older policeman who had searched the farmhouse in summer, and three armed Guardia Civil.

"Your friend has been arrested. We know the whole story so don't bullshit. Tell us where the dope is."

Michael replied,

"His arrest has nothing to do with me."

The big cop punched him hard in the stomach, held him

against the wall, and said,

"With my black belt in karate it's easy to kill little hippies like you. So tell me where the dope is and we'll save some time."

Michael, in pain, scared, and trying to breathe, confessed.

"The suitcase is in the chicken coop."

"Show us."

They walked to the chicken coop and dug up the suitcase.

"Let's go."

Michael and his girlfriend, Janet, were taken to the station near the Ibiza jail. Later that morning the police visited Jim's farmhouse. He and his guests had to drive in to the station for questioning. The cops went to Michael's father and took him in. Each person was separately interrogated.

Jim and his friends were scared and angry, but everyone was released except Michael. For the next three days, he was repeatedly questioned while held in a cell with inebriated men vomiting and defecating into a hole in the floor. Michael had consumed alcohol, smoked hash, and popped pills every day for years. Along with the anguish of confinement and interrogation he was experiencing substance withdrawal. With further physical persuasion, Michael was coerced into revealing the details of his smuggling plan. The police created a confession that he was forced to sign admitting to his guilt in a conspiracy to import and sell illegal hashish. Also contained in the confession was an admission to being a habitual user of drugs, a lesser but serious and separate social crime.

Shocked, shaken, and disoriented, with police

formalities concluded, Michael was placed in the Ibiza jail, where he experienced a mental breakdown. The police transferred him to a Catholic hospital where his legs and one hand were handcuffed to a bed. He was uncuffed to go to the toilet and recuffed after. Once, when the handcuffs were off for a latrine break, he halfheartedly tried to escape by walking out. A nun observing him, said,

"The bathroom's the other way."

Michael remained handcuffed to the bed for two weeks. The restraints were removed one other time for a visit with his girlfriend. Eventually, he was taken back to the Ibiza jail for four more weeks, then transported to the Central Penitentiary in Palma, on the neighboring island, Majorca.

Confession

Sleep released my subconscious mind from confinement to a momentary flight outside the cage. Waking required orientation as the stark reality of captivity confronted me.

Two policemen dressed in suits and ties appeared at the bars. The guard opened the door. The two escorted me from the cell, through the corridor, and up a stairway. We entered a room resembling a study, with bookshelves on a wall, stuffed chairs on a red carpet and a large wooden desk before a bay window that looked down on the courtyard we entered in last night's shadow, now filled with sunlight. A concern that the police would know about my father's fighting with the International Brigades against Franco's forces in the Spanish Civil

War, and use that knowledge for retribution, preyed on my mind. One of the policemen from yesterday was sitting at the desk. Another man stood. They told me to stand. Our conversation was in Spanish.

"You are in the office of the Secret Police. We can keep you for three days without notifying your consulate. Tell me what happened."

"In Kabul, a man in a taxi took me to Peshawar where the hashish was sold to me by a man on the street."

"No, that's not what happened."

While emphasizing a word, my right hand had lifted up. The standing man slapped my outstretched palm.

"*Electricad.*"

He shook his body, miming the effect of electricity shocking me.

"Go back to your cell and think about it. We'll talk later."

This fake story would not work. It appeared that only the truth would satisfy these secret police, and keep me from the electricity and who knew what else. Later, the same two men took me upstairs again.

"Tell me what happened."

"Michael planned for me to meet a man named Ahmet at the Khyber Hotel in Peshawar. Ahmet arranged a taxi to a house where the suitcases were given to me. They were transported to the Peshawar train station, to Karachi, and to Barcelona."

"Good," he said.

"Cigarette?"

The sensation of tobacco smoke entering my lungs, although not my usual behavior, offered a momentary sensation of relief.

"We're going to write a statement that will say you and your friend smuggled ten kilos of hacheech into Spain, and that you're habitual drug users. Then you'll sign it."

The government of Spain granted a wide latitude of conduct to police power, which meant that my guilt was assured by the confession signed, no matter if the police had tortured me or not. No innocent until proven guilty, like back home.

The police walked down to the cell with me. After lunch they returned. We went upstairs where their prepared confession was signed. The mood was noticeably lighter. The police had dropped their serious tough demeanor and were all friendly. No mention was made of my father.

"Get your suitcase and we go."

With my hands again bound with handcuffs we walked out to the courtyard.

"Here's your money. We took some for the food."

"Let me have your pack of cigarettes."

"That's fifty pesetas."

The policeman gave me the money and cigarettes then motioned for me to get in the back of their sedan. With my arrest and confession concluded we departed the offices of the secret police.

Municipal Jail

My captors drove to an old building housing a municipal jail. With my emptied suitcase in hand, they escorted me in, removed my manacles, and departed. A blue uniformed guard led me through a corridor to a large cell. A group of men were inside, playing cards, reading magazines, and conversing. Bunk beds lined the walls. The jailer motioned for me to enter, then locked the iron-barred door behind me. Self-reliance advised me to keep to myself. Most of these prisoners were being held for petty crimes. They had no ulterior motive other than to pass the time as amiably as possible. My crime was more serious and captured their interest when my tale was told.

When a visitor arrived for me the following day a guard walked me from the cell to a meeting room where a round-faced, red-haired, balding man greeted me.

"My name's Joseph McLean, the American Consul here in Barcelona. You'll be in this jail until you're transferred to the prison in Barcelona. You're charged with smuggling illegal drugs, a crime carrying two penalties. You do jail time, and pay a fine. You'll have two trials. Could be in a year. You might get six years. In Spain, there's no parole, but every two days of work gives you a day off your sentence. Good behavior reduces that. If you get six years you'll probably only do half. The fine is for not paying tax on your contraband. It could be a few thousand dollars. You'll need a lawyer. We'll send your family a telegram."

Those pronouncements hit like an iron fist. Years. Confinement threatened to become a long road through a dark forest.

The surly guard escorted me back into the cell. Among those with me was a young man wearing a worn beige suit with a red T-shirt and black and white high top tennis shoes. We were the only ones in suits. Juan was a conversational guy. He got coffees and pastries on my tab and was appreciative. Twice a day a vendor arrived to take orders for outside purchases. Meager jail rations could be supplemented if one had money.

Prisoners were transported out and in, but for me there was no leaving the cell. We slept on the bunk beds attached to the walls, played cards, read magazines, and exchanged crime stories. There was little to do. A small television showed Spanish language programs. The men in the cell were all Spanish, except for me, the lone American.

After ten days of uneventful monotony two Guardia Civil came to transport me, along with Juan and a few others, to Barcelona's largest facility of forcible confinement, the penitentiary. The word was redolent of dingy dungeons, rats, and rot. An apprehensive mood stole over me knowing my destination was prison, likely for a lengthy period. The Guardia Civil handcuffed us and we were ordered into the back of their Land Rover. As we sped toward our dark destination a pronounced contrast was evident between those people in free flow, glimpsed through the Rover's steel mesh window, and us, trapped and inert. Snatched from field and furrow, we observed a fleeting mirage beyond our reach, a dance of light, destined to be but a memory, now rapidly receding from our sight.

Centro de Detencion

The Rover reached the massive dark structure of Barcelona Centro de Detencion por Hombres where it crawled through a large open gate in a high stone wall and slithered to a stop inside a shadowy courtyard. Women were gathered in lines, packages in hand, chattering in clusters while waiting for entrance, to have

a few moments with their family members held within. We were led from the Land Rover and marched straight to the door, where our restraints were removed.

"*Silencio!*"

The Guardia addressed the guards within through a small port on a blue iron door. The portal opened and we entered, leaving the last vestige of the outer world with unrestricted moving beings behind.

Juan had been here before and cautioned me,

"Walk along the wall, not in the center."

"*Vamanos.*"

Green uniformed guards escorted us along a white tiled corridor's edge to a locked barred gate spanning wall to wall and floor to ceiling. A door in the gate was opened and we passed through, finding ourselves facing a pavilion in the center of the prison. From this hub guards regulated access for five large three-tiered galleries extending from the center like spokes of a wheel. Sounds echoed and ricocheted. Metal moving against metal squealed. Men shouted instructions. We were led along the wall through the center to the first gallery, called *Periodo* or *Observacion*. New residents were placed here and observed for five days, receiving evaluation before gallery assignment. After some processing procedures my name was called and a capo, a prisoner facilitating the guard's work, led me to a cell on the second floor, my suitcase still in hand. He told me to enter, watched me pass within, slammed the door shut, and drove the locking bolt home.

The cell was six by ten feet. Two bunk beds along the length formed a corridor between them to the window above that looked down on a dirt yard below. At the entrance was a sink and a toilet. The dreary grey walls were stone, with peeling paint. The chatter of men in the yard mixed with the bouncing of a handball in motion was audible from the window. Standing on the bed one could look down and see prisoners on the yard. They wore ordinary street clothing, no uniforms. Guards were garbed in green, with military trousers, dark shirts, and sweaters or jackets, topped with a captain-style hat.

Eventually a call for dinner sounded. The capo walked the tier releasing locking bolts and opening cell doors. He instructed me to go down to the *planta,* the first floor. Plates and utensils were distributed along with a cup for the ration of wine with the meal.

Men stood in line, first for the wine, drinking the one cup on the spot observed by the guards. No hoarding. Following the alcohol warmth greasy food was doled on our plates and we were ordered back to the cells to consume our meal there.

With the wine and something to eat some relaxation of tension lessened the new unfamiliarity of lockup. Sleep released me from the claustrophobic confine. At seven in the morning a trumpet pierced my nocturnal tranquility, the signal to wake and begin the day. When the metal doors were unlocked inmates were required to stand at attention in the doorway. A guard and one or two capos walked along the cellblock tiers counting, a procedure that was done five times every day. Those guards took their counts to the *Jefe de la Galeria*, the head. The Jefes took their count to the center. The counts were tallied. If the numbers were not in alignment with expectation, the count had to be repeated. When the numbers were correct the trumpet again sounded, activity replaced silence, and breakfast was wheeled into the gallery on carts in large containers. We were released from our confines with our plates to descend and form a line to receive the meal and return to our cells. Morning activities could then proceed but for us in observation there was little to do but remain confined for the five-day duration.

The first day the cell was mine alone. The following day a Spanish man was brought in. He taught me some words and phrases, which were jotted in a notebook that was among the few possessions in my suitcase, now stashed under my bunk. This young cellmate was a complainer. His mistake was griping to the capos and guards too often. After the final count the following night the dissatisfied prisoner was escorted from the cell down to the office where a guard grabbed the man's testicles and squeezed. My cellmate returned in tears, in pain, and humiliated. He stopped complaining. Next day he was transferred and replaced with a cheerful Moroccan, a singer who taught me a popular song of the time.

Ave Maria se fue
buscando solo la playa
con sus maletas de piel
y su bikini de raya
ella se marcho y solo me dejo
recuerdo de su ascencia
con la minor indulhencia
que voy hacer
que voy hacer
que voy hacer
Ave Maria se fue

On the third day a medical examination was mandated. We were marched down to the first floor. The medics were inmates with no medical training, supervised by a doctor. My medic was a young Catalan. Catalonia is an autonomous community of Spain, designated a nationality by its statute of autonomy. It is comprised of four provinces, Barcelona, Girona, Lleida, and Tarragona. Its people speak Catalan, a variation of Spanish, as well as Spanish. Although the region is an autonomous community General Franco abolished its statute of autonomy after the Spanish Civil War because Catalonia had been opposed to Franco's forces. During this period Catalan language, culture, and self-government were suppressed.

While waiting for my exam the medic asked me the circumstances of my bust. My response didn't include specific names, so his next question came as a surprise.

"Do you know Ahmet?'

"No."

Not true.

"He was here before many months. He has visa

violation. They take him to border. France."

In my still fearful state this questioning was suspicious, but my fears were groundless. The medic was a young student, an unfortunate victim of a group cocaine bust. He had been here when Ahmet passed through on deportation charges but was unaware of Ahmet's actual scene in Pakistan.

At day's end, the lights went out. My head hit the pillow. Night imagery lifted me beyond the walls. Sunlight sparkled on a summer sea. Warm white sand met gentle blue waves. Green trees in a gentle breeze. But a strident morning trumpet intruded on my dreamscape. Every time.

A Milestone

My thirtieth birthday coincided with my fifth and final day in observation, a Sunday. After lunch a capo escorted me from my cell through the prison's center to the fourth gallery, where foreigners and those awaiting trial were housed. The second gallery held inmates serving their sentence in Barcelona. *Reincidentes*, repeat offenders, were in the third. Political prisoners and solitary confinement occupied the dreaded fifth gallery. *Maricons,* homosexuals, inhabited their own building, separate from the population. A few hundred men were housed in a gallery and each gallery had a designated yard bounded by the buildings.

The capo led me to an office where the guard on duty assigned me a cell. The capo walked me to a nearby open door.

"John, *un Americano.*"

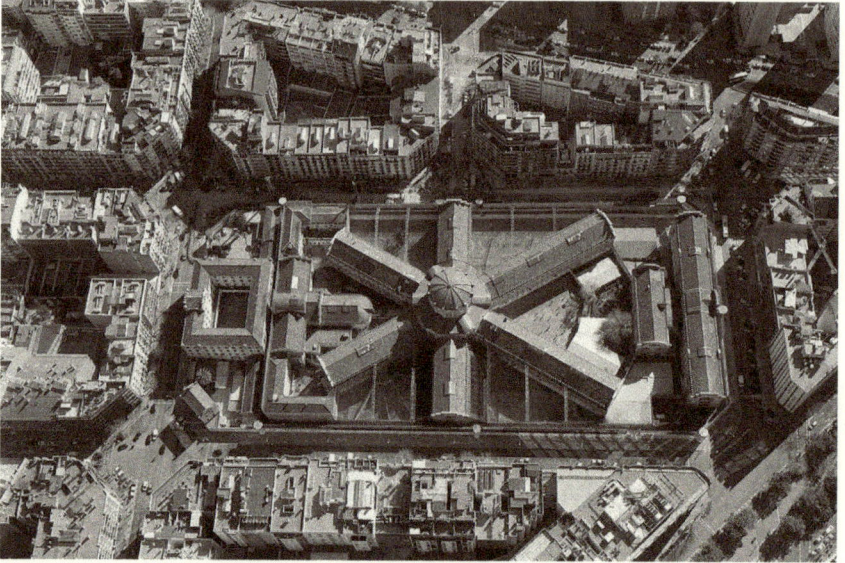

A portly young man was sitting on top of a bunk bed. He wore jeans and a jacket, both of black denim. Looking our way he slid down and landed on the floor.

"Hey, man. Far out. Are you in for drugs?"

"Yeah, hash."

"Me too, man, hash. What's the suitcase for?"

"The hash was in it."

"John immediately examined the interior.

"Hey, man, there's still some hash in here caught in the tape. Can I get it?"

"Sure."

John worked the tape, plucking the small remnants of hashish stuck there.

"They've kept me here for seven months, for a kilo."

He mixed the bits of hash with some of his rolling tobacco and twisted it up.

"My lawyer says my bail should be granted soon. My fine has already been paid. When you get bail you promise to go to trial but you don't. They give you your passport and you split."

He lit up.

"Far out, man."

My living situation was to be with a normal person, a hashish head like me, which was a relief. Being amidst people was good after solitude. Sunday was the only time prisoners were allowed to stay in the gallery during the afternoon, instead of the forced exit to the yard, or going to work in the factory. Cell doors were left open. The atmosphere then was more casual and relaxed. Men in conversation were strolling the floor. A television bolted to the wall at the end of the gallery played a rerun of Bonanza with dubbed Spanish.

A short man and a tall man appeared at the door.

"Hey, this is Sid and Colin. They're British, too. The new guy's American.'

"An American. You're the only one in here."

Sid was the shorter of the two. He looked to be in his forties, with an outgoing demeanor and a strong British accent.

"You can come and work with us, in the hospital. John works there, too. The food's better than what you get in here, that's for sure. We bring it back to the cell."

Colin was an imposing figure, well over six feet in height, with short sandy hair and a pronounced Cockney accent. Sid and Colin shared a cell two doors over. Colin had stupidly smashed up a bar in a drunken rampage, but he appeared to be a regular bloke, as did Sid and John.

After my arrest, detention by secret police, ten days in the municipal jail and five days confined in observation, the atmosphere in the gallery seemed like summer camp. Friendly faces spoke English and we had more freedom of movement than had been my recent experience. The normal street clothing and absence of violent inmates relieved my concern.

Offenders were housed in the fourth gallery while awaiting trial or until getting bail. Once trial had concluded an inmate would serve the remainder of their sentence either in the second gallery or be transferred to another penal institution. Guards often were young men working in prison as alternative fulfillment of military service. For some, particularly the older ones, being a guard was an occupation.

The bell sounded. Relaxing time was over, and the two Brits departed.

"We'll pick you up in the morning to work in the hospital," Sid added.

Sunday was the one night that a proper cooked meal wasn't served. Instead, dinner was a processed cheese sandwich. Later that night, when the final count of the day concluded, doors were shut, the locking bolts were slammed home, and all was quiet.

"Hey, man, you want to see the rats?"

Standing on the bed frames we looked from the window down on the yard. Rodents ran over the garbage cans on carts waiting for tomorrow's collection. Scurrying squeakers. My thirtieth birthday was observed, not in freedom, but, ironically, in benevolent social condition. My apprehension that prison would be a torture chamber subsided.

My motorcycle climbed the winding road to the farmhouse on the hill. A storm dumped water in the dark of night. Holding the bike up was difficult. It went down.

Illuminated by candles in a window above, Buddha looked down at me. A trumpet sounded.

"Hey, come on, man, get up. The count."

Dreams were a mental escape from confinement. No doubt about it, however, this was prison. We rose, dressed quickly, and then took our positions at the open door of our cell. The guards marched by, two guards on each of the three tiers, counting. When the numbers were right, the trumpet blew. Activity replaced the silence. In the prison's center carts of breakfast food were being wheeled into place before each gallery. Capos were calling names of inmates to come to the office for mail.

Hospital

"Let's go to the hospital, man. Get a couple of plates to bring back food."

We left our cell and walked a few doors toward the center where Sid and Colin joined us. We were the hospital crew. Being with these British acquaintances in street clothing on my new job seemed like normal life on my first full day in the second gallery of Barcelona prison.

Our path took us through the center past the barbershop on the left, and the homosexual's wing on the right, then left into the courtyard that led to the hospital. There were no security checks or gates to unlock. We were free to move through our designated areas.

The hospital was no more than a housing unit for aged, infirmed, and mentally ill, with no real medical facilities. Some men were milling about in the dirt courtyard. A man rushed over to us, babbling animatedly, and repeated,

"I'm Bambi, I'm Bambi."

He wore a black motorcycle jacket. His long, greasy, black hair fell uncontrollably into his face as he moved with jerky motion. Another younger man was standing alone by the wall smoking a cigarette. He was dressed in blue jeans and denim jacket with colorful flowers and peace signs embroidered on his clothing.

"Paint it black," he said. He smiled and winked in a conspiratorial manner at me while he did a little shuffle dance.

"That's Tony," John said.

"He's in for drugs, too."

We were there to serve breakfast, lunch, and dinner to the hospital residents. Walking up a stairway to the second floor we found the food waiting for us. As we wheeled the carts into a large dormitory beams of sunlight streamed in through large high windows. Numerous beds were arrayed with small storage tables beside them. Crosses were affixed to the walls along with images of the Mary and Jesus. Here were the older and infirmed inmates.

The ambulatory men formed a line with plates to be served. We went around to those who were bedridden. In addition to the dormitory, a section of private rooms were occupied by inmates who were not in ill health but, through privilege, were able to serve their sentence in the more comfortable surroundings of an individual room in the hospital, rather than in the larger galleries.

"That guy embezzled millions from a bank," Sid related, indicating a well-dressed man with gold-rimmed glasses and a gold watch.

"He's serving three years, but he got to keep the money."

Finishing in the dormitory, we had one more stop where mentally ill inmates occupied individual rooms. Bambi and Tony were among them. At the conclusion of our work we filled plates for ourselves and returned to the gallery.

The Yard

Our plates were taken to our cell. Two long baguettes had been delivered in our absence, a loaf a day each. The gallery was quiet since the occupants had all departed, either to the yard, or to the handbag factory. Outside one would walk, talk, sit, read, and view the apartment buildings that rose up around the prison, from where the residents could look down at us. A few enthusiasts played handball. Everyday but Sunday afternoon we were marched to the yard, morning and afternoon. From there, twenty or so could line up to go to the *economato*, the market, to buy things like yogurt, toothpaste, and espresso coffee, a stronger variation from the mass produced café con leche that came around every morning.

John introduced me to a few other young drug offenders, none of whom had been caught with large amounts. Rafael was a short, prematurely balding, friendly guy with a sardonic sense of humor. He and a group of his friends, including the medic who had asked me about Ahmet, had gone in on a deal to get some cocaine. Something went wrong and the lot were caught, arrested, and tortured to reveal the identities. These were not professional traffickers but young college kids who only wanted to get high.

"Fucking mother," Rafael cursed in English, "the cops pulled out my fingernails to get me to talk. They gave me electric shock, too. Fucking mother."

Rafael took short drags on his cigarette. A few of his fingers had black ends where the nails had been.

"We had coke."

The secret police tortured to obtain confessions from those unwilling to volunteer information. With excessively severe drug laws prevalent in industrialized nations people who would never rob, rape, or murder were treated as arch criminals, to be tortured and imprisoned. Hypocritical governments crushed citizens for getting high while allowing sloppy drunk and dangerous alcohol use legally. Industrialized soul killers. We were innocents in the Garden of Eden with some artificial rapacious judgmental power dictating to us their terms of existence, then abusing us for plucking the fruit growing on the vine.

As we walked the cold prison yard we sometimes fantasized that when the old power mongers fell and our young generation of liberators replaced them we would be considered heroes and pioneers with our names inscribed on commemorative monuments for our bravery in facilitating the acquisition of ancient medicinal material for mental enhancement.

A Brief Guitar

Not long after my arrest, Jim visited. Seeing him on the other side of the Plexiglas window was disconcerting. He was considerate, compassionate and without vindictive reproach. Fortunately my behavior that implicated him and his house through association had no long-term adverse effect. He had written an explanatory letter to my mother in California but there was nothing he could do for my legal situation that had to proceed according to Spanish law.

Jim brought with him a nylon string guitar that he deposited with the facility for me. The instrument came to my cell but not for long. Don Francisco, a serious and strict guard, heard me playing in the cell and confiscated it, saying Barcelona prison regulations did not allow inmates to have musical instruments, although they were allowed in some Spanish prisons. Part of my rationale in planning the smuggling event was that if caught some of the time could be devoted to music.

If addressed at all, and it was more prudent to avoid direct communication with them, guards were addressed by the honorific title *Don,* followed by their first name.

Jim's Letter

November 14, 1974

Dear Madelyne,

I'm writing this letter to let you know what's happening, as I know you must be worried sick. I'll start by telling you the history of the whole event leading up to your son's arrest. You should know that he can't really write you himself, as it takes six weeks to get a letter out of prison (at least that is what he told me when I visited him yesterday).

As you probably know, I left the house in his care and during the summer he played gigs but didn't earn enough to save any money. When I returned in October he had already left and I'm sorry I didn't get back earlier as I'm sure I could've talked him out of it. He told me Michael pressured him into it, but he is his own person therefore it's difficult to put all the blame on Michael. In any case, Michael is in far worse danger than him.

Anyway, he was a runner for Michael. That is, he was paid by Michael to go to Pakistan, pick up two suitcases with false bottoms containing more or less ten kilos of hash and then return to Spain (Barcelona) with them. The plan was for him to telegram Michael when he had returned to Barcelona and for the two of them to proceed to Denmark and sell the hash. Michael has told the police he was going to sell it to American sailors on Palma. There was a hitch, as they say, as one of the suitcases was lost along the trip (in transit in Rome - perhaps there was an informer involved as there are no other explanations for some of the details). He went against the plan (as was explained by the other partner in the deal, a Turk in Pakistan who is well known by Interpol) and brought the one suitcase to Ibiza and gave it to Michael. Michael then phoned the airport in Barcelona and was told that the other suitcase had been found, and your son went to pick it up.

Needless to say, this was a terrible mistake, as the police were waiting for him. He was arrested and told the full story. The next day Michael was confronted by the police in Ibiza and he, along with his girlfriend Jan, his father, and I, along with my houseguests, had to go to the police station, accompanied by the other suitcase. Well, as only Michael was involved, the rest of us were released after making statements. Michael is in jail in Ibiza.

I've talked with the consulate in Barcelona and with your son and with his lawyer. He is working in the hospital ward and thus eating better than most prisoners. He is well, hasn't been hurt in any way, and is thinking very clearly. The consulate is a good man and is doing what he can to help. I got him a guitar, which I'm not sure if he will be allowed to play, and he's biding his time. He will need a lawyer. Interpol is interested in international dope rings and they are running a check. As he has never been a part of anything like this before, there will be no pressure put on the Spanish to prosecute him heavily. He was simply a runner or courier or whatever it's called and there are literally hundreds of people being used in the same way. The authorities are after the organizers, not people who are used because they are desperate.

His lawyer feels it will be a case of money. There is a fine per gram of hashish that your son was caught with. This could be around $5,000. This what is called bail but is in reality a payoff because if they let him out and give him his passport it's understood that he will leave Spain and the money will stay behind. This is standard procedure. I know many who have had this happen to them. They pay the bail, are given their passport back, and told that the trial will be in a few months. Not many stay around. Third, there may be a rehabilitation fine, which the lawyer told me is very little.

The lawyer feels that he could be out of jail within a month or two, providing Interpol doesn't come up with

140

anything. It's for sure they won't. So, it's a matter of money. He has asked me to ask you to ask his father to help you in making these payments. He says that as soon as he is free he will return to California and work to pay it all back, and lawyers' fees also, of course. You know your son and you know he'll do what he says. Money is needed to buy his freedom. There could be more to it, but his lawyer feels this is the way it is and that's all there is to go on right now. Michael will probably be in jail a while as he has admitted to some pretty extraordinary things. Please keep my name out of this. Ask the lawyer to keep me anonymous as I have a lot to lose if the Spanish police feel that I've been getting myself involved in this business, and decide to make my life difficult. Try not to worry.

Love, Jim

Insane Strategy

Michael's solitary observation period concluded at the prison in Palma. He was assigned to a dormitory with eighty other men. As the days progressed and the stark outlook of confinement extended he suffered with fear of a stiff twelve or eighteen year sentence to be meted out as punishment for longhaired foreign dope dealers under the fascist dictator Franco. Possibly the sentence could even be changed to life. Fear overtook his reasoning. As a consequence of his decision to risk endangering himself and those around him with the ill-fated smuggling venture the trauma of his acquaintances had turned to anger. In addition, living on another island, visits were impractical. Michael was abandoned. Even his live-in girlfriend stayed away.

With his attorney suggesting the probability that the case would not go well Michael's thoughts became darker. Periods of irrational fears resulted in erratic behavior. In his unbalanced condition Michael reasoned that the only way out of this predicament was to escape. He heard that at La Clinica Mental de Jesus, a mental hospital in Palma, nicknamed the *manacomio*, or nuthouse, security was less stringent than in prison. Michael developed a plan to feign insanity in order to be transferred to the clinic from which he would effect an escape.

Michael initiated his scheme by simulating freakout sessions. Every morning he went to the doctor to complain about terrible headaches and reported hearing voices. He was prescribed sedative pills to tranquilize him, but the pills made him sick. Nonetheless, he was required to take them for fourteen days. Michael completed the course of treatment and complemented that by making a scene in the dormitory at night, screaming, waking residents, banging his head on the bedpost, and actually drawing blood. After two of these outbursts he was taken to an observation cell. After two weeks he was transferred him to the mental clinic. Michael was faking insanity but his severe depression was real. Contributing to his state was the withdrawal from drugs and alcohol, along with the emotional upheaval of being divorced from regular life, combined with shame, pain, fear, and guilt. But his charade had worked and from the clinic Michael could implement his risky plan of escape.

Two German Bank Robbers

Johann was in the prison hospital when we became acquainted. He and his friend, Hans, were young Germans who ran out of money while living the easy life in Ibiza. In an attempt to reverse their financial slide they hatched a scheme to rob a Barcelona bank. Pacifists that they were, and not wanting to cause inadvertent injury, they decided to facilitate the robbery brandishing toy guns, thinking those being robbed would consider the toys real weapons. Johann and Hans made a voyage to Barcelona, selected a bank and entered, demanding money while flashing their ersatz weapons. They got some cash and were making their getaway when a bank guard drew his real pistol, aimed, and pulled the trigger. Johann was shot in the stomach. He grimly enjoyed showing me the hole. Purple skin tissue covered a cavity five inches in diameter. Sucking in his breath, the tissue pulled inward and revealed a gaping hollow where his abdominal muscles had been. Johann was good-natured and maintained a fatalistic but macabre sense of humor about his situation. In spite of the obvious physical discomfort and disfigurement, Johann was amused at the irony of being blasted way out of proportion to the care he and Hans took not to harm anyone with their fake weapons.

Once healed, Johann was transferred out of the hospital to the fourth gallery. His co-conspirator Hans liked to sing. On one occasion we were walking in the yard singing The Beatles' *If I Fell* in harmony until a gruff and musically unappreciative guard told us to knock it off. We weren't allowed instruments or radios.

The only music was in church on Sunday morning.
After some months, during an improvement project that included a new shower building where there had been only two showers in a gallery, speakers were installed in the yard to broadcast music. After months of songless silence, *Strawberry Fields, Forever* wafted across the yard and into our time warped desolation. Hearing the Fab Four break through the bonds of isolation seemed an act of defiant insurrection. *Nothing to get hung about.*

Sunday

The yard for our gallery was no more than bare dirt with a concrete strip in the middle leading from the center to the factory. In one corner stood a small multipurpose building used for church service and Sunday afternoon movie screening. The films were all in Spanish and were often old Hollywood movies, usually westerns, or crime movies. We watched Johnny Cash playing a good guy gone wrong in *I Walk The Line*. Johnny's dubbed-in Spanish was incongruous, but the film gave me the realization that with Great Britain's colonization of the New World, Africa, and India, English language and culture spread across many a sea and border. American films and music continued that influence.

Sunday afternoon, as an alternative to the forced exit to the exercise yard, we could choose to stay in the gallery with cell doors open to rest, read, socialize, walk the floor, or watch the one small black and white television. Soccer was popular, as were old Hollywood series, some of my favorites as a kid, like *Gunsmoke*, *Wagon Train*, and *Bonanza*, except they all had dubbed Spanish. Ironically, *Pippi Longstocking*, the Swedish girl with stick out braids, was a show that got attention amidst the westerns.

Hair - shining, gleaming, streaming

In 1950 my parents moved us into central Los Angeles on our migration from Detroit to a rented house on Third Avenue near Jefferson Boulevard. Although my father had been in America for twenty-five years he retained an unpolished peasant demeanor stemming from his youth in the old country. Beneath his American veneer his personality embodied an old style European mentality that precluded fashionable long hair on males.

Around the corner on Jefferson Boulevard Dad took my little brother and me to a barber of Japanese descent who enjoyed alarming me by repeating

"Butchie, butchie,"
in his clipped English, with much laughter, referencing a hair style of the time that left the top of the hair short and standing straight up.

"No, no butchie," was my desperate response. My father took the opposite tactic, encouraging him to take off more. At age six there was something about short hair that intuitively was disagreeable for me, like wearing shorts and sandals.

One Christmas my mother gave Dad a barber kit, that included scissors, a comb, and dreaded electric clippers for mowing hair around the neck and ears down to short prickly stubble. My father forced us onto the back porch, with physical persuasion and curses, to cut away as much hair as possible, in a rough manner that often left us, including my mother, in tears. In summer he shaved our heads down to the bone.

Once Elvis appeared on the scene with a pompadour, sideburns, and ducktail, my father's old world destruction began to meet resistance until by sheer stubbornness and much outcry he found the process too much to inflict. With a little hair grease my hair could be sculpted in the rock and roll style. In junior high school my art teacher started calling me Elvis in class.

With the advent of the Sixties the universal acceptance of long hair on men as well as women transformed my Elvis look to long, flowing, shoulder length locks. Hair felt sensuous. For the next ten years my hair remained uncut as barbershops and butchie cuts receded in my memory.

Barcelona Prison prohibited hair growth, whether scalp or facial. Shaving was mandatory. On the yard, guards looked for hair violators and when spotted

approached them with the terse comment,
    "Barberia."
That was the command to immediately go to the barber,
located just off the center. Personal razors were
forbidden. On my first visits barbers, prisoners like us all,
shaved me using a straight razor. But having a man run a
sharp blade across my throat was unsettling. The shop
had safety razors with which one could shave oneself and
that became my procedure, foregoing the ceremonial
aspect. The shop required payment of five pesetas,
accomplished using script tickets in denominations of
one, five, ten, twenty-five and fifty pesetas, a peseta
being equivalent to a penny and a half. Script was
purchased with an inmate's money held in *peculio*, their
account. On one occasion a barber shaved my head as a
concession to prison fashion. Once was enough.

Crazy Tony

    Working in the hospital we sometimes tarried in
their yard on the way back to the gallery. Tony, the paint
it black winker, was interested in communicating with
me when he heard about my musical background. He
dressed in clothing with multi-colored embroidery of his
own creation that included butterflies, flowers, and
astrological images. He had his patented shuffle dance
and spaced out too far gone routine but he confided that it
was an act. Tony was pretending to be mentally
incompetent, thinking his charade would spare him a
long prison sentence. Tony was a guitar playing
songwriter and was the only person in Barcelona allowed
a guitar.

There was a price for Tony's deception. The gambit was risky. There was no guarantee that the court would be lenient and the feigned insanity involved being housed with mentally deficient and unpredictable people. There was always the possibility of shock treatment administered for behavioral anomalies, alleged infringement of protocol, or simply being victimized by sadistic staff. My associate in our ill-fated smuggling venture was employing a similar strategy in Majorca.

Painting Flowers

Concurrent with the practice of imprisoning citizens for civic violation is the development of factories within prisons to manufacture product for profit by utilizing those who are incarcerated for cheap labor. The prison operated a profitable leather handbag enterprise situated in a large brick building at the rear of the fourth gallery yard. Marketed all over the world, the purses are sold with a tag that reads, *Made in Spain, by genuine Spanish craftsmen.* Workers earned up to the equivalent of ten dollars a day. In addition to monetary incentive factory employment contributed a day off an inmate's sentence for every two days of work.

Although my participation on the hospital crew provided better fare it lacked financial compensation. Hanging around the yard every morning and afternoon had no benefit. Being employed and simultaneously reducing my sentence was appealing.

Jaime, one of Rafael's busted student group, was the head of the table in decoration, the painting component of handbag assembly. He arranged for me to take the place of a departing worker. We sat six at a table coloring small petals on embossed flowers stamped on the exterior of a brown leather purse. The slightest amount of color on the tip of a thin brush produced just enough paint to fill a flower petal. Five petals to a flower, five or six flowers to a bunch, a few bunches to a handbag.

The money from employment enabled us to afford small necessities. A radio in our section played lo-fi music. The bakery produced pastries for sale that were brought to the factory and throughout the institution on large wooden trays. My weight increased from lack of movement with a diet of starch, fat, flour, and sugar.

The Eui-Eui

There is a particular mentality that adjusts well to institutional life. Tata was the custodian in the decoration section of the factory. He committed minor crimes in an obvious way so he'd be caught and sent back to serve a short sentence, be released, then repeat the process. Officials kept his job open for him because everyone knew he'd quickly return. Tata liked the structured regimen of prison. Three hots and a cot, they say.

Tata approached me one day.

"Have you ever seen a Eui-Eui," he asked with obvious amusement, as the answer was likely to be no.

"*Es un pajaro.*" It's a bird.

"Well, no, it's unfamiliar to me."

"Look," he said and unfolded a sheet of paper, revealing a rudimentary drawing of a penis and hairy testicles, with wings sprouting from the sides, flying over mountains. A prick flying free. Tata chuckled at his presentation. He was a bird destined never to soar over the high walls to the world beyond.

Two American Attorneys

The American Consul visited on occasion but was unable to offer assistance other than to send a telegram to my mother informing her of my arrest causing her to faint when that communiqué arrived. After the initial shock my mother shouldered the responsibility of financial means to afford legal representation. Her first action was to engage a pair of San Francisco attorneys who convincingly stated that it was to my advantage that they visit me in Barcelona, at her expense, not withstanding the fact that American attorneys have no legal standing in Spain. Representation in a Spanish court had to be from a Spanish *abogado*, a lawyer.

The two flew to Spain and we conferred. They shopped for boots and a warm jacket for me and visited the attorney who ultimately was to speak on my behalf in court, whose name was provided to me from inmates. Finished with me, the attorneys hurried off to Paris, before returning to California and sending their fee, including travel expenses, to my mother.

A Barcelona Attorney

Senor Federico Valenciano agreed to represent me in my legal defense. We conferred in a part of the prison known as *Jueces,* Judges. Inmates sat on one side of a

Plexiglas window and visitors sat on the other. My attorney was a well-tailored, bearded man with eyeglasses. Introductions were exchanged. He informed me that my trial was to be adjudicated in Ibiza in the summer, seven months away. A separate trial would occur in Barcelona for the contraband fine, a fee for illegal undeclared hashish importation. There was no alternative but to wait, prepare, and deal with it.

The lawyer's fee was five thousand dollars, and had been paid already by my mother. My father absented himself from the process, and was to communicate not at all, except one brief moment of parental involvement in a letter with a lecture on freedom, saying,

"Even birds aren't free."

The potential revelation of my father's Spanish Civil War activities against Franco's forces decades ago that might bring retribution stayed in my mind for some time, but came to nothing.

My mother later revealed her fear that her son would be tortured in a fascist prison but the situation for me was free of abuse. The potential painful emotional effect on my mother was not considered during the planning. Mom was to support me throughout the ordeal, with money, letters, and sending books and clothing. She was my beacon of hope, the light in the fog that ever glowed.

The Asylum

Michael had chosen a radical method to handle his legal crisis. Feigning insanity to escape punishment rather than face the consequences directly brought a difficult set of circumstances into play.

Michael was handcuffed to a bed by three limbs and was given tranquilizers. Now he was with the real loonies, the uncontrollable psychotics, all physically restrained to their beds, drooling and screaming constantly. The staff provided a bedpan in which to defecate. With his one free hand he wiped. Two weeks passed. Periods of panic recurred as he attempted to strategize. Conditions were appalling in the hospital and he was paranoid with terror of being tortured in a prison under the dictator Franco. He prayed for the relief of that Valium every night.

Having negotiated his way into a mental asylum Michael feared he could be judged insane and locked away for the rest of his life. He had to convince the authorities that there was enough wrong with him that he didn't belong in jail, yet didn't belong in a mental institution either.

After an interview with the clinic's head psychiatrist Michael was held for observation but assigned to a ward with less acutely disturbed patients who were depressed but not violent or self destructive. Here patients weren't criminals but housed in a city mental hospital, some committed by their own families who didn't want to deal with them. These were developmentally disabled, morose, schizoid, phobic, and manic individuals. Each morning Michael was released into a large patio with six hundred men where he focused on isolating himself from the worst eccentrics. He had to move around. On one occasion Michael was napping under a tree and awoke to discover a patient having a bowel movement on his chest.

Maricons

Maricons, homosexuals, were isolated from the population, in their own wing. These were flaming queens and transsexuals, men who looked like women, or tried, with garish result. On Sunday afternoons, the maricons marched through our yard to the movie, a cause for some amusement. The prisoners formed a gauntlet through which the maricons paraded, a colorful, swishing, mincing display. The inmates jeered and catcalled, and the sashayers hooted in return.

The maricons ran the prison laundry concession. Those who had the financial means to send their clothing and bed sheets for washing had standing orders. Hanging on the wall at the entrance to the maricon's gallery was a huge portrait of a man in women's raiment.

John's Cigarette

Five times each day we were required to stand at attention in our doorway in a neat fanlike configuration as our green-garbed warders walked the tiers and counted us. John was smoking one of his self-rolled cigarettes when the count bell sounded after lunch.

"Put it out," was my suggestion, knowing today's guard, Don Francisco, was strict.

"It's all right. I'll hold it behind me and he won't see it," John said.

Don Francisco walked up and almost passed us when he noticed smoke rising from behind John's back. He stopped the count and approached John.

"Put your cigarette out," he commanded, and resumed the walk. As a result of his violation John was relieved of his job in the hospital. John felt Don Francisco overreacted. He was hurt.

Another guard took a different approach on his count, walking as fast as possible, staring straight ahead, not counting at all. He often played handball in the yard with the inmates and demonstrated an antiauthoritarian demeanor, whether real or feigned.

A month later, John was called to meet with his young and attractive female Catalan attorney. His bail had been issued and paid by his family. He had to get his gear and walk out the door now. His passport was being returned and the idea was to hightail it beyond Spain's border and forget about coming back for the trial. John was out of there like a hurricane through the Grand Canyon, leaving behind only a photo of himself smiling at his pet crow perched on his arm, and his black, white, and red bedspread, acquired when he bought his hash in Morocco. We had become friends and the prison was less cheery for a while.

A Counterfeiter

Sidney was one of the British men who had worked with me in the hospital before my departure for the factory. Sid said he had a criminal mentality. He came to Spain in a camper van with his wife and another couple, carrying a large amount of counterfeit Spanish money they planned to spend while touring the country. Their ruse was inadvertently revealed when a suitcase full of the bogus bills fell out of their van and opened during a routine traffic stop, surprising the officer by the inordinately large amount of cash that, on subsequent inspection, was determined to be forged. Sid took the rap, getting his wife off the hook, and was given a twelve-year sentence that began in Barcelona before his eventual transfer to the penal institution in Santander.

Sid refused to speak Spanish, not that he could not, but he would not, that being a small way to retain control and keep him out of conversation with guards. He had previously served four years in Brixton, a British penitentiary built in 1820, with small cells and poor living conditions that contributed to its reputation as the worst prison in England. His stories of life in that Draconian facility were unsettling. Sid said he'd rather do eight years in tranquil Spain than four years in vicious Brixton. The British penal system was harsh, with professional career criminals maintaining an underworld hierarchy, controlled by those in positions of power who utilized violence to enforce their code. Rolling Stone Mick Jagger was imprisoned in Brixton for one day on a marijuana charge, but his short stay was an exception to the rule.

My impression of prisons, gleaned from stories about American institutions like San Quentin, Sing-Sing, and Folsom, was one of brutal tattooed gangland gladiators stabbing, raping, and brutalizing victims. Barcelona was unlike America, with no racial divisions, Spain being a country of one ethnicity, although regional conflict did exist. Although not in fear of dangerous violence, we were confined in small cells, enduring unsanitary conditions in an old cold stone fortress with poor nutrition. Incarceration was deprivation.

Barcelona prisoners were for the most part normal

civil people working through their time without making things harder than they already were. Ironically, prison in a fascist country employed humane treatment, at least for us foreigners and first timers.

In my high school if a boy was caught with a shirt that wasn't tucked into his trousers teachers and staff were allowed to inflict corporal punishment by compelling the offender to take off a shoe, hand it to the staff person, bend over, and receive swats on the butt with the shoe. Similar remedial behavior was implicit in the prison environment, although with potentially more serious consequence. From the threat by the secret police to use electricity on me and from the blackened ends of Rafael's fingers where the same police removed his fingernails, there was no doubt in my mind that physical abuse was employed by the prison staff if they chose. But one would have to go out of their way to flaunt the rules and offend. If one conformed to the plan, they got the easy way. If not, they got the hard way. Though the institutions differed, the message of both high school and prison was similar. Abide by the rules or get physically punished. Prison entailed more severe consequence. Most people followed procedure.

After John's departure, Sid asked me to move in after Colin, his previous cellmate, had received bail and left. With me, Sid would have a reasonable person in his cell, diminishing the likelihood that an unknown commodity would be assigned. In a small room that might hold up to four people space was restricted and behavioral anomalies became an imposition on the others. We of like style and similar custom did best to live together to avoid unpredictable troublesome conflicts being imposed by unknown persons in the tide of turnover, although we weren't always successful. There was no official protocol to changing cells. One just informed the capo of the transition, and he in turn informed the guards in their office.

Execution

Every day, without fail, the trumpet sounded at 7:00 am to wake us and be counted, so it was with surprise that one morning we woke slowly, without being called to do so. 10:30 came around and we were still locked down.

"It must be an execution," Sid said.

"To avoid a reaction they keep us locked in until

it's finished."

When the trumpet sounded and after the count was taken, the capo told us that an execution had taken place in the fifth gallery. The executed man was a member of Euskadi Ta Askatasuna, or ETA, as the Northern Spanish Basque nationalist and separatist group is known.

The method of execution was the garrote, a capital punishment of Spanish origin in which an iron collar is tightened around a condemned person's neck until death occurs by crushing the neck, causing strangulation and injury to the spinal column at the base of the brain. It took an execution for us to sleep in.

African

Moroccans and Africans passed in large numbers through Barcelona for deportation, mostly on visa violations. Among them was a young man from Kenya, a country in East Africa whose population speaks both Swahili and English and wherein lies Lake Victoria, the world's second largest fresh water lake.

Victor had been arrested for possession of some pounds of hashish. Short in height but large in intellect and humor, Victor asked us if he could move into our cell, having tired of the company of some of his less educated fellow countrymen. We represented an American British union and after John and Colin left Sid was the only Brit rooming with the only American. Our attitudes and English language appealed to Victor. We agreed. Victor was gracious, with a ready smile and infectious laugh. He was still tight with the African contingent located at the end of the cellblock. Our cell was at the beginning of the block, a preferable location.

Victor's sister lived in Barcelona and regularly brought him packages that included her home cooked meals. Her peanut sauce chicken and rice was a welcome piquant addition from prison food. Victor was required to share his sister's deliveries with other Africans, this having to do with some hierarchy of their culture, but there was enough for us as well.

Only one other American came to Barcelona during my time there. Patrick had been busted with a small amount of hashish, enabling him to get bail after a couple of months. After Sid received his official penal assignment and was sent on to Santander, in the north of Spain, Patrick moved in with Victor and me.

Dining

For a vegetarian, prison food was a punishment in itself. We consumed animal fats and starch, with little garden vegetables or fresh fruit. A sense of irony imbued the tasting ceremony that took place in the center prior to every meal. When all the food had been transported from the kitchen in vats on carts to the gates of the galleries, all action ceased and a hush descended. A proper valet in a tuxedo with white gloves marched forward all pomp and proper to the head guard on duty. He carried before him a silver tray, upon which were small samples of institutional food, on china plates with silver service. The guard sampled the smallest portion possible and with a dismissive wave always signaled approval. The trumpeter then sounded the call to dinner, the gates opened, and serving commenced.

Before lunch and dinner the wine call was shouted. Wine is an essential European taste. Deprivation of wine with meals was considered to be too inhumane. At the call, we took our plastic cups and formed two lines to receive the only high allowed within the walls. A precise ration was ladled out and consumed on the spot under the guard's watchful eyes. To avoid any personal accumulation for a grand drunken event we weren't permitted to take wine back to the cell.

After being dished out with large ladles from barrel-sized containers by the capos as we held out our plates our meals were taken in the cells. After eating we cold-washed plates and utensils in our cell sink. There was no hot water.

Capos coordinated events in the gallery. They called us by name to collect mail, led marches to the showers, and did the duties assigned to them by the guards. One capo seriously beat a man who had informed on another. It happened while we were all locked in. The capo, having access to the cell keys, unlocked a door and wreaked havoc on the guilty individual by repeatedly slamming him with a chair. For this violent infraction, the capo received two weeks solitary confinement in the fifth gallery. In addition to punishment cells political prisoners were housed here that included members of the Northern Spanish Basque nationalist and separatist group ETA. They weren't allowed to work in the factory or mix with the general population. The fifth gallery was a prison within a prison. Executions were conducted here. The capo was relieved of his position afterwards as a consequence of his behavior. That beating was the most serious violence during my stay.

Double Vino

Being in bed except at night was forbidden, but rarely enforced. After lunch, augmented with a glass of wine, one might be inclined to recline on their bed for a few moments. On one occasion we were having a post-lunch rest when the door was flung open by the capo. The little guard who always worked with Don Francisco accompanied him.

"Sleeping in the day is against the rules."

The capo took our names. We expected some reprimand but Don Francisco needed to acquire a crew for cellblock cleaning and selected those who were caught in the rack. We mopped, scrubbed, scoured, brushed, and polished to exhaustion for the rest of the afternoon. Feared for his stern manner of dealing with inmates, Don Francisco gave us a reward along with our punishment.

That evening at dinnertime we heard a call,

"Those who worked on the cleaning crew today, extra vino."

Adjustment

Michael's first months in the mental facility were difficult, but he found a method, walking around the patio all day at a fast pace, doing exercises, and talking to himself. He contorted his face in a frown and wrinkled his brow simulating mental anguish when he saw guards but he stopped short of violence. The guards were big gorillas who could jab a syringe into an offender to tranquilize those who got out of control. The institution administered scary electroshock therapy, an accepted therapy for depression, so Michael played his act to not appear dangerous in avoidance of that extreme. He faked taking the pills that were prescribed from fear of what they might do.

After some months away Michael's girlfriend Janet began monthly visits, bringing him a liter of orange juice mixed with vodka. She managed to slip him some Dormadinas. Once they tried to get it on in the bathroom but their romantic liaison was foiled when a nun saw them enter the bathroom together.

The planned escape was designed to happen during visitation with Janet. That room was outside the bars but Michael's attempts at convincing her to get him a counterfeit passport and money failed. She reasoned with him that an escape could be worse and his sentence might not be that bad. He should do the time

With Janet's refusal to assist him, and because the sensible thread of her urgings wove slowly into the maze of his thought, the escape failed to materialize. She brought him his guitar, which he played in the patio, but the music drew a crowd. Some of the loonies enjoyed the show but some got carried away. To avoid arousing the wilder nature of Michael's audience the guitar was confiscated.

Michael Gets His Groove

As winter transited to spring and acceptance replaced shock Michael was learning how to deal with sick people and how not to be noticed. Once managed, the hospital was a more comfortable situation than the prison. The one-on-one visits with his paramour in the same room were superior to the separation in prison with a plastic window between them.

His trial was to be in Ibiza in June. He and his coconspirator were to be judged together. Michael was apprehensive about that confrontation but hoped that his incarceration in a mental hospital would be to his benefit. The court might lessen a judgment of criminality and gratify his choice of mental instability as a defence.

Contraband Trial

The day destroys the night. Night divides the day. Weeks became months. The vernal equinox relieved winter's chill with welcome warmth. Although unable to break on through the stone walls and metal doors of prevention a routine was established that enabled me to tolerate the disadvantage of confinement. Work in the factory occupied the day, letters from friends and family arrived, and the occasional book or article of clothing reached me. A copy of Rolling Stone magazine was delivered with female photos blackened by the prison censor.

The day of my trial for contraband arrived in April. Surly municipal police escorted me and Crazy Tony along with a few others out of the prison to a waiting Land Rover in the courtyard. We were manacled for transport to the court. Once inside the hall of justice our restraints were removed but we were made to stand in wait. Overly serious police eyeballed us while fingering their rifles. Tony displayed the weird mannerisms of his

mentally unbalanced act but that behavior threatened to push the overly attentive cops into retaliatory action. With my looks of admonishment he wisely desisted.

Each defendant was separately escorted into a small courtroom, and in few minutes returned. My attorney arrived and when my name was called the police walked us into the court. A group of judges dressed in suits and ties sat at a table. Senor Valenciano pleaded my case but there was little that could mitigate the fine levied for the avoidance of the proscribed tax amount on imported contraband. My penalty was assessed at four thousand dollars. Along with the five thousand dollar fee for my attorney, and the two thousand more for the American attorneys, the legal cost was eleven thousand dollars for what was intended to be a two thousand dollar payment for my effort.

Sex

The absence of female stimulation stopped my sexuality completely. There was nothing. No thoughts, no fantasy, no actions. A void. Physical gratification and pleasure did not exist within those walls. The feminine is the origin and female interaction had been more than adequate before incarceration. The state of withdrawal from the outside world stimulated an inward meditation that affiliated more with thought process than with a physical realm. Take care of business later.

Suicide

Not everyone adjusted to prison. One despondent man killed himself jumping from the third floor tier on Christmas Eve. The head African in our gallery drank bleach in a suicide attempt. Instead of death, the caustic chemical burned his intestines and stomach.

Bhagavad Gita

Books provided a form of engagement. My brother sent me a thick copy of the Bhagavad Gita, the Indian text that came into existence in the third or fourth millennium BC, explaining life and how to manage the human condition. The Gita informed me that karma was the creation of a reaction to my activity. Action had consequence. Turning off your mind, relaxing, and floating downstream, as John Lennon suggested, left me vulnerable to log jams. We do well with direction. Instead of looking *for* myself the work *on* myself proceeded. Prisons and monasteries have common ground. The isolation provides an opportunity for contemplation. The slate was wiped clean. A beginning was underway.

Changes

"Your trial will be in three weeks. You'll be going to Ibiza by boat. And, good news, the prosecutor is only asking for six years and a day."

My attorney regarded me through the window that separated visitors from prisoners. His eyeglasses had thick lenses. His beard was neatly trimmed. He wore a sweater vest under a wool sport coat in the June warmth.

In Spain, sentences were grouped into three categories of up to six, up to twelve, and up to eighteen years. The prosecutor chose which was appropriate for the crime and requested that sentence. Six years and a day was the maximum in my case, but the court might give me fewer, depending on circumstances. The case would be tried before three judges.

A sense of excitement began to brighten the daily routine. Going anywhere was a stimulating prospect. After eight months in Barcelona a summer voyage to Ibiza.

In the factory we talked about the trial.

"What did your lawyer tell you, " Jaime asked.

"My trial is in three weeks, in Ibiza."

"*Conyo*, that's good. They give lighter sentences there"

"The jail there is nice."

"They let you have women in the cells."

"Si, and hashish."

Old Juan coughed hard and spit into his handkerchief. There was blood in it.

"*Joder*, when Paco dies we'll all be free."

Paco was the Spanish people's nickname for

Generalissimo Francisco Franco, their autocratic dictator and head of totalitarian Spain. Earlier in Franco's forty year rule he had established repression characterized by concentration camps, forced labor and executions against political and ideological enemies that caused the deaths of a quarter of a million Spanish people.

When Franco died, the *indulto*, the pardon, was supposedly going to set us all free. That was the hope. In Spain, there was no system of parole as there is in America. An inmate could work in prison enterprises and receive a day off the sentence for every two days of labor. Some time was reduced for good behavior. The only other method of sentence reduction was by an irregularly declared pardon of varying numbers of years that was traditionally granted to prisoners by the rare coronation of a new king, which in this case, would be King Juan Carlos Alfonso Víctor María de Borbón y Borbón Dos Sicilias, the grandson of the previous king, Alfonso XIII.

General Franco had already chosen Juan Carlos to be the next head of state. When the general died the new king would have a coronation. Immediately after assuming the throne, in a gesture of grand benevolence to his subjects, the king would grant the *derecho de gracia*, the right of grace, or indulto, pardon, an act defined in the Spanish Constitution as an act of renunciation of the state's part of its punitive power founded on reasons of equity and public interest.

Being a Catholic country, Spain might also give a pardon on the installation of a new pope. The pardon would be a commutation, or lessening of the penalty for a crime, while its beneficiaries were still considered guilty of their offense.

Return To Ibiza

A capo came to my cell the night before the voyage to escort me to the first gallery, the transit point where inmates both entered and departed the prison. He expressed some enthusiasm for my trip to Ibiza. My wounded bank robbing German acquaintance Johann shared the cell with me that night. His trial was to be in Ibiza and we'd be traveling together in chains to the playground of the hipster world. My guitar was returned to me for the trip.

Our excitement for the impending journey kept us chattering in anticipation late into the night. In the morning we were escorted to the front gate. Two Guardia Civil met us and applied the manacles that were to be on our wrists throughout the voyage. The guards had rifles as well as handguns. We were driven to the port where the first night of my arrival in Spain was passed five years previously.

As we waited in the terminal travelers observed us with noticeable curiosity. We were outside of cold dead walls among free people on a sun-drenched summer day for the first time in eight months. Children chattered. Women walked. A rush of sensory stimulation.

We were escorted on board our ferry and below deck to our cabin. Passengers continued to take notice of us as we passed, manacled and under guard, eliciting curious glances. Once situated in the cabin, the guards cuffed us to the beds and left us to go about and throw down a few shots of cognac. Through the open door, a group of passing inquisitive female travelers looked in and initiated conversation, questioning us about the nature of our situation. The stimulation to be once again in public reminded me that there was a world of endless variation beyond the monotony of painting flowers on handbags while confined in grey stone.

These Guardia Civil were more easygoing than most. They recognized our love generation hipster demeanor and guarded us in a relaxed and friendly manner. On deck, one of them left his rifle by my chair as he went for a drink.

Our ship arrived in the port town of Ibiza in late afternoon. The sky was exploding in radiant orange surging into bright yellow with purple and violet edges. The swirling waters reflected the light with evanescent translucence. Seabirds flew through this landscape as salt-tinged air holding them aloft in feathered flight carried the aroma of the sea's vastness with freedom implicit in the wind. We took it all in, a feast of the senses at this world's beauty, overwhelming us with light and pleasure after so long in the ancient tomb.

Hotel Naranja

Spain's Guardia Civil is a federal military status police force founded in 1844. The Guardia were omnipresent throughout the country, distinguishable by their green uniforms, and distinctive black patent leather tricome hats. One of their responsibilities is the safeguarding of prisoners and in this regard the Guardia transported us on each movement between jails and prisons. The force obviously was a steady customer of Rover Motors, as Land Rovers seemed to be their exclusive vehicle of choice. One was waiting with a driver to transport us to the Ibiza jail located up the hill at the top of the old town.

On arrival, our handcuffs were removed. We were registered. The Guardia bid us good luck and took their leave. We were in the main building that housed offices on the second floor where the jailers could look out to monitor activity. Our new jailers escorted us down a staircase where we were released into a dirt courtyard bordered by two wings of right-angled low-roofed structures with blue doors.

A group of men observed us. One of them was Michael. He cracked a smile seeing me.

"Hey, it's you. Welcome back to Ibiza. Man, it's good to see you."

We embraced. In spite of our incarcerated situation we had been long acquainted and still capable of civil communication.

"Michael, hey man, how are you?"

"Well, not so good. It's been hell in the mental hospital in Palma, really been rough. My idea was to fake insanity to get me out of this situation. It might not work. Things are better here, though. What about you."

"It's been all right. Barcelona won't let me have my guitar. The factory keeps me going."

"Hey, man, it was a mistake to get us into this."

"Yeah, it didn't turn out to be such a good idea. Hey, Daniel. What are you doing here?"

Daniel was an American who lived in Formentera.

"Hash, man. Sold some to the wrong dude."

We were happy to see each other even under the restriction of our circumstance and pleased to be in Ibiza where the quarters were much more relaxed and open than Barcelona, or Michael's prison in Majorca.

The jail was nicknamed *Hotel Naranja*, The Orange Hotel, from an orange tree that grew in the courtyard's center. There were no cells, but unlocked rooms with wooden doors that allowed us the freedom to move around the area at will, and change rooms if we desired.

Our trial was a few days away. Weather was warm. With small, quaint quarters the change of pace felt like arriving at summer camp. Michael's girlfriend visited and surreptitiously brought him hashish and Dormadinas as well as large bottles of orange juice mixed with vodka. The lackadaisical guards didn't bother searching packages thoroughly. With a minimum of concealment Janet got inebriates to him. Being stoned in this confine was of no interest to me. Michael was still in an emotional and frightened state, and his habitual behavior enabled the seizure of an opportunity to numb himself.

With low security and easy procedures of the Ibiza jail the guards left us to ourselves. There was no trumpet to wake us. The warm days were without schedule. We American acquaintances chose to share one room together, where we socialized, played music, and slept. It was summertime and the living was less controlled than Barcelona's stricter precision.

After one of Michael's visits with Janet, he told me Astrid was intending to visit. But my full moon goddess failed to appear, made no visits, and sent no letters. My expectation crash-landed, but it was best that she not get ensnared in the wake of my misjudgment.

Making music with a guitar was enjoyable again, although feeling the strangeness of the strings biting into my now un-calloused fingers was a new sensation. Still, the music engendered a free flowing quality that had been missed in the absence created by Barcelona's policy, and we relished the pleasant interlude whiling away the hours until our date with justice.

The big cop who punched Michael when he was busted came to the jail office and looked down at us while we were in the courtyard. He said something insulting and Michael, remembering the sting from the beating received at the hands of this brute, couldn't resist loudly cursing him. Enraged, the cop initiated a rant and demanded of the jailers to be let down into the yard to work Michael over some more, but he was restrained and wisely not permitted to descend among us to vent his anger.

Our fellow prisoner Daniel had a son of eight months with the improbable name of Lightning. The easygoing guards allowed the opportunity for the child to have an afternoon with us in the jail. The mother delivered the boy to his father who was greatly gratified, as the baby was a sweet and gentle reminder that new beginnings were still possible.

Trial

The day of judgment arrived by authority of the Spanish government for the crime of being in possession of illegal hashish. Having survived these eight months of captivity with no ill effects, my mood was optimistic, and a sense of confidence gave me determination. Whatever storm was hurled at me in that hall of justice would be weathered.

Michael was apprehensive. His months of faking insanity confined in a mental hospital had increased the discomfort of his incarceration. The pretense of incompetence in the hope of that condition precluding a severe sentence had been difficult to maintain and might conclude as a failed attempt to avoid the inevitable.

Prepared to meet the inquisition, we were summoned by our warders to the jail office. Municipal police put handcuffs on our wrists then escorted us to the adjacent court. Our attorneys were waiting outside the courtroom. Our restraints were removed. The police stayed with us. Senor Valenciano was dressed in a brown wool suit, white shirt, and red tie. He was in a chipper mood, clapping me on the back with assurance that he would mount a vigorous defense. The facts that this was my first offence, and that the instigation was not mine, would be viewed favorably.

Michael's attorney was a less imposing figure. Short, bald, with thick-lensed eyeglasses, he dressed in a black suit and black tie. He would attempt to establish that Michael's intention was not to sell the twenty pounds of hashish, but keep it for his personal stash.

Our case was called. We entered the dark oak-wooded courtroom. Three black-robed judges sat at a massive desk on a raised dais with red velvet drapes behind them.

Proceedings were conducted in Spanish. The prosecutor made a preliminary statement informing the court of the crime we committed by smuggling an illegal substance into the country. He requested a sentence of six years and a day.

"Did you carry two suitcases containing twenty pounds of hashish, into Spain?" The prosecutor called it *hacheech*.

"Yes."

"Did you plan the operation?

"Yes."

Our attorney's followed with statements affirming our lack of criminal history. They painted a portrait of us as naïve, first time offenders and asked the court to be merciful.

The short proceeding concluded. The police came forward to escort us from the courtroom to the hallway where our manacles were reapplied, and our attorneys joined us, cheerful and optimistic. The verdict would be rendered within a day or two.

Night's comforting cloak enveloped us in her opaque grasp. Stars glistened. Dreams drifted unhindered until the eastern glow revealed morning's bright revelation. The earth continued its revolution on its orbit around the blazing ball of fire through the vacuum of eternal unending space. Playing guitar, singing, reading about karma in the Bhagavad Gita, doing yoga, and changing the effect of unconscious behavior occupied me. Michael played music, drank vodka, smoked hash, and popped pills while awaiting the court's judgment.

Verdict

Two days after the trial our jailers called us into the courtyard. From their office above they dropped two envelopes out the window. Our verdicts fluttered down to our outstretched hands. The prosecutors had been met halfway by the mercy of the judges who saw fit to apply a measure of leniency. The court had sentenced us to a term of three years.

With eight months of my sentence behind me, and by working to reduce the time, the most for me to serve would be another year.

Michael was less sagacious. He was afraid to return to the mental hospital where feigned insanity had no bearing on the outcome. The posing, the time strapped to a bed, and being in the company of real lunatics was for naught. Two days later, Michael, along with Daniel, was transported back to Palma de Majorca.

With his sentence pronounced the need to feign insanity was unnecessary and Michael discarded the act. Doctors determined he was not mentally ill and he was transferred from Palma by boat to the prison in Alicante on the mainland. On the journey the guards removed his handcuffs and sat with him at the bar while Michael was allowed to consume enough alcohol to satisfy his need.

The Guardia Civil arrived for my transport on the ship back to Barcelona. They assured me that a three-year sentence was a breeze, that luck was on my side. They called my arrest *mal negocio*, bad negotiation. No wrong, just bad planning.

Our interim in Ibiza, along with a reasonable sentence, had lifted my spirits. There was to be an end to this restriction of my activity in another year or so. The course of events, however, was to unfold in a different and unpredictable direction.

Four

Redemption

Home Again, Jiggety Jig

After my summer vacation Barcelona's prison aura, though dreary, lacked the fear and uncertainty of my previous arrival. That tension was replaced with familiarity.

Time in observation passed without incident but for one trick Michael taught me.

"Say you have colitis and they'll give you hospital food," he advised.

His ruse worked. During the medical examination the medic noted the condition on my chart and assigned me the better quality diet. After five-day isolation a capo arrived to escort me back to the fourth gallery, envious of my visit to Ibiza and enthusiastic in conversation about the island. My quarters with Victor and Patrick and my work in the factory were waiting. My official sentence would soon arrive with an assignment to a penal institution.

The Priest

Within a week of my return, the prison priest, Padre Pablo, came to see me at the factory. He summoned me outside to speak.

"They tell me you are a musician. Would directing the chorus be of interest to you? My musical director is going to another prison and we need someone to play guitar and coordinate the music."

My response was immediate.

"Yes. Piano was part of my studies as well."

"Good, you can play the organ, too. "

"It sounds like a good opportunity for me. Thank you."

"Bien. We get your guitar."

With more than a little spring in my step, we walked from the factory to a door in the center, where the guard on duty granted us access to a large storage room. Shelves were filled floor-to-ceiling with items the inmates possessed when they were arrested. There my guitar rested. The priest instructed me to take it. We walked back to the center where Padre Pablo retrieved a key. We wheeled about and within a few steps he stopped before a wooden door, unlocked and opened it, and led the way into a chapel. In contrast to the random sounds outside, there was tranquility within the sanctuary. A raised dais stood at the far side with pews before it. To one side was an organ beside a piano. Padre approached a dark wooden closet and opened its door.

"These are my robes for the services. You can keep your guitar here and get the key for the chapel whenever you want to come here and learn the music and practice. Rehearsals with the choir are Wednesdays and Thursdays, after dinner. We do two services on Sunday. We're happy you are joining us."

Church Music

The priest gave me access to my previously forbidden guitar, along with a quiet room to play, the only place in the prison where being alone was possible, other than solitary confinement. My presence in Barcelona had been unnoticed, but the transition to being a musician for the church instigated a change. My cellmates, Victor and Patrick, agreed that the gig was a beneficial experience for me. My fellow workers at the factory perked up as well. Celebrity was thrust upon me.

At the first rehearsal, the chorus was effusive in expressing notable enthusiasm at my participation, like they were with an American star engaging in cultural exchange. The twelve singers were all Catalan, as was the priest. They conversed in that language, spoken in Barcelona and in the Balearic Islands, sounding like Spanish with a lilt.

Setsa jucha menchan fecha d'un panchat.

Seven judges ate the liver of a hanged man.

Padre Pablo chose the material for each Sunday's service and provided charts to prepare the instrumentation. Six years had elapsed since music school, where piano was required for all students, but reading and learning the music was not difficult. With my private time to go over the selections, and the two rehearsals, we were ready in time for Sunday services. The church welcomed me back for the first time since high school, when my girlfriend Tamara had occasionally been able to convince me to attend.

Padre Pablo was a short, bald, cheerful man. He had a habit of cursing at little things by saying,

"Me cago en Dios,"

meaning, I shit on God. The expression is a common utterance in Spain but the irony was lost on everyone but me.

The experience of working with the Catalan chorus was unique, and one that put me in touch with Spanish people, as opposed to my previous experiences with only English speakers, where we were foreigners in the countries we visited and moved in our own insulated social sphere. My involvement with the chorus was an honor for me, and they felt the same. This interaction would not have happened in the real world.

In addition to choral songs, the priest liked interludes of music to accompany liturgical events. For these, whatever melodies popped into mind were played, bits of pop songs, *Scarborough Fair, The Boxer, You Can't Always Get What You Want*, Beatle songs, anything. Young attendees recognized the music from the pop repertoire and were entertained with their inclusion in the services. The chorus sang three and four part harmony arrangements accompanied by guitar or organ. It proved to be great fun for us. Church attendance had a noticeable increase.

Being the only American, with some history as a musician in Hollywood, and in the service of the Catholic Church, brought me respect from the authorities and a growing stature as the prison pop star. My guitar still couldn't be brought to my cell, but the chapel served as a sanctuary where bluebirds flew over the faded rainbow and troubles melted like lemon drops in a place of privacy. Within the limits a prison imposes, the administration began to give me the run of the place.

Day Of Saint Mercedes

Spain is a Catholic country in which every day of the year has an associated patron saint. Spanish people celebrate their birthdays and their saint's day. If your name is Vicente, on Saint Vicente's day you take all your friends out and buy them drinks. There are saints for every manner of the human condition. Saint Mercedes, Our Lady of Mercy, is the patron saint of prisoners. On her day prisoners are put in the compassionate spotlight to be honored, albeit briefly.

In preparation for *El Dia de Mercedes*, Padre Pablo planned a program for the general population in church and a separate performance in a private chapel for the director of the prison, the guards, and their wives. In addition to favorite church songs, the music included a show-stopping choral work entitled, *Patrona de Barcelona*.

Preparations began two months prior. The complicated organ part for *Patrona* was learned. It had a powerful conclusion, not unlike Beethoven's *Ode To Joy*, but with a Neapolitan sixth cadence. The cadence is used at the end of *O Sole Mio*. It sounds dramatic. The chorus rehearsed. Padre stressed the importance of delivering a good performance.

Meanwhile, we prisoners were planning a talent show to be held in the yard in two shifts since not all of the population was able to fit in one yard at one time. The coordination was assigned to me. Prisoners auditioned. A stage was constructed for the event.

On the morning of El Dia de Mercedes the chorus did two inmate services then, under guard, walked outside the iron entrance door to the outer courtyard for the staff performance. The chapel was resplendent with stained glass windows and marble statuary. Guards were garbed in white dress uniforms augmented with gold braid. Their wives were attired in elegant dresses with wide-brimmed headwear. Senor Director wore his white uniform with an increased amount of gold braid and racks of medals pinned across his chest. His rotund wife sat beside him in a black dress with large white polka dots. Her effusive white hat erupted with a decorative artificial floral arrangement.

Padre Pablo addressed the assembly, reminding attendees that prisoners were not to be forsaken, that their souls had the possibility of redemption and beyond punishment was the opportunity and hope of improvement that the patron saint of prisoners, Saint Mercedes, offered. At the service's conclusion the chorus delivered the knockout punch, a powerful rendition of *Patrona de Barcelona*, emphasizing in music and in words Saint Mercedes' faith in criminal's moral resurrection.

Senor Director congratulated the priest and thanked the chorus for our participation. We were treated to chocolates and told to return to the galleries. We were not under escort. One could have fled and made a getaway from that less guarded chapel but we strolled back into captivity with chocolate dissolving in our mouths, uplifted with the success of the performance.

For lunch, the kitchen had prepared paella, the traditional Spanish dish of saffron rice with shrimp, rabbit, sausage, and chicken. The guards were arrayed in their dress uniforms with shiny medals, and clean white gloves on their hands. Instead of the inmates distributing lunch, today the guards served us. They went to each cell offering Coca-Cola, which they poured while they exuded politeness. We fell in line to receive our paella. We were allowed to lounge around the gallery for a time with cell doors open. Then it was show time.

We paraded into the yard for the performances. Crazy Tony did *Paint It Black*, playing guitar, singing, twisting, and moving like a spastic Elvis, in keeping with his feigned insanity. My choice was a fingerpicking gospel song by Reverend Gary Davis called *Samson and Delilah* with the refrain, *If I had my way, I would tear this building down.* If they only knew.

At the show's conclusion the prisoners stood as the director and his retinue exited. Senor Director approached me. He acknowledged my performances and my work on the shows, shook my hand, and expressed his appreciation. Though brief were the moments full was their measure. Love was the force and great was the treasure.

Riot

Stringbean was dead. The macho guard entered his cell and beat him to death in a fit of sadistic rage. *Habichuela*, Stringbean, was mentally unbalanced. He approached me once, babbling and repeating himself, wearing a jacket with prison script pinned all over the outside like Boy Scout merit badges. The Bean didn't belong in the third gallery with the habitual repeaters. He needed to be in the mental unit of the hospital. The guard who killed Stringbean was known to be a mean character that looked for trouble and enjoyed the power he carried to dish it out. Whenever he was in my vicinity my response was to avoid eye contact and glide by invisibly. This guard wasn't in our gallery often. He worked the third gallery where Stringbean had been housed.

The news of the death spread throughout the prison. The third gallery was reacting with spontaneous insurrection. The men refused to come down for dinner. The next day none of them left their cells when the doors were opened in the morning. Now, they were shouting and throwing the contents of their cells out onto the floor.

Control is the most salient aspect of prison life.

Its loss was bad and troublesome for the rest of us. The authorities tried to go on with the routine for everyone else. We had breakfast, as usual, and when the bell sounded to announce work we went out.

Walking to the factory took us through the yard between our gallery, and the third, where, in addition to the disruptive shouting, we could hear things being thrown around. We fell to working while an uncomfortable sense of apprehension escalated as the unruly uproar continued. Eventually, Don Francisco, the head of the factory, instructed us to leave our places and go out into the yard. Shouts were continuing from the third gallery. We could see smoke from fires that had been lighted in some of the cells. Some men had made their way into the center where they were out of control fueled by rage at the murder. A few ran into our yard shouting encouragement at us to storm the center in an attempt to take over the prison. Some began throwing whatever they could find toward the doors. Some dashed in. As fast as they ran in, they ran back out shouting. Now, we heard gunshots.

"They're shooting us."

Most of us in the yard weren't participating but we found ourselves being engulfed in a riot. The entire group in the yard ran back into the factory through the still open doors for protection from the shooting that continued in the center. We nervously waited while Don Francisco phoned to ascertain the situation. He told the authorities that we were peaceful. An arrangement with the guards in the center was negotiated. We were to go to the factory door, form two lines, and put our clasped hands on our heads. Don Francisco was to lead us calmly back to the fourth gallery where order had been restored. We assembled at the door. Don Francisco led us across the yard to the center's entrance. We crossed the threshold and were confronted by the sight of a phalanx of heavily armed riot police standing shoulder to shoulder with shields in one hand and clubs in the other. With their reflective facemasks and helmets they looked like death invaders from outer space. We eased silently past and into the gallery where the gate was closed and locked behind us. As we passed, some of the police took random swings at the passive inmates.

The three of us were back in our cell, shaken but unhurt, while some heads had been cracked. The prison was in lockdown. Authority has limits. Even prisoners have power.

Mother

The usual hum of activity was absent. In its stead was silence. We were back in the cage and weren't being allowed out. Meals were distributed one door at a time by the capos. The metallic sound of our cell door bolt moving in its channel followed by the heavy iron door opening pierced the tranquility. A capo had been sent to inform me that my presence was required in the visiting area. My mother was here. Mom had arrived in Barcelona on the day of the riot. She had not told me about a European visit.

Walking through the silent gallery, we saw shoes, clothing, and debris that lay scattered on the floor where they had fallen during the melee. The capo explained that one consequence of the riot was the cancellation of all activity, including visits, but since my mother had come all the way from America an exception was made.

In the visiting room the guard pointed out my mother's familiar face smiling on the other side of the plastic in the subdued room gloom. Mom had been shocked and fearful at news of the riot. Relief in seeing me unscathed brought her to tears.

After the violent events of the previous day and the months of incarceration the moments together were reassuring. Mother was the rock in my sea of turbulence and now she asked for my promise to return home to California. Six years of travel had expanded my knowledge of the world and my place in it but the exploration had reached a conclusion. It was time to go home.

The guard in the visiting area conversed with me regarding the riot.

"Here in prison, there are two ways, the easy way and the hard way. If you want the easy way, you get it, but if you want the hard way, we have that, too. It's your decision."

That was the message of the Bhagavad Gita. Karma was the reaction to one's action. We get what we give.

Lockdown continued for a few days, during which the active rioters were identified and placed in new solitary confinement areas converted from cells in each gallery. Normal behavior was restored, and routine resumed.

The Priest's Offer

Five months after my trial Padre Pablo told me my sentence would soon be arriving. He offered me a choice, to stay in Barcelona and he would make things comfortable for me, or go to whatever facility the authorities designated. Although appreciative of the better condition my church work provided, a change of scene was preferable. The priest was supportive, without reservation. Our groove was guided by grace but when the highway calls you got to move.

Orders arrived for my transfer to the prison at Santander on Spain's north coast of the Atlantic Ocean. This facility occupied a rural area containing a dairy farm. Thirteen months had elapsed confined in Barcelona's detention center, nearly the same time as my living on Ibiza, an equal balance between paradise and captivity. It was time for the last leg of my Spanish vacation.

Journey

Late autumn brought cool days when leaves would become brown and crunch underfoot, if there were any trees to drop leaves in our midst. The shortening sunlight produced the darker, deeper colors of fall. The moment for my transfer from Barcelona to Santander had arrived. A capo came to my cell door.

He waited for me to gather my few things then escorted me to the observation gallery for the night, from where those in transit would depart. Barcelona was an education, not the book learning at the desk type, but lessons in real life, conquering adversity, with an acquisition of internal understanding. In another year my debt to Spain would be paid. Incarceration would conclude.

The last time that any structured discipline had been applied to my life had been in high school. Lacking any military or real employment experience, apart from music performance and writing, the course of my journey flowed without regard to conforming to rules, until Barcelona. Here the routine was strictly observed with regimentation, factory work, and regularity without exception, one day like any other. The time was the first in years that drugs had not been a part of my everyday experience. My body was cloistered but my mind was freed from the debilitating effect of habitual dependence.

The distance from Barcelona, on the northeast coast of Spain by the Mediterranean Sea, to Santander, in the northwest by the Atlantic Ocean, is 336 miles. We would travel in stages. The first night out we would stop in Zaragoza and sleep in the city jail. The next day's journey was to Carabanchel in Madrid, the largest of Spain's prisons, where a few days might pass before continuing northward to Burgos. Santander was my final destination, on the Bay of Biscay, where the city's beaches were a popular surfing location, one of only a few in Europe. Our expedition was to be by bus and Land Rover.

Franco

Inmates often talked about General Francisco Franco, Spain's head of state. In 1936, while he was chief of staff for the Spanish military, Franco led a successful revolt against the democratically elected government of Spain, and in October of that year, he was appointed Generalissimo of Nationalist Spain and head of state. A month later, Nazi Germany recognized Franco as the legitimate ruler of Spain, as did France and England. By 1939 the United States granted recognition to the military general.

In 1940, Spain declined Hitler's request to join the Axis powers in World War II. From this point, Franco was a dictator. His rule was law. Spain displayed all the characteristics of a right wing dictatorship, ruthlessly crushing all opposition. The nation had to endure the activities of a secret police force. All the aspects of politics that would have been taken for granted in Europe, such as fair elections and political opposition, were not tolerated in Franco's Spain. In 1947, a law was passed that made Franco head of state for life. Planning for posterity, Franco decreed that at his death the monarchy would be restored and Prince Juan Carlos would become head of state. Later, during the Cold War, Franco was seen as a safe bet against any spread of communism in Western Europe.

Inmates discussed Franco for one reason above all others. Since there is no parole in Spain, the only way to have a sentence reduced, other than the work two days, take a day off your sentence reduction, was by an *indulto*, a pardon. The pardon was usually declared as a gesture of benevolence when a new head of state took office. Inmates sometimes discussed state pardons as an imaginative exercise in wishful thinking. The king designate was not head of state as long as Franco remained alive. Franco's death, therefore, was the inmate's only hope. But the old ruler had been in power for so long it seemed that the time would never arrive.

The End Begins

Three Spanish robbers accompanied me in a ground floor cell on my final night in Barcelona, in preparation for the morning's departure. They discussed their favored methods of robbery and their desire to find valuables, particularly diamonds, in the homes of their victims.

While the four of us in our observation cell waited for the night to pass, a capo came to the door and excitedly reported that Franco was hospitalized with rapidly deteriorating health. The story was dominating the news.

When morning arrived, we were escorted from the Center of Detention for Men in Barcelona onto a waiting bus, where we were handcuffed to the rails of the seats for our day's journey to Zaragoza, a city that had been Roman in 25 BC, a Muslim state in the eleventh century, conquered by Aragonese in the thirteenth century, and the site of martyrdoms during the Spanish Inquisition. My prolonged confinement served to enhance the new and pleasurable sensation of rolling down the highway. Cooped in small cells, everything visually is close. Viewing open country, trees, rivers, and villages as we sped past, enlarged my dormant field of vision.

When our bus arrived in Zaragoza in the evening we were moved into the jail. We dined and were given bunks for the night. News of Franco's worsening condition increased a palpable excitement.

Gloria!

Early on the morning of November 20, Generalissimo Francisco Franco, age 82, the fascist ruler of Spain from 1939 to 1975, died from numerous health problems and Parkinson's disease. Some hours later that day, unaware of the general's death, we prisoners were herded back onto our bus, handcuffed to the rails, and our journey resumed. While passing through open countryside moving toward Madrid, one of the guards, who had been listening to a portable radio, announced,

"Franco's dead!"

"*Gloria zanahoria*," someone exclaimed, which translates to glorious carrot, meaningless but for the rhyme. Seeking reassurance that, in fact, the dictator had expired, he added,

"Look for the flags to be at half staff."

Navigating the outer regions of Madrid, we did begin to see Spanish flags flying at half-staff. It was true. Franco was dead. The coronation of the king and the pardon could not be far away. Our bus left the rural district, threaded its way through the outskirts of Madrid, and arrived at Carabanchel Prison. We observed black bands around the right arms of the guard's green uniforms. The atmosphere had become festive with smiles, excitement, relief, and joy. Sorrow was in short supply. In the hearts of the Spanish people there was a long held desire for change, a simmering hope that the old fascist methodology defining Franco's era would transit to a new democratic beginning, one that entailed freedom and an entrance to the common union of Europe.

Although larger than Barcelona, Madrid's Carabanchel was built on a similar design, that of the Panopticon, a name derived from Panoptes, a hundred-eyed giant in Greek mythology known to be an effective watchperson. The design consists of a circular structure with an inspection house at its center from which the staff is able to observe the halls of the massive galleries that are attached to the center like spokes of a wheel. Between the galleries were yards for prisoners to congregate. Unlike Barcelona, Madrid allowed musical instruments, long hair, and beards.

A temporary cell was mine alone. All eyes were transfixed on television while Spain observed the coronation of King Juan Carlos on November 22, followed a day later by a national funeral for the deceased head of state, General Franco.

Heady optimism permeated the atmosphere. The solemnity of what was to have been a year to complete my sentence gave way to expectation of immediate release. The pardon was imminent, but when, and for how long? We waited, with anticipation.

Burgos

The day following the coronation of Spain's king two Guardia Civil loaded me and two others in a Land Rover for the next leg of our journey to Burgos, the capital city of Castile, a medieval kingdom of the Iberian Peninsula that had participated in the reconquest of Iberia from the Moors in the 1300s. Castile is the origin of the Castilian language that is referenced as Spanish. When Ferdinand II of Aragon wed Isabella I of Castile in 1469, the union led to the creation of Spain.

Castile is a high plateau and at 2800 feet elevation the climate of Burgos is noted for cold and windy winters, always with snow and below freezing. The city is on the Camino de Santiago, a pilgrimage route since the Middle Ages. Walking the Camino provides holy indulgence, spiritual tranquility or just a good hike in the country. The route covers a distance of almost five hundred miles, usually from the French Pyrenees to Santiago de Compostela in the northeast.

At the conclusion of a grey chilled day of travel our Land Rover arrived at the dreary prison. Shaded under a perpetually shrouded sky, the earth held accumulations of snow, bunched and icy in an atmosphere of benumbed shivering and inhospitable bitterness.

We were escorted to an old, musty, cold dormitory. Staying warm required lying in bed with layers of blankets for insulation in this frigid, damp room. Quartered with other inmates in transit, either from or toward Madrid, we weren't allowed out of our moldy enclosure. We occupied ourselves with reading, chess, talking, and waiting. An itch developed on my left inner thigh, turning my skin red. My one time out of the dormitory was to the infirmary, where the inflammation was treated with a topical medication that began to clear the problem.

The Pardon

Two days after my arrival, while in my bunk slathered in scratchy woolen blankets to ward off the cold, an excited shout pierced the gloom. An enthusiastic animated voice from a prisoner outside the building repeated,

"Tres anos, tres anos, tres anos."

Three years. King Juan Carlos had demonstrated his benevolence toward the country's incarcerated by bestowing the *derecho de gracia*, the right of grace, the long discussed *indulto*, a pardon of three years from each prisoner's sentence. In that trancelike frosty netherworld, enclosed in a decrepit building, among people of a distant dimension, far from my origins, a realization flashed with lucid clarity. Three years *was* my sentence. It was over, cancelled, null and void, completed. Fourteen months had been served. The rest was no more. The end had arrived.

In a dormitory in what was once the medieval Kingdom of Castile, in the country where my father had in the late 1930s fought the fascist Franco and his troops, who, without benefit of a fair trial by jury, or even evidence, sent his Republican Assault Guards to assassinate the poet Federico Garcia Lorca, and a couple of hundred thousand more, in a country like many nations where longhaired love generation youth were confined to ancient cold stone fortresses for possessing hashish, while being detained against my will and transported between the country's houses of detention, the rare gesture of government leniency for which we had been waiting was granted, communicated to us through the sealed door of our incarceration, that would cancel my debt and conclude my confinement.

In lieu of the option of walking out the door now and heading down the road there remained the necessity to finish the journey to Santander, a day away, and await official procedure.

Some, with shorter sentences, were ecstatic. Those, however, with longer terms to serve, were complaining that three years wasn't enough. There had been cases of twelve-year pardons, and considering that Franco had control of the government for decades and pardons were rare, some expected a more magnanimous gesture.

The political left in Spain viewed the amnesty as minimal, extending to only thirty per cent of the prison population. Common criminals benefitted but only two hundred thirty-five political prisoners were released of the four thousand that were incarcerated. While Juan Carlos was being crowned riot police were handling demonstrations outside the country's prisons that called for full amnesty while protesting the pardon's paucity.

That afternoon those prisoners who had received packages of home-made edibles combined that with the institution's food to create a celebratory version of a last supper in the dormitory dining room with what decoration they might muster, for as elegant a presentation as could be managed. The call for lunch went out and we arrived at the festive table to discover the moment of victory enshrined in gastronomic glory.

That afternoon we lingered long, in a conquering mood about our sudden unexpected good fortune. For me the pardon signified impending freedom, and the end of my restriction through ego and ignorance. No more would my behavior allow taking a chance that wagered my liberty, no longer to be taken for granted. Freedom's value was learned the hard way, the only way that we really understand.

Michael's Release

Michael had adjusted well in Alicante, associating with the few Americans while working in the prison leather handbag factory. Six months after his trial he received the pardon granted by the incoming head of state, King Juan Carlos.

During the course of his incarceration he was declared an undesirable social misfit and persona non grata in Spain. An expulsion order was issued declaring that he was *en busca en captura,* meaning that if he was apprehended on Spanish soil he was to be arrested on sight. Instead of simply putting him outside the prison walls in Alicante, he was deported to Marseilles, France.

Michael took a train to Barcelona the next day, making his way to Ibiza under an assumed name. On Christmas day he took a taxi to his girlfriend Janet's house, where he saw someone slipping out the back when he was seen arriving. It was Jack in bed with his Jill. He and Jack later had a coffee and talked about it but such was the state of his new reality in Ibiza. That one hurt. The next day, two Ibicencan farmers with whom Michael was well acquainted escorted him on back trails, armed with shotguns, to see his father. Ibicencans were no strangers to smuggling. The islands' many sea caves have long been ideal hiding places for sea folk who desired concealment while transporting contraband. Therefore, a certain sympathy for Michael's plight ensued.

The trio approached the old man's house, calling him out for a surprise. Michael's father was an alcoholic who had lived alone in the country for years. The old man didn't recognize his son. He had been in bed with his bottle and was intoxicated with a five-day beard. After two or three long minutes his jaw dropped and recognition came. He cried with joy at the reunion and eventually went inside to clean himself up, but didn't hug his son.

With an expulsion order in effect there was nothing more Michael could do. Sadly, he had to leave Spain and his father, whom he never saw alive again. Michael returned to California to start over, leaving father, house, and unfaithful girlfriend behind.

He made an effort to get permission to return to Spain, where he owned the house in which his father lived, but to no avail. It was increasingly evident that he was to be denied.

Two years later Michael received the news that his father had died. A neighboring farmer decided to investigate after not seeing the old man for a couple of weeks and found him dead in his bed, bottle of cognac in hand. Michael was notified and was able to return to Ibiza on a special visa to bury his father and sell the house.

Eventually, his persona non grata status expired. He returned to the island, gave up drugs and alcohol, built a house, and got a real job teaching English. Michael journeyed from a childhood in Los Angeles, passing through the psychedelic sixties in San Francisco to old world Spain and a drug induced haze that resulted in incarceration. In the end he rejected that numbing behavior for a good life on the small island that has hosted travelers for centuries. Michael traveled far to discover what he sought, a peaceful place in the sun.

Santander

The day after Spain's king bestowed his magnanimous grace, a number of us were manacled, led from our chilled quarters, escorted onto a waiting bus, and departed frigid Burgos, newly pardoned and warmed within.

Our bus left Castile and made its way to the province of Cantabria, the northern region bordering the Cantabrian Sea on the Bay of Biscay, a gulf of the

Atlantic Ocean where depths reach three miles. The bay also contains shallow waters of the Continental Shelf, resulting in rough seas and some of the Atlantic's fiercest weather, known to cause merchant vessels to flounder, take on water, and sink.

We descended from a mountainous route and entered Green Spain, the land between the bay and the mountains, with lush vegetation from the moderate and wet ocean climate. In this region, rich with archaeological sites, are found cave paintings from 37,000 BC, at Altamira, the first cave where these prehistoric works were discovered, thirty kilometers from our destination.

Santander is a port city noted for its beaches and seaside resorts that swarm with sun- basking tourists. The prison is located on a strip of green land with walls that touch the beach on one side and snuggle into hills on another.

Our bus stopped in front of the main building where a group of men gathered to view the unloading. My former cellmate, Sid, had been transferred here months before. He stood among those greeting the new arrivals. First thing he said was,

"You're a free man."

Sid's sentence of twelve years was partially reduced by the pardon but he still had years to serve. Undeterred, he was as chipper as ever and took advantage of the moment, once formalities were complete, to show me around the grounds and pastures of Santander.

By comparison to Barcelona's urban and military environment Santander was rural, less strict, with smaller buildings, and spacious. In the operation of the farm and the dairy the residents were granted much freedom of movement.

Each man had a private cell. There was a uniform of sorts. We wore blue jeans and a grey prison coat. The vibe was looser. One could even store the daily ration of wine. It was unfortunate that the majority of my time had been in the more crowded urban setting. The facility allowed more privilege and comfort than Barcelona. There was little time for me to take it in.

The Last Walk

On my third day a summons instructed me to go to the conference room where inmates met with visitors. A guard sat there at a desk, attentive to papers spread before him. He took my summons, read it, and looked back at me.

"Your order for release has arrived."

He presented documents to me.

"Sign these papers. Here is the money you earned working in Barcelona. The money you had at the time of your arrest is still there. It will be sent to you later, through the American Consulate."

"Thank you."

"Go get your things, then meet me back here. You're leaving now. Going free."

My few articles of clothing, some drawings, a book or two, and my guitar, were gathered. The guard was waiting for me.

We left the enclosure of the main cellblock and walked down a grassy slope toward an iron door in the stone wall a hundred yards away. The day was cloudless and warm. A light wind carried the scent of wildflowers and the salty sea. Wooly white sheep grazed in the verdant fields beyond the walls. Rippling splashes of blue water at the edge of the vast Atlantic Ocean sparkled in the sunlight. Gathering waves of exhilaration washed within me. The enclosure of prison began to slip away like a serpent's discarded skin.

Fourteen months on Ibiza and fourteen months of captivity in Spanish jails balanced in illustration of both the natural world and captivity. Freedom is too valuable to be gambled. My journey had been by tempest tossed but survived. Time to return to that far off shore where the lamp was lifted beside the golden door.

We reached the final gate. A guard opened the portal that straddled the gateway between restriction and the open road.

"The next time you come to Spain, no drugs."

We laughed and extended our hands in goodbye salute.

"Adios"

"Adios"

The wide world waited.

Barred Window Blues

He told us what's happening outside the bars
he told us our friends are wishing on stars
brothers and sisters and all of their love
hoping for freedom on the wings of a dove

Some have to suffer some have to sing
for those who are growing the bell's going to ring
freedom or innocence no judge can declare
sooner or later we're all going there

No place to run no place to hide
the only good vibe comes from inside
life's an experience and kind of a joke
i thought it was funny when i was taking a toke

Freedom came and found me today
i hate to go but it's just to play
from the island of travelers and masters of space
it was lightning who emptied the dark from this place

Best to be cool when you want to stay high
time moves quickly here in the sky
sunrises red sunrises gold
handle life gently nothing's foretold

Hey baby let's go back to where you were born
we'll meet again but not on the spanish magic carpet
play your guitars but don't forget
mister businessman can never dress like us

Part 2

Five

Pilgrim

A Marine

Harrison was the son of Bavarian immigrants who settled in the foothills of California's Sierra Nevada Gold Country. The family thrived on their bountiful fruit orchards until the depression brought them down. As a young man Harry worked three jobs in high school to pay for his coveted college education, then he received a basketball scholarship at University of Oregon. At the start of World War II he enlisted in the Marine Corps.

While stationed at Camp Pendleton, California, awaiting shipment to the Pacific theater, twenty-two year old Harry attended a dance where he bumped into his future bride, seventeen year old Patricia, a daughter of English and Irish immigrants, by inadvertently stepping on her toes. Despite the initial painful beginning, a romance bloomed and they were married in a military ceremony. Shortly after the wedding Harry was shipped out to the South Pacific, where the war was horror, but Harry was heartened by the knowledge that his bride was waiting back home. He fought at the battle of Bougainville in the Solomon Islands, was promoted to captain, and awarded a medal for bravery while evacuating wounded comrades under enemy fire. But from mosquitos Harry contracted Dengue Fever. Because of the continuous joint pain, Dengue is also called Breakbone Fever. Ironically, the disease probably saved Harry's life, when his division fought and died without him in Guam, Guadalcanal, and Iwo Jima.

Harry was sent home to recuperate in San Francisco, first in a hospital and later at his uncle's Sea Cliff mansion overlooking San Francisco Bay, where the new Golden Gate Bridge offered a welcome view for battle weary soldiers.

At war's end Harry became a supervisor for Del

Monte Foods at the company's fruit and vegetable canneries in Yakima, Washington.

Three years after the close of the war, Patricia presented to the world a son, given the name Robert, in Old High German, Hruodberht, meaning bright with glory. In our first name world Robert became Bob.

Harry was transferred to headquarters in San Francisco on the fast track to being an executive and the family moved to the new suburb of San Mateo, on the bay, south of the city.

Warm San Franciscan Nights

In 1967, Bob was 19, enrolled in Menlo College and experiencing the Summer of Love in San Francisco, attending concerts at Speedway Meadows, and walking Hippie Hill in Golden Gate Park. The Fillmore auditorium opened, featuring bands like the Grateful Dead, Quicksilver Messenger Service, Jefferson Airplane, Moby Grape, and Country Joe & the Fish. Admission on Tuesday night was one dollar. The exploding new music scene lit a fire in Bob's searching soul nourished by acid-dosed sugar cubes while psychedelic lights pulsated to screaming guitars.

Buddhism

Hip love philosophy was influenced by Eastern religion, with Buddhism at its apex. Alan Watts, the British-born philosopher, writer, and speaker, was the best-known interpreter who popularized Eastern philosophy for a Western audience. Watts gained a large following in the San Francisco Bay Area while working as a programmer at KPFA radio station in Berkeley and writing more than 25 books and articles on subjects important to Eastern and Western religion, introducing the burgeoning youth culture to *The Way of Zen*, the first bestselling book on Buddhism. In *Psychotherapy East and West*, Watts proposed that Buddhism could be thought of as a form of psychotherapy rather than a religion. His writings and recorded talks still shimmer with a profound and galvanizing lucidity. In the 1960s, Watts began to experiment with psychedelics, including mescaline and LSD. Marijuana, he said, was a useful and interesting psychoactive drug that gave the impression of time slowing down. Watts' books of the period reveal the influence of these chemical adventures on his outlook. He later said about psychedelic drug use,

"When you get the message, hang up the phone."

Eastern philosophy began to turn the key in the lock that opened Bob's mental door to a transformative revolution of thought.

Reincarnation? Bob thought we're supposed to go to a place called Heaven and sit on somebody's lap while celestial harpists soothed our newly transplanted soul, but with his mind rampaging and Buddhist thought rushing he gleaned a broader scope of human potential than he previously had conceived.

While beginning an exploration outside the confines of his family's middle class corporate-directed household in San Mateo, Bob was introduced to Watts through an artist, Jean Varda, who hosted gatherings at his Sausalito-berthed ferryboat, The Vallejo. Bob was meeting intellectuals, poets, artists, and musicians who were part of creating the new age Sixties renaissance. Most of these people were ten to fifty years older, while Bob was representative of the younger generation. There were so many creative minds in the Bay Area who were influencing people to look deeper into these newly resurrected philosophies. His mentors wanted to know where he was politically, spiritually, and how the scene was affecting him. As Bob was meeting the people who were shaping a generation, he was evolving from the insular, stultifying middle class attitudes of his family where he previously knew little, except for surfing and sailing.

Surfing

For centuries surfing was a central part of Polynesian culture. Europeans first observed surfing in the late 1700s, when British sailing vessels visited Tahiti on expeditions to the South Pacific Ocean, where Tahitians were riding waves on planks and single hull canoes. In the early twentieth century land baron Henry Huntington brought the practice of surfing to the California coast. Looking for a way to entice visitors to the area of Redondo Beach, where he had real estate investments, he hired a young Hawaiian surfer to ride the waves. Surfing caught on and became immensely popular in California and Hawaii, and subsequently any place in the world where there are waves.

During Bob's youth his father built a small sailboat from a kit and began teaching his son the fundamentals of sailing. Bob took to sailing and in a short time discovered surfing. He began riding waves and having fun in the warm California sun. The communion with water and the beach contained elements of its own subculture, an alternative to the uptight forty hours a week workaday world that constituted the central core of Bob's family's values. Bob surfed the Half Moon Bay breakwater, went down to Santa Cruz, and visited Big Sur to find quality waves in majestic surroundings.

Surfers were already hipsters, of sorts, and the blending of the beach lifestyle and the Human Potential Movement gave impetus to Bob's impending rejection of corporate culture in favor of a path of self-discovery.

Bob acquired a white 1963 Volkswagen bus with a bed in the back. He kept the VW stocked with ten pounds of rice, his board, and his wetsuit. When the surf was up he was on it, hanging ten, smacking the lip, trying not to wipe out, and staying loose as often as he could on the beaches, where the California girls were popping out of their bikinis and the dudes were transfixed on the horizon waiting for the next big set.

Higher Education

Bob was being groomed to be corporate, go to school, go to college, and get a degree. He didn't consider Harvard because his grades were just average and there were no surfing scholarships in the Ivy League. He was having too much fun and wasn't interested in the corporate credo, particularly after having watched his father go from being a war hero to being a sacrificial lamb in a vicious work environment spearheaded by a mean-spirited boss. The depersonalization in the big business culture dulled his enthusiasm for any foray into the corporate world.

Still, whether for his father or himself, Bob attempted some structure in school, but Menlo College embodied everything he found wrong with institutions. Thinking the only way to deal with the system was to have a voice, he ran for freshman class president and won. It was clear to Bob that he wasn't cut out to go along the old accepted roads. The student body representatives weren't asking for anything more than a relaxation of the rules. Could they meet with the girls in the afternoon despite being an all male college? Could they have a dance with the girls from another college? The social structure seemed arcane, with some of the teachers having been there since the 1930s inculcating a suppressive old world atmosphere that was at odds with social changes afoot during the late sixties in America.

Far from having a voice in the system, the entire student body government, and Bob in particular, was asked to leave the college. Mister Munsterman, the dean, felt that Bob was becoming a beatnik, as he put it. In conversation with the dean, Bob informed him.

"Mister Munsterman, I'm not a beatnik. I'm a hippie, and proud of it."

His statement of identity did not improve his standing with school officials, and, having had enough, shocked but relieved, Bob accepted the dean's request to depart the college.

Still, Bob tried yet again as a student, enrolling for another year and a half at College of San Mateo, CSM, lovingly referenced as the College of Small Minds. He studied liberal arts but felt his time was being wasted. Too much outer knowledge was percolating in his head at the edge of, and beyond, the classroom.

Flight

The moment had arrived for Bob to make decisions independently. He knew he had to find something different from his father, yet he still faced a transition from being a kid raised in the comfortable suburbs, where there was little or no threat, to going out into the world alone with no safety net.

Bob's high school friend Michael was planning to go to Europe. Bob determined that he, too, would take the plunge and see what was on the other side of the Atlantic. They agreed to meet in Europe and left the United States separately in 1969. Bob secured passage on a freighter from San Francisco bound for Rotterdam via the Panama Canal. Traversing the canal during a tropical rainstorm, Bob dropped acid and made his way to the highest deck on the ship to better appreciate the full fury of the raging tempest and lightning-filled sky on his enhanced consciousness.

The two friends met in Amsterdam and traveled to Scandinavia, where the summer sun lingered long in that land high above the equator. Their attention was captured and enraptured by the old world ambiance and stunning blonde Nordic women.

On the Atlantic coast in southwest France is the city of Biarritz, thirty-five kilometers from Spain on the Bay of Biscay, formerly a whaling settlement, now known as the European capital of surfing. Bob harbored a strong desire to visit the world-class surf spot. It came down to did he want to further pal around with his friend or surf with the French chicks? Michael, see you later.

Surfing in France

In Biarritz, Bob encountered high school acquaintances, two guys and a gal with four surfboards, a Volkswagen van, and a plan to drive to Greece after two months of French waves. Bob was asked to join them. The group rode the Atlantic swells, visited the Asiatica Museum with its collection of Indian, Nepalese, and Tibetan artifacts, observed the sharks and seals at the Museum of the Sea, was awed in Saint Martin's Church and the Russian Orthodox Church with its famous blue dome, nibbled sweet confections at the Museum of Chocolate, and marveled at the Hotel du Palais, originally built as a summer palace on the beach for Empress Eugenie, the last Empress of the French, and wife of Napoleon III. The asteroid 45 Eugenia was named for her.

Compared to year after year in classrooms, traveling in Europe was beginning to unwind the tightly wound spring of Bob's middle class corporate-aspiring thought process that was expanding toward a new realm.

Yugoslavia

Having caught their quota of Biarritz waves, the group broke camp and made their way through France, Switzerland, Austria, and into Italy. In Rome they snuck into the Colosseum at midnight, walking the pitch-black corridors where Christians long ago awaited their gruesome demise. Then it was on to Yugoslavia and the beauty of the Dalmatian Coast.

As they were driving along a highway on a quiet and balmy summer night police cars with sirens wailing and lights flashing descended upon them. The van was stopped, and with their Uzi machine guns drawn, the police ordered the occupants out and forced them down on the pavement on the empty highway. Bob was thinking,

"They're going to kill us right here on the damn road under the cloak of darkness."

The kids hadn't scored any real hash yet but they had their own little stash strategically hidden on their bodies. The cops took everything apart, throwing possessions out of the bus and on the roadway while machine guns nervously twitched in the still of the night inches away from the travelers' heads. For sure the cops would invent a story, plant some dope, and whisk them away to a grimy grey stone prison to be chained to the walls and tortured until death, never to be heard from again.

The search produced no incriminating substances, and as quickly as the police descended, they departed. Stars glittered and a bright moon glowed. The kids watched the cars and motorcycles disappear down the road into the hushed night. Clothes, wetsuits, and surfboards were strewn around them. Released from the verge of being busted and jailed, the young travelers gathered their scattered belongings and departed, fearful but relieved. Dictatorial government abused youth, using the herb as a scare pretense.

Greece

From Yugoslavia, the Californians entered Greece, the cradle of Western civilization, at the crossroads of Europe and Asia. The birthplace of democracy, philosophy, the Olympics, and The Odyssey was suffering under a military junta, with considerable tension. In Athens, underground revolutionaries approached them, desirous of enlisting help in their struggle against the military rulers, but Bob and his friends were peace and love children from the Golden State, desirous of no more than a good joint and some waves in the next town. The travelers denied the freedom aspirants any assistance.

Having scored a pound of Red Lebanese from an Israeli in Athens they thought unmarked Lincoln Continentals were following them. Male long hair and Volkswagen vans constituted a *Come And Get Us* sign for authorities. Bob was able to ditch the trailing cars once, and in the break they stashed the dope at a construction site, then departed to Crete, returning to Athens a month later, in the same van, this time without a police tail. Back at the site after some digging around the stash was found and retrieved.

Having to return home for school at summer's

conclusion, Bob's compatriots bought leather sandals, took them apart, pressed their hashish into the soles, glued it all back together, and mailed the lot to one of their grandmothers in America. When Bob returned home a year later to handle his army induction situation, one of those friends queried,

"Guess what I have."

"Ah, the red Leb."

There was still some of the smoke left.

Since Bob intended to stay on in Europe, he bought his friends' van for $150, and shortly thereafter received a letter from his schoolmate Michael, saying,

"Come to Spain. I have a house for us, on an island called Formentera."

Island

Retracing his route, Bob drove without incident to Spain. In Barcelona he loaded the van on the ferry to Ibiza, then went on to Formentera, to Michael's house on the western side of the island. With tranquility and beauty there so appealing, Bob plunked down ten dollars for a month's rent on his room.

Arrival on Formentera after so many miles freewheeling in Europe, traveling the highway and decompressing from his urban skyscraping horn honking environment, created an immediate sense of peace and safety. Occupying a quaint little stone cottage nestled near blue water was like being in an Impressionist painting. Bob's continued association with a growing melange of international travelers expanded his world view and increased his interest in spirituality.

Westerners were responding to Eastern culture. If you want to live the life of an ascetic then off you go. No test needed to become a monk. Things were on his mind already. Early on as a youth, walking home from school, Bob contemplated. What brought me here? What is my essence? Cause and effect. Something occurred to make this existence happen. Priests and elders couldn't answer his questions, giving him the old unconvincing cliché theory instead of an experiential answer.

After a few months in his friend's company, Bob intuited that his goals would best be accomplished without the necessity of sharing other people's karma daily. Desiring independence, he searched for and located a small house, with enough space for a bed and a table and not much more, on *La Mola*, the less populated higher elevated side of the island. He was alone, and that suited him. He acquainted himself with the local farmers and fishermen. No longer in need of need the wheels, he traded the Volkswagen for twelve ounces of hash. Driving was done. The inner journey began.

Island police knew the growing population of foreigners smoked hashish and were tolerant as long as people were peaceful, but they did not require a warrant to enter and search a house when they wanted to learn about its inhabitants.

Bob was in his garden where, in spite of the poor soil and dearth of water, he was able to coax a few vegetables to grow when he spied a coterie of police motorcycles and cars approaching. Quickly dashing in before the police, Bob jammed all the hashish down the front of his pants ahead of the storming troopers brute entrance. The cops were looking for the daughter of Barcelona's mayor, or so they said. A search was conducted, but nothing was found, and the officers departed. As they walked out the door Bob moved, causing the hashish to fall from his trousers to the floor.

It was good on La Mola for four months until a letter was forwarded to him from his draft board with a date for examination in preparation for induction into the United States Army to fight in the Vietnam War. He would have to return to the United States to handle that situation.

On his last day in Formentera Bob walked to the clear waters of the Cape where he found four female acquaintances swimming naked in the clear water as the sands in his voyager's hourglass were emptying toward the moment to board his boat, depart this place of unique calm, and return to California in an attempt to be released from conscription at the hands of a military eager to sacrifice him to a jungle war. His last vision of Formentera was of the frolicking mermaidens immersed beside the rocky shore in aquamarine water reflecting shimmering sunlight beneath a deep azure sky where the blue of the blue meets the blue.

Selective Service

Bob faced an uncertain outcome with a draft board, hungry for young men to serve as canon fodder for a Cold War military conflict that ultimately claimed the lives of 3,000,000 Vietnamese and 58,000 Americans. Registration for the draft was compulsory for males eighteen to thirty-five years of age. Failure to register could result in a five-year prison term.

Back in California for his appointment, Bob went to the Oakland Induction Center with three hundred other potential conscripts. Most were trying to avoid the 1A classification that meant available for military induction. Some were stoned, some hadn't slept in days, and one had even shot off a toe, all to escape compulsory military service. When a man was accepted by the military he received induction orders to report for basic training at Fort Ord. Thirteen weeks later the conscript shipped out to Vietnam's killing fields. A draftee who failed to report for induction faced a prison term. Kill or go to prison was the government mantra for a misguided policy that finally ended when the unpopular war was abandoned.

Bob received a deferred classification excusing him from service due to injuries sustained at an earlier age. Released from military obligation Bob's traveling fires were rekindled. After a brief inner debate, the spiritualist in him took precedence over the sensualist. The opportunity had arrived to visit the birthplace of Buddhism, in India. School obligations had faded, and he had dodged the war bullet. The doorway to the mystical East, the goal of late twentieth century hip sojourners, was open, and Bob was ready to walk through to the new ancient world.

East

Fueled by exposure to the San Francisco bands at the Fillmore Auditorium, Bob's burgeoning interest in music inspired his purchase of an excellent Martin D18 guitar for his return to Europe and beyond. Jetting back

to Ibiza, he stayed the summer with Michael, who was caretaking a farmhouse on a high hill overlooking the Valley of the Moon. When autumn leaves drifted by his window Bob traveled to the Canary Islands off northeast Africa for an attempt to crew on a boat taking one of the commonly followed sailing routes, from the Canarys around the Cape of Hope at South Africa, to the Seychelles, and hopefully find another boat the next thousand miles to India.

Bob arrived to find only one lone sailboat in the harbor. He had arrived during the off-season. That led to an alternate plan, a flight from Paris to Copenhagen to Bombay for $150 with the Jimi Hendrix Charter. The plane departed one week after his arrival in the Canarys, so he had to hustle directly to Paris to catch the plane, without a proper visa for India.

Landing briefly in Copenhagen the temperature was a temperate 50 degrees Fahrenheit, but when the doors opened in Bombay, passengers gasped at the heavy, hot, and humid conditions. Along the road from the airport into town were the homes of the Harijans, the lowest caste people, residing near a dump where they could gather what useful items they might salvage from the fetid trash heaps to sell and earn their meager sustenance.

In Bombay it was common to see people with two, three, and even four limbs missing who functioned as beggars. Bob discovered later that there was a beggar's union to coordinate activities. One could go to the union, then be driven to a designated spot for the day's begging. Renting a malformed baby was helpful to increase donation due to the sympathy factor. Union administrators received fifty percent or more of the beggar's earnings.

Bob first stayed at an old hotel with a Victorian look, but no air conditioning. Out the window on the first night he saw an old man in a bed being pushed down the street by two men. He asked the concierge what was happening, and was informed that they were Jains. The Jain Dharma religion, one of the oldest in the world, prescribes a path of non-violence towards all living beings and emphasizes spiritual independence and equality between all forms of life. Practitioners believe that non-violence and self-control are the means by which they can obtain liberation from the cycle of reincarnation. The Jain diet is one of the most rigorous forms of spiritually motivated diet found either on the Indian subcontinent or elsewhere. It is completely vegetarian, excludes onions and garlic, and may exclude potatoes and other root vegetables. For Jains, lacto-vegetarianism represents the minimal obligation. Food that contains even small particles of the bodies of dead animals, or eggs, is unacceptable. The production of dairy products is perceived to involve violence against cows. Strict Jains do not eat root vegetables, such as potatoes and onions, because tiny organisms are injured when the plant is pulled up, and also because a bulb or tuber's ability to sprout is seen as characteristic of a living human being. Jains rarely go out at night when trampling insects is more likely. In their view injury caused by carelessness is like injury caused by deliberate action. Eating honey is outlawed, as it would amount to violence against bees. Jains avoid farming because it inevitably entails unintentional killing or injuring of small animals, such as worms and insects, but agriculture is not forbidden in general and Jain farmers exist. Additionally, because they consider harsh words to be a form of violence, Jains often keep a cloth for a ritual mouth covering, serving as a reminder not to allow violence in their speech.

The ultimate deed of good karma, as Bob saw first-hand, is a ritual sacrifice of themselves to bugs that infest their body. The infested person is pushed through the streets of cities as their body is being eaten alive by bugs while being witnessed by a sympathetic alms-giving public. In comparison, college might be looking better now.

Bob wasn't worried about his lack of a visa when he arrived in India. He reasoned,

"They'll love me, with my long hair and my yoga. They'll welcome me with open arms."

Naively thinking that he would be liked because of

his hair, the opposite was the case. Kids threw stones at him from rooftops because of his appearance. Some longhairs had conducted themselves inappropriately, fornicating in the temples and making a generally negative impression. Bob determined that sacrificing his shoulder-length locks, symbolic of his American liberation from square conformism, would allow him to move about without attracting undue derisive attention. He no longer needed to be a symbol, so the Love Generation look was eliminated. Bob went on to pursue his quest for Buddhist knowledge free from unnecessary encumbrance. To divest himself of extraneous weight, he gave away his guitar.

Attempting to obtain a visa, Bob discovered the process required leaving the country and reentering. The authorities gave him a choice.

"You can go to Bangladesh, or you can go to Ceylon."

Bangladesh was undergoing the Bangladesh Liberation War of Independence, resulting in the secession of East Pakistan from the Islamic Republic of Pakistan and establishing the sovereign nation of Bangladesh. The nine-month war pitting East Pakistan and India against West Pakistan witnessed large-scale atrocities, the exodus of 10 million refugees, and the displacement of 30 million people.

Ceylon

Thinking he would obtain his visa for India in Ceylon, then return, Bob boarded a train from Bombay and traveled through jungle, mountain, and desert, down the west coast of India before turning to Madras on the east coast, then down to the southern tip of India, to Rameswaram, considered a holy pilgrimage site, with the Ramanathaswamy Temple dedicated to the Hindu god Shiva, in the south Indian state of Tamil Nadu, noted for numerous and elaborately carved temples, particularly those depicting sexuality. The town is located on Pamban Island, separated from mainland India by the Pamban channel, and is fifty kilometers by ferry crossing to Ceylon, today's Sri Lanka.

Ceylon is farther south than India and every bit as hot and humid. The oppressive, persistent heat drove Bob to the tea estates in Nuwara Eliya at 3000 feet, where Queen Elizabeth has her tea plantation. In 1954 the queen and her husband, Prince Philip, flew to Ceylon for an official state visit. The royal couple was invited to the Pedro Estate Tea Plantation in Nuwara Eliya. To commemorate the occasion Philip was given the opportunity to plant his own tea bush, which subsequently flourished. Cuttings taken from this bush have been propagated on the estate, resulting in an exclusive royal tea. The British are excellent gardeners and dedicated tea drinkers.

Riding a bus on a winding and terrifying mountain road, Bob arrived at Kandy, the ancient capital of Ceylon, nestled in the central mountains. This second largest city in Ceylon has a small lake in its center, and lies in the midst of hills in the Kandy plateau, which crosses an area of tropical tea plantations. Bob first stayed at the YMCA by the lakeside, surrounded by mountains that are covered with clouds, monsoon rains, birds, and snakes. He paid a dollar a day.

Monastery

Eric Boedeker, a British monk who had left England before World War II, was an ordained priest in Buddhism and Hinduism. Once they became acquainted, Eric introduced Bob to the hierarchy of the Buddhists in Kandy.

At the top of the surrounding hills above Kandy sits Udawatta Kele Sanctuary Forest Hermitage. When Bob arrived, in addition to Eric, there were two German and eight Ceylonese men living as monks and studying Buddhism.

For the next six months Bob lived in the monastery, wore the novice robe, and studied Buddhism. His main teacher was Venerable Nyanasiha, a German who had fled East Germany shortly after the end of World War II, ahead of the Russian occupation. He become a monk in Ceylon. Nyanasiha was knowledgeable about the Love Generation, and interested in the western sacraments of peyote, mescaline, and LSD.

One of Nyanasiha's favorite stories described a Buddhist monk who took LSD. After a few hours he was asked,

"What do you think of acid?"

He responded,

"Weak."

Six months after his arrival, Bob was ordained. Having reached the first stage, Reverend Nyanasiha, took Bob on a four month walk throughout central Ceylon, visiting hermitages and caves where he had previously resided, often in outdoor situations, sometimes in the company of cobras and viper snakes. The viper's spit, alone, if ingested in the mouth or eyes, caused death, as did being bitten. Everywhere they went there were animals from bears to bugs that annoyed humans persistently. People were part of the food chain. Bob and his teacher walked through Ceylon barefoot with one change of robes and a begging bowl. They took one to two meals a day, but nothing after noon, to allow for a clearer meditation at night, when the temperature cooled.

The light diet freed the monks from being laden with food that would induce sleep. A monk's life was passed with considerable time in quiet meditation. In twenty-four hours meditation occupied at least twelve. One slept for a couple of hours, woke, meditated, slept a couple of hours, and woke again for more meditation. Monks eat from alms, food given by townspeople. Their life was all quietude and self-contemplation. There is nowhere to run, no dope, no alcohol, no sex. There's no escape, just dealing with one's self, raw.

For a year Bob lived as a celibate initiate with 254 rules of conduct. He was not allowed to look a woman in the eyes. Life was dedicated to meditation. Meditations go through periods of just being tired of oneself. The biggest enemy was boredom. A few months earlier the most important thing was getting laid. Now that whole dynamic had changed. No surfing either. Bob saw some beautiful waves in Ceylon but surfing was forbidden. He semi-cheated once and went bodysurfing naked.

The Buddhists had temples and hermitages comprised of ten to twelve monks living in straw huts in jungle. Once a day the townspeople provided them with food placed in their alms bowls. For this the monks either went into town or the people would come to them.

Buddhists consider this lifetime to be but one

among many, and many lifetimes are required to evolve into a state of enlightenment where one stops being reborn into realms of suffering. Buddhism is the way out of suffering.

Buddha attempted to practice Hinduism but found it too radical. He found something halfway between being a prince and being a radical ascetic. His practice was more tolerant of self-introspection without having extreme deprivation. Buddha became adept at meditation, and experienced changes in his consciousness, about which he wrote. Buddha lived a normal life. He worked during the day, waking at three in the morning, to meditate for two to three hours, then he went to work, meditated at lunch, came home after work, and meditated another two hours. That was the everyday life of what they call a householder, a breadwinner. Buddha was married and had children. He wasn't a celibate living in a cave.

Bob's teacher was well known for achieving enlightenment through meditation, even though he wasn't celibate. He was a rebel within the structure of Buddhists and Hindus.

On occasion Bob attended holy festivals where thousands of religious followers, monks, ascetics, sadhus, and holy men congregated. Some performed penance of an extreme nature, eating glass, hanging by fishhooks in their backs for hours, eating dirt and rock, even lying on a bed of nails. At one festival Bob visited Austrian Heinrich Harrer, author of the book, *Seven Years In Tibet,* recounting his experiences escaping from a British internment camp in India and walking to Tibet where he became a teacher to the Dalai Lama. Harrer had residences in both Ceylon and Nepal.

Bob received a one-year visa to stay in Ceylon as a religious worker to see if he was suited for the meditative life. He encountered adept practitioners living in hermitages and caves throughout Ceylon. Reverend Nyanasiha was revered for his disciplined practice as well as his ability to live in the jungle despite the many varieties of mostly venomous snakes. He taught Bob meditation and, importantly, how to avoid stepping on a snake. Look where you walk. Meditate for an hour, walk for an hour, meditate for another hour, and walk some more. At day's end twelve hours of sitting had been completed.

To the Himalayas

By the end of Bob's visa year it became evident to him that, as holy as it was, he couldn't continue to live as an ascetic. He was twenty-two years old and on the verge of taking a serious lifelong vow, including that he would never touch, think about, and never have carnal relations with a woman again. Bob had come to the East with a preconceived notion of Shangri-La, where everybody sat peacefully in meditation for hours on end, and there was certainly that, but the lifestyle was rough. There were annoying snakes and mosquitoes that could not be killed since Buddhists kill nothing. Bob made the decision that he was not cut out to be a one meal a day meditator in the forest for the rest of his days. There was still too much living to do. He abandoned the robe, hoisted his backpack, and boarded the third class section on a train bound for northern India.

After three months reacquainting with urban life in

New Delhi, Bob set out for Srinagar, Kashmir, renowned for the glass-like waters of Dal Lake that reflect the surrounding snow-capped mountain peaks of the Veil of Kashmir in the Himalayan mountains. Kashmir sits at 9,000 feet with surrounding mountains going up 20,000 feet. Bob traveled in a style reminiscent of the 1700s, where one carried a letter of introduction. When he left Ceylon, Eric Boedeker, known as Swami Ramaji, gave him letters of introduction and addresses of people to see in India, Kashmir, and Nepal. The letter said,

"This is my friend, he's traveling throughout India, he has no schedule, and when he will arrive is unknown, but please treat him with kindness and show him your life."

Bob went to these addresses, knocked on the door, and introduced himself. Even if a year had elapsed they'd say,

"Oh yes, we've been expecting you."
He was welcomed, given food, a room, a shower, and was considerately treated.

On Dal Lake people resided on ornate Victorian-styled houseboats. Bob rented a small floating residence called *The Young Persian Palace* and studied with meditation teacher Gopi Krishna for three months. His meditations were meant to quiet the restless mind and experience his being, without thoughts racing through his head. His practice was enhanced by the influence of his evolved teacher along with deep breathing exercises, known as prana yama.

Bob traveled on to Kopang Monastery outside of the Nepalese capital of Kathmandu, residence of a dozen Tibetan monks who had fled Tibet because of the Chinese military invasion in the 1950s that murdered monks by the thousands, and people by the tens of thousands. Bob stayed at Kopang for a month, along with a small group of fellow westerners, while learning Tibetan meditative practices. Unlike other sects in India these teachers allowed women to take ordination. In the spirit of compassion the practitioners took a vow to be continuously reborn until every sentient being on earth had achieved enlightenment and was no longer subject to the endless cycles of birth and death.

The majesty of the Himalayas was a revelation. One hundred miles from Kathmandu stands mighty Mount Everest. The glowing, white-capped mountain glimmers in a deep blue background of pure sky, its peak reaching nearly 30,000 feet. An ascending trail was clearly visible until it vanished in the clouds. People took the path up Everest, seeking the thrill of climbing or a meditative life.

Along the trail to the base camp of Mount Everest are outdoor hot springs at 15,000 feet, with steaming sulfur-smelling water bubbling up to the frozen surroundings. At night the heavens were vibrant with stars, with the Milky Way seemingly at one's fingertips, clearly, with no houses and no lights, just the self and the universe, sitting in a hot pool in natural formed rock, freezing cold out and crystal clear, no distractions, no television, no social media, no conflict. It took a while to adjust to the solitude and the tranquil nature of life at 15,000 feet, but in time Bob's restless mind became more disciplined and more at peace.

Everything must be exciting in the Western world. There has to be good against bad, right versus wrong and always the struggle, the pull of dualities. In the East, one could experience a different life, free from conflict.

There was only one's self, and the daily discovery of who one is in mind, heart, and soul. The more one meditated, the more one became involved in experiences that were extraordinary and unexpected, like leaving the body, and having past life experiences, or the simplicity of just being still.

Bob eventually left the Himalayan area and traveled to Benares, today's Varanasi, on the Ganges River in India, where funeral pyres burn bodies to ash to be swept away in the river of eternity. Benares is the spiritual center of India and is one of the oldest continually inhabited cities in the world. Hindus believe that death in Benares brings salvation and many come there to die. Lengthy stairways lead from the Hindu temples to the Ganges with people bathing and washing their clothes next to the melting bodies waiting to be recycled once again.

A majority of Benares inhabitants rode bicycles with old-fashioned bells rusting in worn handlebars. There was little outside noise of cars with their horns honking and engines running. One hears a rhythm through the bicycle bells, an underlying musical dance in the ancient city. Benares is not far from Bodhi Gaya, the location of the 2500 year-old Bodhi tree under which Buddha became enlightened.

Back in the USA

After India, Ceylon, Kashmir, and Nepal, Bob's physical health was compromised. Having profoundly experienced both Europe and the East, but depleted with pneumonia, he determined that he would return to his own land. Bob boarded a flight from New Delhi to Frankfurt, changed planes, Frankfurt to New York, and caught a bus to Memphis, Tennessee, where his father now lived. Ironically, after so long as a chaste monk, devoid of female company, one of the two women with whom Bob entered into conversation on the bus was sufficiently moved by both his persona and tales of Eastern enlightenment to perform fellatio on him in a discreet manner en route.

Refreshed, Bob arrived in Memphis, clothed in full Tibetan regalia, looking like a transplanted Himalayan yak herder, with multicolored woven boots, baggy pants, rope belt, and traditional oversized herding shirt, unusual attire in conservative Memphis. He would shortly have a reunion with his father whom he had not seen in five years. When they had parted in 1969 they were on different sides of the political fence, but time and distance were to help heal the divisive wounds of the tumultuous Sixties with a single embrace.

Harry, divorced from Patricia, had married an opera superstar with six children. The family lived in a well-preserved thirty-two-room plantation-style mansion with a carriage house behind it, down the road from Elvis' Graceland. From the Memphis bus station, Bob was driven in a taxi to the antebellum dwelling's front porch. He walked up and rang the bell. Opening the door, a while-clad maid looked the lad up and down, and taken by Bob's far out clothing inquired,

"Wha, what do you want?"

"I'm Harry's son."

The maid about-faced, ran back down the hall, waving her arms, and with agitated tone exclaimed,

"Mister Harry, he says he's your son. You have to see this."

Harry rose from the dinner table to confront his Tibetan-garbed, backpacked, mountain man son, returned from Eastern outer space. The two embraced, and like that, Bob was back home.

The first thing his father did the following day, to make his son sociable, was to take him straight to Brooks Brothers and put him in a checkerboard pattern suit with a white shirt and tie. Sri Pee Wee Herman San.

There was some adjustment to experience in the rapid transition from Himalayan stargazing to shopping at the mall. Bob was so much slower than everybody else, waiting for his sojourning soul to catch up with his body. Now he had to adapt a traditional path with a modern path, because he wasn't going to live like a holy man in the caves of America.

Maintaining the roots of what he learned was his challenge. So much of Buddhism is about giving up attachment to things, and so much of America is about consuming things. Complete opposites. Returning gave him insight, tested him, and revealed that he was not yet free of his attachments. That's the idea, to break the cycles of birth and rebirth through enlightenment, or, like the Tibetans, work until all sentient beings on earth had achieved enlightenment and were no longer subject to the endless cycles of birth and death.

Six

The Hashish Trail

Immigrants

The 20th century saw more technological and scientific progress than all the other centuries combined since the dawn of civilization. Accelerating scientific understanding, more efficient communications, and faster transportation transformed the world in those hundred years more rapidly and widely than in any previous century. It was a century that started with horses, simple automobiles, and freighters, but ended with high-speed rail, cruise ships, global commercial air travel and the space shuttle.

In the early 1900s, Salvatore and Sara both came to America from the same village in Sicily. Salvatore was a fisherman. He went to Mississippi where he had relatives, but the fish weren't big enough, driving him to set out for San Francisco where he got on the crew of a sister ship of the famed Balclutha, a three-masted, steel-hulled, square-rigged sailing ship that searched the big fish in Alaskan waters.

Despite their common origin, Salvatore and Sara were unacquainted until they were introduced at an Italian community event in San Francisco's Noe Valley. They married and had four children, one of whom was a daughter, Camille.

At the same time that Salvatore and Sara were a part of the immense wave of Europeans immigrating to America, Antonio left his birthplace at age sixteen in The Azores, the island chain some 800 miles west of Portugal in the Atlantic Ocean. Antonio immigrated to America where he found work on a dairy farm in Petaluma, California, forty miles north of San Francisco. Here he met and married Mary, an American-born woman whose family were also Azorians, and owned property in Northern California that included a dairy farm. Mary gave birth to six children, one of whom was a son called Anthony, named for his father.

In 1918 the first of two influenza pandemics infected 500 million people across the world, killing 50 to 100 million. It was one of the deadliest disasters in human history. When Antonio died from the epidemic Mary had to sell their farm but managed to retain five acres of pasturage to rent out for animal grazing and thus was able to survive financially.

During World War II, Anthony and Camille met while both labored in California on the construction of Liberty Ships, he in the Richmond shipyards, she in Sausalito. Two Liberty Ships were finished every day to help the war effort. Camille and Anthony married in 1941 and gave birth to two daughters, Isabel and Donna, and two sons, Renaldo and Joaquin.

After the war Anthony became a mechanic for the Marin Dell Dairy that operated an assembly line system for filling milk bottles. In 1954 they bought a house for $13,000, just north of the Golden Gate Bridge in Marin County. Camille raised the children and was active in the Catholic Church and in the schools. Although her daughters demonstrated demure behavior, Renaldo, called Ron, and Joaquin proved to be prone to pranks and had a love of things mechanical, particularly cars and motorcycles in their teen years. When occasion demanded they could best most in boyhood battles.

Joaquin Travels

Joaquin was eighteen in 1966 and enrolled in college, doing well scholastically but enjoying the party atmosphere that often prevails when young adults congregate. His enthusiasm was enhanced by the presence of young women on campus, with one of whom Joaquin had established a steady relationship. However, as youthful romance often does not sustain beyond the initial satisfaction of nascent urgings, he and she ended their liaison.

It was at this juncture that Joaquin's wanderlust took flight. Airfares from America to Europe were low. He had some money saved and, along with a friend, he chucked college and departed for what was to be a higher education on a six month sojourn to Europe and, fatefully, to Istanbul, Turkey, where the higher part came in.

In Turkey, Joaquin and his associate met numerous travelers, including Japanese, Australian, and European. Many congregated by Sultan Ahmed, the spectacular Blue Mosque, built in the seventeenth century, with one main dome, six minarets, and eight secondary domes. By comparison to California, where stiff penalties prevailed for marijuana possession, the scene in Istanbul was loose. At the time, hashish and opium were legal in Turkey, and the two travelers joined the trend to avail themselves of the intoxicating substances selling cheaply for those with American and European funds.

Hashish Star

Along with his friend and a new acquaintance recently discharged from the US army while stationed in Germany, Joaquin scored a kilo of hashish that he eventually brought back into Europe. Some of the hash was sold in Germany to American army personnel. The proceeds helped the travelers financially. Joaquin hid the rest of the hash and brought it back to San Francisco in 1967, in time to encounter the city's Summer of Love. At the famous Human Be-In, held at Golden Gate Park, Timothy Leary expounded the philosophy that was to become the rallying cry for the age. *Turn on, tune in, drop out.*

At this moment Joaquin was a somewhat geeky guy with glasses, although he had been an athlete, but that doesn't mean much after high school. His return to the Bay Area with his ball of Turkish hash accorded him close to rock star status. Everybody had shoeboxes with poor quality Mexican weed, all stems and seeds, while Joaquin had high quality Turkish hash. The instigation for his entry into the entire hashish trade that was to characterize Joaquin's next nine years was born in the sudden influence that the possession of the intoxicant gave him with his peers.

Fugitive Kind

While Joaquin hung around his hometown soaking up the love and good vibes, it happened that an acquaintance absented himself without leave from his station on Treasure Island after two years of otherwise devoted duty in the service of the United States Navy. As a deserter the man faced dire legal consequence if apprehended. Under the duress of his fugitive situation, he appealed to Joaquin to provide him with a hideout.

By this time, Joaquin had dropped out of college, and, as a consequence, lost his student deferment from the draft, conferring upon him a 1A classification, of prime physical and mental status to be conscripted. The United States Army required the involuntary obligation of military service to enable a steady source of men to prosecute the deepening armed conflict in Vietnam. Joaquin's status likely would result in his being called and placed in the fighting legions of the American Army prosecuting the war. Some who were drafted chose to flee the United States for Canada or Europe to avoid being sent to the deadly fields of that unnecessary military confrontation. It appeared that Joaquin was about to be next in line. Being a love child did not include participating in the slaughter of innocent people far from home, or sacrificing one's life as a pawn in some misguided power game. Joaquin initiated a plan of escape to Europe, but one that would last longer than his first innocent Eurailpass experience. Meanwhile, he helped to hide his AWOL acquaintance, but after some months, law enforcement seemed to be zeroing in on the situation, requiring the man to be moved to neighboring towns on three separate occasions.

In this, the pre-computer 1960s, it occurred to Joaquin that the possibility existed for his fugitive acquaintance to obtain a passport, in spite of his perilous circumstance. The seaman was persuaded to go to the Federal building in San Francisco to apply for the document. Ten days after application, an envelope arrived at the house of the man's parents containing his newly issued passport, in spite of his being in arrears and wanted for desertion. Joaquin coordinated the fleeing serviceman's flight to relatives in New York. The plan was for him to go there and wait, while Joaquin and another friend, who was in a similar predicament with a 1A classification, sold their motorcycles and cars, and divested themselves of possessions in preparation for extended stays overseas. They intended to meet in New York, and depart for Europe, but part of their plan was undone when the seaman crossed the Connecticut state line for a romantic rendezvous. The authorities stopped him and his status was revealed, leading to incarceration in a Brooklyn naval brig.

Exodus

When Joaquin and his friend arrived in New York and discovered that their acquaintance was being detained there was nothing more for it but to get on with their part of the European sojourn. The two boarded a plane bound for Lisbon, a city chosen at random, from where they traveled by train up to Germany and bought a Volkswagen van, the choice of travellers in Europe and beyond. The young adventurers proceeded south to Morocco, because Joaquin had learned from his earlier trip that one could actually, maybe not make a huge living, but at least get by transporting and selling hashish in Europe. Northern Morocco manufactured excellent green hash in the area of the Rif Mountains.

Further free flowing in England, Joaquin was part

of the crew at the 1970 Isle Of Wight Music Festival. There he applied his knowledge of things mechanical, helped build the stage, and schmoozed with Jimi Hendrix and other musicians present at that historic event. While being interviewed for *Message To Love,* a film about the festival, Joaquin expostulated.

"It's just groovy, man. There's a new species emerging, and the new species has different forms of culture. It's a whole new thing. When you see things like this happen it's far out. We're upsetting the system that's been around with western man for two or three thousand years, and the whole thing's flipping out. Arriving in England, they threw me in jail for about four hours, right off the bat, for not having a lot of cash and not looking respectable. It's like that. I've been to jail in a lot of countries. They don't like the way I hang out. They don't like my lifestyle. I smoke a little hash and I just hang out. I don't like to work too often unless it's for something groovy."

In 1971 Joaquin went south to the Balearic Islands in Spain where his friend Jim had purchased a farmhouse on Ibiza. Joaquin was lulled with the laidback atmosphere on the islands. While enjoying Jim's hospitality he took advantage of his friend's guitar skills to learn some fingerpicking techniques.

The emerging alternative thought processes of the Sixties counter cultural movement included examination of the nontheistic Buddhist religion that encompassed awakening and enlightenment of sentient beings, to end their suffering by eliminating ignorance and craving through understanding that all things are dependent on causes and conditions, with the possibility of liberation through realization that had previously been unattainable by heretofore accepted Christian-based theology. Joaquin had been reading and discussing Buddhist teachings and beginning to study and apply them to himself.

On Formentera some friends gave him hospitality and laid a hit of mescaline on him from California, origin of the best psychedelics on this teardrop of a planet.

Vision Cave

Joaquin hiked alone to *La Mola*, the highest part of the island, carrying his guitar and hoping to trip all night practicing some of his music techniques in one of the island caves. He climbed the trail to the north by northwest-facing cave at the edge of a 600-foot cliff. Perfect, not a soul around. Joaquin gathered the driest wood he could find, stockpiling it at the edge of the cave.

As the sun set, he cooked his brown rice and arranged his sleeping bag on boughs of pine, though he didn't anticipate sleeping at all on this special night. He smoked a bowl of hash and ate his rice, chewing each mouthful fifty times, as Buddha instructed. The fair weather was deteriorating rapidly as Joaquin tuned his guitar. A tempest began to rage a few hours later. The cave entrance faced Ibiza, twenty miles away, an emerald jewel in a lapis sea, now invisible behind darkness and the developing power of the storm. At midnight, with the elements raging ferociously, Joaquin dropped the mescaline. Not long after, the guitar seemed to be playing itself. He was just a witness. The storm became a rhapsody of violence, lightning flashing and thunder crashing, roaring out a symphony of raucous heavenly power dominating earth and sea. This display of nature's strength, with rain flying in every direction, even upward from below, Joaquin welcomed like a moviegoer watching an epic production in his cave theater. The safety of the cave, the warmth of the campfire, overwhelmed him with waves of pleasure. Even his insignificance while the heavens erupted with massive power was reassuring and comforting. The cave was Joaquin's shelter from the storm. He felt like he was transported back in time, man in cave, animal ensconced in cave, primordial, magical, elemental. Cave, fire, deafening thunder, billion volt lightning bolts, rain, wind, inky black night, a violent harmony.

While the tempest raged outside Joaquin's mind churned and burned. He chanted a Tibetan mantra, thanking nature for this awesome existence and his small, infinitesimal part in it. Tears of joy flowed softly, contrasting with the ferocious tears of the fierce storm. He fell into a reverie of quiet chanting, occasionally poking the fire and adding a log now and again. The contrast of elements raging without, calm warmth within, brought to him a completeness, a mystical union. Fierce yang thunderbolts, calm yin cave, a communication, a dialogue between the dualities of life was occurring. He was merely a witness. Fire and water, life and death, instant flashes of brilliant, thunderous light, deep swirling blackness. There was no conflict, nothing to be resolved, only a crystallization, an integration, and a completion. Nature is perfect, balance is everywhere, eternal, only our minds fail to perceive it. Thus is born the illusion of confusion, of separateness. This lifting of the foggy veil of obscurity revealing nature's eternal perfection washed over Joaquin like a baptism, an epiphany, staying with him the entire night.

With the dawning of morning's faint light on the eastern horizon, the storm abated. As pale rose color heralded the imminent sunrise, Joaquin discerned undulating clouds billowing and shape shifting in the western winds. He sat by the cave entrance, leaning against his backpack, watching as the foamy sea, the sky, and the island of Ibiza made their appearances.

Lord Buddha

A cloud, about the size of Ibiza, drifted into view, floating like a billowing mountain of pink cotton candy. There, perfectly clear, the cotton candy cloud mountain was not a mountain at all. As Joaquin focused his attention he perceived a perfect sitting Buddha on a lotus throne. He was dumbfounded, awestruck. The hallucination was so real and delineated. Buddha was in the full lotus, eyes closed, hands lying one on top of the other in his lap, holding a flower.

The wind was rotating the Buddha cloud in a clockwise direction as it moved to the east. The cloud, at first directly facing Joaquin, slowly turned to profile. Although conditions were blustery the wind didn't alter the Buddha cloud at all. Joaquin then perceived the perfect profile of another Buddha. The two were sitting back-to-back, identical in every minute detail. This vision made Joaquin stand, throw some wood on the fire, look away for a moment, and splash some water on his face from his canteen. He walked out to the very edge of the 600-foot drop, watching the white-capped sea throw large waves against La Mola's sheer base.

Looking back at the Buddha cloud, Joaquin

observed it rotating 180 degrees, the second Buddha still a carbon copy of the first, full lotus, eyes closed, hands holding a flower in its lap. In the twenty to thirty knot winds this just isn't possible, but there it was.

Joaquin flashed on the lyrics to the Donovan song, *First there is a mountain then there is no mountain then there is.*

The mescaline vision continued its rotation as it flew easily east, farther away, but retaining its shape, in the endless expanse of turquoise sky.

This vision became a portent of where Joaquin's life might be going. The experience planted a seed that grew into a conviction that he would make a life change that involved a pilgrimage to the birthplace of the Buddha, in the little town of Lumbini, at southern Nepal's border with India.

Eastern religion, mysticism, meditation, and yoga, originating in the ancient cultures of the east, were inextricably woven into the fabric of the Sixties counter cultural movement. In addition, the use of mind altering substances, particularly marijuana and its product, hashish, originated in the Cannabis fields at the foot of the Himalayas, where the wisdom of the East developed and the weed grew wild.

Going East was a goal for many Europeans and Americans, to complete the journey to the ancient world, the source of eastern philosophies, among them Confucianism, Taoism, Hinduism, Buddhism, Sikhism, Zoroastrianism, Jainism, Islam, and more. Numerous people that we admired, like The Beatles, had already made their trip to India to meet with their guru. When *Sgt. Pepper's Lonely Hearts Club Band* was released in 1967, the music influenced people. *Within You Without*

You. India. Air and overland automobile travel enabled our generation's direct experience of the ancient world's knowledge.

Afghanistan

Inhabited for over 50,000 years, the vast country of Afghanistan's location on the Silk Road connected it to cultures of the Middle East and Asia. Numerous civilizations have interacted and fought in this land for centuries.

Arab Muslims brought Islam in 642 AD and in 1219 Genghis Khan and his Mongol army overran the region. In 1870, the British exercised influence and controlled the state's foreign policy. After the Third Anglo-Afghan War King Amanullah Khan attempted reforms in 1919 , such as abolishing slavery, mandatory elementary education, abolition of the burqa for women and co-educational schools. These actions alienated conservative tribal and religious leaders. The country's religion is Islam, practiced by 99% of its citizens. 90% follow Sunni Islam and the remaining are Shias.

Numerous tribal groups occupy Afghanistan that include Pashtuns, a warrior and martial people originally from eastern Iran who follow Sunni Islam, and Hazara, a Mongol people who are Shia Muslims. There was a big Persian influence in Herat. Persia held Herat for a couple of centuries. In the north of the country live the Turkmen, the Uzbeks, and the Kochi people, the nomads, who migrate from the mountains to the valley of the Indus annually to trade produce of their goats and sheep for products of settled life. When Alexander the Great and his Macedonian forces arrived in Afghanistan in 330 BC their army contributed to the mixture of ethnicities by fathering children with indigenous women. Afghanistan is the world's largest producer of opium and is a major source of hashish.

Kabul

In May, 1971, Joaquin hitchhiked from Barcelona with the intention of getting to Nepal and India on the road that passes through Afghanistan, and Kabul, where Joaquin first settled. He established residence at The Friends Hotel on one of the main streets in the Shar-e-Nau district. All day through the window of his room the jingling of bells around horse's necks on their halters and harnesses were heard as the steeds pulled the small carts that served as the taxis in town. He had finally arrived in the magical, mystical, old part of the planet. The city was a unique and compelling place much to his liking.

Kabul was the capital, and largest city of Afghanistan, over 3,500 years old. Numerous empires have fought over Kabul's valley for its strategic location on the trade routes of South and Central Asia.

Shar-e-Nau was the new town. Paghman was outside of town on the way up to the road that goes to the Salang tunnel that the Russians built through the Hindu Kush mountains to get up to Mazar-i-sharif. Kabul was an incredible place in the early seventies. Maybe there was an undercurrent of violence but at the time it wasn't apparent. Afghanis weren't upset at foreigners. They were friendly and always liked a great joke and a good laugh. On occasion, Joaquin even slept on the front porches of some of the chai shops and he always felt safe.

The main event in Kabul was his acquaintance with Afghani hashish, the benchmark for hash at that time, with the highest percentage of THC Delta 9, the active component that creates the high. Afghans have been growing Cannabis and producing hashish for millennia.

Joaquin could see immediately from the hotel clientele, and from the number of westerners in Kabul, that the hashish trade was thriving. Nearly every westerner had a smuggling angle. The city was bustling. King Mohammed Zahir Shah was trying to modernize one of the most primitive, backward countries on earth, but change was anathema to many, particularly for the clerics, who practiced old Muslim law.

Joaquin settled into a pattern of living in Kabul but he took opportunities to explore other areas of the country. He set out for Mazar-i-Sharif, the largest city in Afghanistan north of the Hindu Kush mountain range, accessible from Kabul by the Salang Tunnel, a link between northern and southern Afghanistan. The tunnel crosses the Hindu Kush mountain range under the difficult Salang Pass at 11,000 feet elevation.

A day's journey from Kabul brought Joaquin to Mazar-i-Sharif. He walked from the town's center to *The Balkan Nights*, a hotel contained within eight-feet high walls of a caravanserai. Ali, the proprietor of the hotel, sensed that Joaquin might be a dealer checking out the possibilities. The hotel had garages built into the walls inside the courtyard that allowed guests, or dealers, to drive past the gate to park in one of the three garages. There, the vehicles were kept off the streets while the stash of hashish from the nearby production areas was hidden. Ali had a one-stop shop; a dealer could score, stash, and never be seen on the streets of the city until driving away.

Joaquin stayed in the hotel on his first night. The following day, he left his backpack in his room with traveler's checks and hundred-dollar bills hidden in the tubes of the pack's frame. In his pockets were two $20 traveler's checks and 1500 Afghanis. His passport hung from his neck in a cloth pouch. He carried a Rajastani bag for incidentals that included a Swiss army knife.

Joaquin caught a bus out to the nearby river, a tributary of the Amu Darya. Here the desert spread before him to the north, where camel caravans from Xian met with caravans from Asia Minor, with some trade items making the 4000-mile journey to the Mediterranean Sea.

From the river Joaquin continued on to the ruins of the ancient city of Balkh. Only the foundation of the oval city remained, amidst tan rubble and blue tile chips. Legend states that Zoroaster was born here, and the city was the origin of the Pashtus, the Baluchis, and the Persians. Thousands of years later Alexander and his Greek army passed this way, followed by the Kushan Empire. By the 9th century, the Arabs had settled in Balkh. In the 13th century the Mongols destroyed the city, which was rebuilt, then again destroyed by Timur in the 15th century. The building and destroying was like an extended extra-innings baseball game where the lead continually changes.

This once great city had teemed with people from all over Asia who traded silks, lacquerware, slaves, and porcelains for spices, myrrh, saffron, dates, precious stones, and glass, along with philosophies, weapons, and diseases. It was now a deserted and dusty ruin. Even the river had abandoned the site, having changed its channel through this now treeless expanse.

Back in New Balkh, Joaquin scored a half-kilo of hashish for about four dollars, half the price of the best quality hash in Kabul. It was beautiful, light-green pollen that smoked very smoothly, trippy, with an almost hallucinogenic quality. Outside the small town, cannabis fields bloomed and production boomed. Joaquin hung out awhile in town, sitting on a rope bed in a chai shop, drinking glass after glass of sweetened hot tea while digging the lazy local vibes. The Tajik people were relaxed and friendly. Joaquin noticed a few Eurofreaks. They looked French.

On the bus back to Mazar-i-Sharif, two French travelers were smoking hash. As the bus arrived at the main station, two plainclothes Tajiks grabbed them and hauled them off the bus, cursing and shouting. Joaquin exited the bus slowly and began walking toward the Balkan Nights Hotel, but a grizzled Tajik grabbed him from behind. The man showed Joaquin some photo identification as his associate rounded the corner. Ali had warned Joaquin that the locals would try to shake the freaks down, but Ali's hash samples weren't near the quality found in Balkh. Joaquin realized too late that he should've asked Ali for the best quality product.

The men escorted Joaquin to a small jail building enclosed in a dusty garden with a low mud wall. None of the men had uniforms. His bag was searched and his passport examined. The men were mellow with no violence in word or deed. The Frenchies were nowhere to be seen. They must have paid off and left already. That was a good sign.

Joaquin pleaded ignorance. How could hashish be illegal in Mazari and legal in Balkh?

"Hashish khoobas Balkh, hashish no khoobas Mazar-i-Sharif."

Joaquin had about 1300 Afghanis left with the two traveler's checks, and his bag with the Swiss army knife. The bargaining began. Joaquin acted all humble and contrite, as though they were the nuns and he was the Catholic schoolboy caught red-handed, but the process was simply a matter of *baksheesh*, a bribe. He pays and he goes, standard operating procedure in these parts.

The police were arguing amongst themselves about the knife. Surely, the chief would get that. All Joaquin really needed was his passport and he'd be fine. Obviously the hashish was forfeit. Joaquin wondered how many times the same half-kilo would be sold and then confiscated. This is how food was put on their table.

After some discussion and bickering the police informed Joaquin that he would be free to go if he signed and surrendered his traveler's checks, gave them 1000 Afghanis, and surrendered his knife (concealed weapon), and his Rajastani bag (a pleasant gift for a girlfriend or wife).

Joaquin gladly handled over the bounty and with many polite salaams he departed. A good gig, just shake down the tourists returning from Balkh on the bus.

Back at the Balkan Nights Joaquin discussed the day's events with Ali.

"You told me to be careful, Ali, and that was my intention. The hash was good, very good."

"You no ask Number One. You try," Ali said, and tossed Joaquin a piece of Afghani flying saucer. A squeeze and a sniff revealed that it was dynamite.

Joaquin eventually went to buy large quantities of hash in Mazar-i-Sharif and brought it down in pollen form in huge sacks into Kabul. There he would hire hand pressers. All they did was press the pollen into the famous Afghani flying saucers sought by every hash smoker on the planet. These were maybe an ounce or two, thicker in the center and thinner out to the edges. The presser's hands were callused, even on the tender part of their palm in the middle, from a lifetime of pressing.

Joaquin's extensive knowledge of automobile mechanics allowed him to facilitate the secreting of hashish in westerner's vans for transportation back to Europe. In this manner he earned enough money to exist in the underdeveloped economy.

Smoking Afghan Style

Afghans love to smoke hash, and did so in a unique manner. They liked to smoke and inhale so much hash they would pass out at the pipe or fall on the ground in a stupor. They were the hardest of the hardcore, smokers par excellence. Joaquin previously thought westerners were extreme hash smokers but when he got to Afghanistan, forget it. Afghans smoke hashish straight, no tobacco. They had a huge chillum, or bowl, that went inside a massive crockery hookah three feet high half-filled with water with a long bamboo stem that went down inside that was sealed by a wet cloth. When the hookah was prepared the participants placed slices of pure Afghani hash in the bowl, then dropped a glowing red-hot coal on top of the hash.

A smoking stool was used because the top of the stem of the hookah was about five feet high and the device was so large and heavy it couldn't be leaned over. Smokers stood on the stool to reach the stem. Some were so short they were on their toes.

Smoking began with the men inhaling and exhaling, hyperventilating repeatedly, drawing in then releasing huge amounts of the smoke of burning hashish. The process would go along, with ten or twelve smokers in a circle waiting to step up, with everyone chanting and clapping with every inhalation. It was a counting contest to see how many hyperventilated breaths of pure hashish a person could take before they had to come off the pipe. In the process, some became so dizzy they would fall off the stool.

Hash smoking was an event where the toughest man in the room attempted to outsmoke everybody else, every time it was done. This was the Olympics of hash smoking and a daily event. It would conclude where the party ends because everyone's passed out on the floor. This is not smoking and then going out and doing something creative. This was oblivion unlike how it's done in the west where someone wants to function. With one little hit in the morning one can handle a busy day with a little lift and a little high. But in Afghanistan there's not much to do. They're out in the fields and back home at night. There were no theaters. This was a form of entertainment, but only for men. Afghan women did not participate in these gatherings.

Dog Fights

Kuchis are huge, ferocious, powerful mastiff dogs, bred by Afghans for both flock and home protection. The Kuchi resembles the Saint Bernard, but with longer legs, bobbed tails, tan heads and bodies, and black mouths and noses. These massive canines are courageous, fearless, and loyal to their own family. They are outstanding guardians and are ferocious against wolves, leopards, or any prey that try to approach their flock or their people They can be willful and stubborn, over-protective and territorial. The mastiff guards its family and property. In addition to their domestic uses, Afghans have a tradition of engaging the aggressive creatures in sport fighting.

Joaquin was in attendance at some of these dogfights and occasionally wagered on the result. Contests were held in a gravel pit wherein around thirty Kuchi dogs were gathered in the company of a couple of hundred men and boys. Women were excluded. The arena is some forty feet in diameter with attendees ringing the fight area.

A referee calls two dogs to the center, with two trainers per dog, each holding a leash. Sometimes one dog will wither when brought nose-to-nose with its competitor and in that eventuality another dog is quickly brought to take its place. When both dogs demonstrate their eagerness to battle they're separated momentarily while bets are placed.

Once the wagering concludes the dogs are released. The canines immediately go into battle mode, leaping for the jugular, attempting to bite hard into the neck while standing on their hind legs. Like two wrestlers, each attempts to throw the other to the ground. The first to achieve three throws is declared the winner. In the event of a kill the survivor is victorious.

The moment the beasts begin the crowd becomes boisterous, shouting, cursing, jostling their neighbor, even throwing punches in the heat of passion, as the onlookers immerse themselves in the blood sport.

Usually, after three throws, the trainers rush in to separate the fighting combatants before the winner pummels the loser to death. Grudge fights often break out between owners, trainers, and onlookers. The average Afghan male is like a bantam rooster, ready to duke it out at the drop of a turban.

At one fight's conclusion, a mustached and goateed man presented a small black bear with a bell around its neck that had been taught to ride a bicycle in circles. Before the crowd dispersed the bear's routine induced no little delight, particularly when it finished the show by dancing to the rhythm of a drum on which the trainer hammered out a beat. Coins and small banknotes were thrown into the arena and gathered by the trainer. The matinee thus concluded, the commencing enervating afternoon heat forced the crowd to seek shaded shelter elsewhere.

Bamiyan -World's Tallest Buddhas

With Joaquin's intensifying interest in Buddhism he was intent on visiting Bamiyan, the paradise valley at an altitude of 9000 feet, 100 miles northwest of Kabul. Here Hazara people have lived for centuries in one of

Afghanistan's most resplendent and lushly green settings. The Hazaras are a Shia tribe, the second largest denomination of Islam. Shia is the short form of the historic phrase *Shiatu Ali*, meaning followers of the prophet Muhammad's son-in-law and cousin Ali, whom the Shia consider to be Muhammad's successor. Like other branches of Islam, Shia Islam is based on the teachings of the Quran and the message of the Islamic prophet Muhammad. Unfortunately, rivalries with other factions of Islam, such as the Sunnis, have created conflict and disparities between them.

The Afghan Hazara have Mongolian features and have endured continual persecution by the Pashtu, who are Sunni. The Hazara are not misogynists. Women participate fully in all aspects of life, in contrast with the Pashtu who subjugate and restrict females. Hazaras were the friendliest people Joaquin encountered in Afghanistan.

Bamiyan, translated as The Place of Shining Light, from Sanskrit *varmayana*, meaning with color, was the site of an early Hindu-Buddhist monastery. Numerous statues of Buddha are carved into the sides of cliffs facing Bamiyan city. The site was found to be the home of the world's oldest oil paintings, discovered in caves behind the statues.

The Bamiyan valley marked the most westerly point of Buddhist expansion and was a hub of trade for much of the last millennium. It was a place where East met West and its archaeology reveals a blend of Greek, Turkish, Persian, Chinese and Indian influence found nowhere else in the world. Situated on the ancient Silk Road, Bamiyan was at the crossroads between the East and West when all trade between China and the Middle

East passed through.

On the cliff face of a mountain nearby, three immense statues were carved. One of them is a 175 feet high standing statue of Buddha, the world's tallest. The images were created in the fifth century. At one time, two thousand monks meditated in caves among the sandstone cliffs.

When Joaquin traveled to Bamiyan with friends they made their way up the cliffs to the top of the tallest Buddha where they smoked hashish and reflected on the valley's history. They imagined what the area was like a thousand years ago, when Buddhists were the inhabitants and the statues were decorated with bright colors, surrounded by the golden-hued cliffs.

Observed from the Buddha's head, the afternoon light on the lush fields sparkled and shimmered. It was spacious up there on his crown. The enormity of the project made the mundane details of daily life appear insignificant while the idea of the massive stone depictions of Buddha blessing the Hindu Kush for over a millennium seemed wondrous.

Lumbini

Although the first pleasures of Kabul were compelling, Joaquin was in transit. He still had to get to the birthplace of the Buddha, but along the way he wanted to stop and see how hashish was grown and consumed. Eventually Joaquin made the journey to Lumbini but instead of monuments to the Buddha he found nothing there except a decrepit stupa, a mound-like structure containing Buddhist relics. The village was gone. There once was a huge palace, but now no real remnants, no markers, no Buddha Bar to acknowledge the birthplace of the founder of Buddhism. Joaquin said you can never get lost if you don't know where you're going. His trip east was inspired by a desire to be in Buddha's birthplace but when he arrived nothing was there. The journey was a quest for what was revealed to be gone, which is life, in a way. The adventure produced not a preconceived result, but an alternative wealth of unexpected and enriching discovery.

Tribal Area

The British East India Company was an English joint-stock enterprise that pursued trade with the Indian subcontinent, particularly in cotton, silk, indigo dye, salt, tea, and opium. The company received a Royal Charter from Queen Elizabeth in 1600 and went on to eventually account for half of the world's trade.

The British system of governance in India was instituted in 1858 when the British East India Company transferred rule over India to the Crown in the person of Queen Victoria, who, in 1876, was proclaimed Empress of India. The British *Raj,* in Hindi, rule, began in 1858 and continued until 1947, when the British Indian Empire was partitioned into two sovereign states, India, and Pakistan.

The British also controlled the foreign affairs and diplomatic relations of Afghanistan. In 1893 the British drew a line on a map and established a 1,640-mile international border between Afghanistan and Pakistan. This artificial divide was called The Durand Line, after

British diplomat Mortimer Durand, who negotiated the concept with Amir Abdur Rahman Khan, ruler of Afghanistan. The Durand Line cuts through the Pashtun tribal areas and through the Balochistan region, a western province of Pakistan, dividing the Pashtun tribe right in the middle, along with the same for the Baloch people, and other ethnic groups living on both sides of the border, considered one of the most dangerous in the world. Since the 15th century Europeans were conquering, claiming, colonizing, and dividing the globe. This rule wasn't the local people's idea.

After leaving Kabul, Joaquin headed north and crossed the border into Pakistan to visit the hash growing areas in Chitral, on the western bank of the Kunar River, in the Kunar Valley. The valley has direct access to Kabul, but the Durand Line prohibited the valley from being used as a route between Kabul and Peshawar, in Pakistan, and farther south. The other routes are over the longer mountain passes.

Joaquin left the government area, and went into the wilder tribal parts that no power has ever been able to conquer. He was staying at the only hotel in Chitral, in a spectacular region at 4000 feet elevation, some thirty miles from the astounding snow capped peak of 25,000 feet high Tirich Mir in the Hindu Kush range that has numerous mountains of similar height. One is astonished to look beyond verdant fields of green to see Tirich Mir's majestic pyramid of snow and ice further up the valley.

There once were runners who carried baskets loaded with ice, with the trump line over their foreheads, and ran them down the mountain to Chitral, the main village in that area. One was able to get snow cones, or ice in a beverage to have a cool drink down in the village, just as Alpine snow and ice was once brought down to Rome.

Smoking With The Mayor

The mayor of Chitral owned the only hotel. He often came to the balcony on the second floor to visit with guests. Joaquin was friendly with a couple, an American woman and an Italian artist who painted exceptionally well. They sat on the balcony, smoked hash, and watched the town go by, the camels, burros, and horses. There were few vehicles. It was tough even for a four-wheel drive to get up to the village. The mayor usually arrived in the afternoon to socialize with his guests. He had bandolero bullets over his shoulders and his AK47 that he'd set on the table. He issued a jovial greeting.

"Good afternoon, you are today well?"

The mayor always brought chunks of hash to give. They sat and smoked together. Every day he'd present a selection from maybe a different farm. Joaquin was collecting these. The hash was free, staying at the mayor's hotel. The visitors brought some money in to the mayor, and, in return, the mayor gave these little gifts of the local produce.

Arrested

After three weeks in Chitral Joaquin left tribal territory. Reaching the government area authorities stopped his bus. An official boarded and asked questions in the local language.

"Are there any foreigners here?"

All the people turned and pointed to Joaquin. He was told to get his pack for the shakedown, unaware of the process. His pack was searched and all the bits of hash that the mayor had given him were found.

Joaquin attempted to explain.

"This was given to me by the mayor of Chitral."

Joaquin's explanation held no weight for these heavy handed government men. He was removed from the bus, shackled, and escorted to a nearby jail with manacles on his ankles and wrists and a chain between those. He was held in a decrepit jail for two days before he was transported to the town of Mardan.

To escort Joaquin and other prisoners to town a jail warder walked onto the road with a sawed-off shotgun and waved down the first bus that came along. The bus driver hit the brakes and stopped the bus.

There were eight prisoners, manacled and chained together, and on each right hand there was another chain that went down their side. Among them was a young kid and a couple of old men with big beards. The guard opened the back of the bus and pulled nine people out, telling them to get their luggage off the top. These travelers were put on the road in exchange for the eight prisoners and the guard. The bus departed and the offenders were on to Mardan to face trials.

Joaquin had to wait two more days before being taken in front of a judge, who also was a military officer. In excellent English the official summarily inquired,

"Please tell me what happened."

Joaquin replied,

"While staying in Chitral for a few weeks the mayor gave me some hash. It was thrown in my pack and forgotten. My presumption was that the rules must be the same and hash was legal here."

The judge laughed.

"Oh, ho, ho, ho, you have a lot to learn about our country. Where are you from? My schooling was in the United States at Georgetown University."

Joaquin replied,

"Wow, that's Washington, D.C. My hometown is in California. Your English is perfect."

The judge rendered his verdict.

"All right, you're free to go. We're sorry about this."

Joaquin escaped further consequences. He wasn't trafficking. The mayor gave it to him. What was he going to do, throw it away? But the inconvenient detention realized the need for circumspection to avoid further legal entanglement.

Joaquin determined that he was ready to go on to India, but the Bangladesh war was under way between East Pakistan, later to become Bangladesh, and India, against West Pakistan. Joaquin went to the border of India, only open once a week, where numerous people, including westerners, waited to cross.

The Psychic Lady of India

The Punjab is a geographic locale comprising vast regions of eastern Pakistan and northern India. Punjab means *The Land Of Five Waters*, referring to the Jhelum, Chenab, Ravi, Sutlej, and Beas rivers. All are tributaries of the Indus River, with courses in western Tibet and Kashmir. The word for the strain of Cannabis, *Indica*, derives from the river's name. The country of India owes its name to the Indus.

At a border crossing into the Punjab region a woman was employed to detect hashish being brought into India. Attractive, under five feet tall, the woman had an ability to ferret out hashish simply by looking at people. She became well known as The Psychic Lady. Those crossing the border would be brought into a room, twenty at a time, escorted by Sikh guards. Sikh refers to adherents of Sikhism as a religion, not an ethnic group. Male Sikhs have *Singh*, Lion, and female Sikhs have *Kaur*, Princess, as a middle or last name. Sikhs have uncut hair, wear a cotton undergarment, and carry a *kirpan*, a small sword or knife tucked in a strap, and a *kanga*, a small wooden comb. Baptized male Sikhs cover their hair with a turban. Discrimination of Sikhs by Hindus has created tensions.

The psychic lady walked in the room and approached everyone, gazing directly in their eyes, saying nothing. The westerners were perplexed by her tactic. The lady approached a Sikh guard and whispered.

She'd pointed to certain people. They were the ones that had hash. Those who weren't selected could continue and cross the border into India.

Outside Peshawar, at the customs house crossing into Afghanistan, hashish was on the shelves for sale. It was here that a border guard inquired of Joaquin,

"Are you wishing to purchase the quality hashish?"

Joaquin was taken aback at the prospect of an official offering the herb for sale. He thought this was a trick, that he would buy hash and be busted by the next official down the road, but the customs man said,

"No, not to be worrying. We don't do that, this is tribal area."

It was different between Pakistan and India, where the psychic lady pointed out the stoners. India put resources into preventing importation of the herb.

By then, Joaquin had developed a method to hide small amounts of hashish for his own use while traveling. He had taken the hash and worked it into rounded and rolled lines sealed in plastic wrap, then inserted it down the tubes of his backpack. The hash was well hidden and couldn't be smelled. The psychic lady still suspected he had hash but it went unfound, being so cleverly stashed.

Joaquin stayed in India for two and a half years on a three-month tourist visa but no official ever confronted the discrepancy. Travel between Nepal and India did not require a visa. Movement between those countries was uncomplicated.

Finance

Joaquin's skill with mechanics afforded him the opportunity to profit by assisting smugglers with hiding hashish in parts of vehicles that made discovery by customs officials challenging. After facilitating the process a number of times he earned enough to return to Germany where he purchased a Peugeot van to take out East. But he first traveled down to Ibiza where it took him a while to get a *carnet du passage*, the card needed to drive across all the borders. While waiting, he made a couple of runs down to Morocco, bought hashish, transported it back to Europe and sold it there. Everyone loved the Afghani but Moroccan was good as well, and a shorter trip to Europe.

Joaquin determined that with his own van and his skill and experience he could make the eastern run. A lot of western vehicles were coming out. So many westerners were driving from Europe to India to score that the road came to be referenced as The Hashish Trail. Even those double decker busses would make the trip all the way from London to Kathmandu. Joaquin saw a lot of those. But Joaquin only dealt in psychedelics, and things he thought were good for the planet. We can use drugs for any purpose but we did want to use hash for a love vibe, uniting people.

In the early 1970s in Afghanistan the cost for a kilo of hashish was seven American dollars. Kabul was a significant money market in Asia, run by Sikhs. The official exchange rate in India was five rupees to the dollar. On the black market in New Delhi the rate could be seven or eight rupees to the dollar, but in Kabul one could get more than fifty or even seventy Indian rupees to the dollar with a large amount of American money when the official exchange rate was five. In Kabul, one was able to exchange more than ten times the amount of rupees than in India.

Amsterdam was a loose and tolerant European city where hashish was sold openly in places like the rock clubs Paradiso and Fantasio. Most of the dealing was done in Dutch guilders back then, but one was able to ask for American dollars or trade guilders for dollars before leaving to go back out East on another run. Guilders were worthless in Afghanistan, they were unrecognized, and the Deutschmark wasn't used for some time until it became accredited in India and Kabul.

A variety of goods came from India to Kabul and were purchased with Indian rupees. Afghans had their own money but it was worthless outside of Afghanistan. In doing any kind of international trading the rupee was far more valuable than the local currency but it was without value outside of India, Sri Lanka, and Nepal. The dollar was the internationally recognized currency and, with them it was so easy to live in underdeveloped India. Knowing how to go to Kabul to trade currency could profit, but then it was necessary to find a place to stash all those bills because there are people who were ready to waylay those known to have cash.

Hash Oil

Hashish oil is the resinous substance obtained from the Cannabis plant by solvent extraction. The psychoactive constituent of the plant, tetrahydrocannabinol, THC, can be as high as 60-90% in oil, whereas the THC content of hashish ranges from none to 60%. Hashish in large quantities is bulky but hashish oil can reduce the bulk substantially while increasing the THC content, and thus, the high.

Young westerners in Kabul began a practice of transporting hash oil by swallowing numerous doubled condoms containing the oil, then flying to Europe and America, where the material was excreted and could then be used. This technique has been used for smuggling substances like opium, heroin, and cocaine.

Joaquin got involved in making hash oil when that became the craze. He had the van, and hash oil manufacturers needed to get pure alcohol for the distilling process. The only place the alcohol was available was Tehran, a thousand miles away.

Joaquin drove from Kabul to Tehran, acquiring three fifty-five gallon barrels of the highly volatile alcohol, and returned with it to Kabul. All his friends loved him. That's when he met the people that were flying hashish out in containers on airplanes to Southern California, the beginning of importation of large quantities to meet the increasing demand. People knew each other only on a first name basis for discretion.

Hash oil was in vogue for a few years. Manufacturing the oil involved the construction of distillers with copper coils to recover the alcohol that was only available in faraway Tehran. The manufacturing process involved mixing pollen with alcohol and stirring on low heat. Care was required to keep the mixture from exploding. A couple of manufacturers with a big distillery weren't attentive and allowed the mixture to overheat and explode. That brought the cops right across the street from Joaquin's place in Shar-e-Nau, where he had a couple of stills going as well. He worried that authorities might do a neighborhood sweep instead of just going for the men whose distillery was destroyed.

Afghan Vibrations

There was always underlying tension with illegal activities, underground action, and subterfuge, but it's like Bob Dylan said, to live outside the law you must be honest. In Afghanistan caution was necessary. When Joaquin traveled to Kandahar, site of one of the oldest known human settlements, he found it be a reactionary part of the country. The Pashtuns there could be hard, dangerous, and challenging. Two young Frenchmen, new to arrive, weren't being careful, and conducted themselves in a loose manner. They wanted to buy hash, quickly. A Pashtun gave them a little bit of hash and the French men unwisely showed him the equivalent of three or four thousand dollars, which to an Afghan in 1971 was a significant amount of money. The Pashtun consulted his mullah asking what he should do. The Frenchmen were looking to score twenty kilos of hash and had a lot of cash. The mullah told the Pashtun to get them really stoned on opium then cut their throats and take the money. The Pashtun did as his mullah suggested but carelessly left the bodies in an open drainage ditch. The crime was discovered in a matter of days and the Pashtun and the mullah were hung. But the French kids were gone. There were serious repercussions in the smuggling trade in this wild, untamed land. One had to exercise discretion and caution in affairs of a clandestine nature.

Tariffs

On the way to Afghanistan, at more or less regular intervals on the highway, were homemade tollgates across the road with a counter weight at the other end and a man there with a shotgun that would inform drivers,

"This my territory. Must to pay money."

Busses, cars, and motorcycles were required to stop while the toll taker approached vehicles with his hand out and charge, maybe ten Afghanis. It was two dollars or so, not much, but one had to pay. This was not government but local people collecting in tribal areas.

India is a tribal country with many states, languages, and ethnicities in one realm. In the fall foreigners could go up to Manali, a hill station in the state of Himachal Pradesh at an altitude of nearly 7,000 feet, and run through the Cannabis fields wearing leathers where the pollen would accumulate then be scraped off to make hash. In this way the locals acquired tourist money.

Wild On The Trail

The Ganges River is really the ganja river. Ganja is a term of Sanskrit origin meaning Cannabis. At the headwaters of all the Ganges tributaries wild marijuana grows. When Joaquin was trekking in the Himalayas, especially over the Annapurna area, he would have to chop down fifteen or twenty feet high wild marijuana plants just to get an area where he could pitch his tent. Some places were so extremely steep, that when he found a level area it usually was covered with marijuana. While trekking, especially in autumn, Joaquin could chop *kolas*, marijuana branches bursting with buds. They were always seeded because nobody's tending these wild plants. He'd put them in his backpack, let them dry for three or four days, and have a decent smoke. When Joaquin arrived in Nepal and began trekking in the Himalayas and saw that there was wild marijuana everywhere he thought maybe Lumbini wasn't where he was supposed to be going. Maybe it was further up in Nepal. When he reached Nepal he met both Nepalese and Tibetan people, who, by comparison to the wilder Afghans, were of a more tranquil, peaceful countenance.

In Northern India Joaquin became acquainted with Tibetan Buddhism, which ultimately became his religion. The Dalai Lama lives in Northern India in Dharamsala, the seat of the Tibetan political administration in exile. The city is in a majestic setting among steep forested mountains at 7000 feet elevation. The population swelled as Tibetans, fleeing the invading Chinese, increasingly arrived to ultimately create a Tibetan state in exile. Joaquin went there thinking that the Dalai Lama might give him an audience but was content instead to absorb Buddhist teachings with less revered but capable representatives.

Kathmandu

In 1971 Joaquin went to the Eden Hashish Centre in Kathmandu on Freak Street. The Tibetan proprietors let people sample hash or opium before deciding what to buy. A striking seventeen year old Tibetan woman with a baby was giving a sample of product to try, when her baby began fidgeting and needed some milk. The woman took her top down, bared her breast, and fed her baby. She was looking at Joaquin and smiling. This would never happen in an Islamist country. Another woman with a baby came in. The two mothers talked while Joaquin was smoking hash. When the second baby became hungry the first woman took her friend's baby and put it on her other breast. This behavior exemplifies how much more mellow the Nepalese and Tibetan cultures are than the more aggressive Afghans.

When Joaquin got to Kathmandu he decided that Afghani hash is good and it is superior to Nepalese but he would rather deal Nepalese because these people are so cool. You never had to look over your shoulder when dealing with the Nepalese and Tibetans. The more gentle people in Nepal demonstrated the search that all of us in the West were doing to find a more peaceful existence. They practice Buddhist philosophy and the Hindu philosophy of the Nepalese Newar tribes. It was a revelation. After that, Joaquin wanted to deal only with these people. Why put up with the headaches, the underlying tension, even though he had great experiences in Afghanistan and met many wonderful people?

Afghanistan was difficult for women. Afghan men are the worst misogynists on the planet. Getting to Nepal and dealing with Nepalese and Tibetan people was a significantly more mellow experience.

The Pakistanis and the Afghans are armed and can be fierce but the Nepalese can be fierce too. The Ghurkas are people of different clans in Nepal who have had a powerful reputation for centuries. The British used Ghurka regiments in military campaigns from 1857 onward. One detachment even served with Lawrence of Arabia. The former Indian Army Chief of Staff Field Marshal Sam Manekshaw, once stated,

"If a man says he is not afraid of dying, he is either lying or is a Gurkha."

Gurkhas carried *khukuris*, curved knives that are the signature weapon of these naturally warlike and aggressive-in-battle soldiers.

Calcutta

Although inhabited for over two thousand years, the recorded history of Calcutta, East India's principal commercial port, began in 1690 with the arrival of the British East India Company. The British constructed Fort William in 1712 and engaged in frequent fighting, first with French forces, followed by East Indians, led by The Nawab of Bengal. The Nawab with his army attacked and captured the fort, imprisoning and killing British soldiers in the infamous Black Hole of Calcutta, a dungeon so small that 123 prisoners out of 146 died overnight from suffocation, heat exhaustion, and crushing. British troops led by the famous Major-General Robert Clive, known thereafter as Clive of India, recaptured the city the following year and established the military and political supremacy of the East India Company that secured India, and the wealth that followed, for the British crown.

Joaquin visited Calcutta during the Bangladesh war. The city was designed by the British for three million people but there were already seven million inhabitants and another thirteen million refugees from Bangladesh as a result of the West Pakistani's engagement in the systemic genocide of, and atrocities toward, Bengali citizens. There was no place to sleep. On arrival, Joaquin realized this was a mistake during the Bangladesh war. He wanted to see Calcutta but the city was overwhelmed with refugees. Finding one sheet of newspaper and a bit of a sidewalk upon which to sleep was difficult.

Joaquin was fortunate enough to have some money and went right back to the train station but it still took him ten days to leave Calcutta during that terrible time.

Joaquin & Stanley Go East

In the winter of 1974 Joaquin drove his van from the East back to Europe and the Spanish island of Ibiza, planning to stay through the summer in those bucolic surroundings. While residing first in the elegant farmhouse of his friend Jim, Joaquin became acquainted with the American musicians there who were assembling their band. The group, being in need of a bass player, and Joaquin, being decently skilled playing guitar, joined forces. Joaquin was attracted to the concept and began learning bass guitar. He eventually rented his own house and performed with the band, using his van to transport the group and their equipment to their engagements. The months on the island provided a refreshing transition from Himalayan rigors and Eastern culture to a more tranquil Western environ. Performing with the band brought great satisfaction, but, once autumn arrived and the tourists departed, the band finished its work and Joaquin decided to return to the East, and to the hashish trade.

He attempted to engage Alicia, a Spanish woman that he had met while he was surfing up north, to join him on the trip. He sent her a letter stating point of view but her return missive informed him that she had met a man, had a baby, and was otherwise occupied.

Joaquin was planning to drive by himself but, in a casual conversation over coffee in town with Stanley, the band's harmonica player, Joaquin asked if he wanted to go along. Stanley responded with an immediate yes.

The two hit the road and headed toward the rising sun, keeping pedal to the metal all the way to Kabul, where Joaquin connected with his friend, Oscar, another trader in kind. When Oscar flew in with a surfboard the Afghans flipped. A week of effort was required to get the board out of customs. The Afghans were suspicious that there was something wrong.

"What do you using these thing?"

"It's a surfboard to ride ocean waves."

"Why bringing these thing to Afghanistan? No water. No ocean"

"Well, we're heading down to Sri Lanka for the surf there"

Afghan customs relented, releasing the wave riding board to the California surfer in landlocked wild mountain Afghanistan. Eventually, the two did go down to Sri Lanka, surfing for a season, before going back up to Nepal. Joaquin even took Stanley on a Himalayan trek but Stanley was on too much opium and the rigors of the trail proved too difficult.

Joaquin smoked opium when he first got to Bombay but he was so stoned with the dreams and nodding that it felt wrong for him. It only took one experience and that was all. He was a rarity among a lot of westerners who would not refuse getting high on opium. But the drug was a downer and so addictive that one lost normal function. A musician on Ibiza accidently died high on opium when he fell off the tower by Vedra, the mysterious island off Ibiza. Joaquin much preferred a natural consciousness and was known, and admired, for this attribute.

Arriving in Kabul, Joaquin received an aerogram at poste restante telling him that two of his former band mates had been arrested for smuggling and were on a government sponsored vacation paid by the Spanish authorities. Joaquin didn't know where they were but he knew there had been a problem. He also intuited that the two had hatched a risky plan that was less than capable of success.

Joaquin went back to Mazar-i-Sharif and acquired the best hash, the kind that would guarantee sale in Paradiso or Fantasio in Amsterdam where dealers openly sat at tables hawking their wares and would buy the prime Afghani for their personal stash.

After secreting a substantial amount of hashish in the van Joaquin planned to head down into India with Oscar, leave the van there for a time, and surf in Sri Lanka. The van was parked in Bombay inside a walled compound for security at a hotel to later be shipped to

Italy, avoiding the long drive to Europe.

Trekking

Surfing in Sri Lanka warmth was a pleasant interlude for Joaquin and Oscar. Stanley joined them there before the three went back to Bombay in preparation for the shipment. But there was a delay when the ship's propeller had to be replaced and the shipping date was delayed for two months. That's when Joaquin said,

"Up to the Himalayas."

Spring had arrived and with it trekking season. There are only two seasons, spring and fall, April and May, then September, October, and November. The season depends on when the monsoon ends. Storms pack the clouds right up against the Himalayas, the trails become muddy, and trekking is too mucky and dangerous. Treks are multi-day hiking trips through rural and often rugged terrain, where walkers have close views of the scenery. With spectacular mountain vistas the Himalayan area is a particularly popular trekking destination. With a backpack, high quality hiking boots, warm clothing, first aid kit, a supply of food and water, sleeping bag, and tent, treks can be extensive enjoyable outdoor enterprises.

Stanley attempted the trek, but got so ill, due to his use of opium and general lack of tone, that he had to be carried down by a Sherpa porter, and he returned to Kathmandu. Joaquin trekked up to the Langtang area, a region in Nepal to the north of Kathmandu and bordering Tibet. It is protected as Langtang National Park with a number of high peaks including Langtang Lirung, at 23,711 feet, the highest peak of the Langtang Himal, a subrange of the Nepalese Himalayas.

By the time Joaquin returned to Kathmandu, Stanley had developed a relationship with a striking Nepalese woman whom he planned to marry. He wanted to stay and make a family. The two intrepid travelers' directions diverged and they parted company, never to meet again.

End Of The East

Joaquin returned to Bombay and supervised the shipment of the van, then flew to Florence to await the arrival. By 1975 Interpol had computers and because of previous busts, Oscar in Denmark, and Joaquin in Holland, the authorities' suspicions may have been aroused. Oscar met Joaquin in Florence. When Oscar went to the shipping office the woman at the front desk informed him that customs would not release the vehicle since there was a suspicion that hashish or drugs may have been hidden in it. The woman's revelation was a fortuitous breech of protocol that enabled an alternate plan.

Oscar told Joaquin,

"It's registered in my name so it's time to get out of here. It's better not to go back to get it."

Joaquin gave the matter some thought.

"Saturday the warehouse is open for only half a day. They might release it to me then."

Oscar left Italy. On Saturday, Joaquin presented himself at customs with a full gas can, because vehicles must be shipped empty. The two customs officials on duty wanted to thoroughly examine the van. Joaquin said,

"Go ahead. There's no contraband here. We're coming back from a great trip in Asia. We bought carpets in Afghanistan. You can search the whole thing."

While the inspectors were working, Joaquin poured gas into the tank and reconnected the battery. He got the engine running and asked,

"Are you done?"

"Ah, no. We've done a small inspection but our workmen are coming back on Monday, so you'll have to return then."

The customs inspectors had been searching in the area where the contraband was hidden. Joaquin thought when he got out of there,

"You know what? They'll come back with electric drills, and they're going to get really serious, so it's time to split, and this will give me Sunday to leave the country."

When confronted with the obvious awareness of being discovered in this situation it's better to just leave it alone because we may be willing to take chances but we also have to be prepared to cut it loose when things don't go our way. No monkey grip. Know when a bust is imminent. Fortunately, this one came with a preview and not an arrest.

Joaquin left the van with the contraband that was discovered but he and his associate had departed and escaped arrest. The van, shipment, and impending profit were lost. We were all improvising. Transporting contraband wasn't a system that anyone knew. There was no manual, no book of Smuggling for Dummies. The

Hashish Trail from the East to Europe was mostly lone travelers moving a few kilos at a time. In a few more years the overland route would be no more, leaving in its wake political instability and closing societies.

Santander

Having abandoned the hashish laden transport in Italy, Joaquin traveled to southern France, in the foothills of the Alps, where a welcoming acquaintance gave him shelter in his country estate. There he might relax, transit to the European side, and plot a new course. He had lost everything in the Italian debacle, and had little in reserve considering all the years he had been in the trade. Risk began to outweigh reward.

Joaquin received a letter from his friend Jim who was on his way to Santander, on the Atlantic Ocean in Northern Spain. Joaquin felt that some moments in communion with the ocean waves might apply a soothing unguent to the recent abrasion he suffered. Santander was not far south from his shelter in the French Alps. The town had good surfing breaks at Somo and Liencres, and a surf shop there had supplies.

Joaquin and Jim met and camped on the sand dunes above the beach. Joaquin was considering his next move. The two friends recounted travel tales and were present at a surf shop soiree, attended by an international group of waveriders. Both Joaquin and Jim were interested in a French woman at the event, but Jim made a stronger impression with a superior command of French. When they ultimately were married Jim returned with his new bride to America.

North Africa

In conversation with a South African at the surf party, it became apparent that they both had an awareness of each other's involvement in the trade. The South African had a problem in that he couldn't get back in to Morocco but he had a van. Joaquin had no van but he could go to Morocco and knew the hashish producing area of Ketama well. The two came to an accommodation. The South African would supply the vehicle and money, and Joaquin would drive to Morocco, score the hash, and return with it. The two agreed to acquire ten kilos and split the merchandise equally.

Hashish smugglers had become familiar with certain safe routes between North Africa and Europe with specific ships and customs routines from Morocco, Algeria, and Tunisia. Joaquin had done the Tunis to Palermo ferry route. Score in Morocco, drive through Algeria and Tunisia, put the truck on the Sicilian ferry, Tunis to Palermo, where there was no customs at all, and drive off the boat. It was still necessary to go all the way up the boot of Italy but the extra road trip was worth the decreased risk.

European kids tried to carry hashish back home on a British ship plying the waters on round trips between Southampton and North Africa. Every time the boat docked in Southampton customs found substantial amounts of herb. *The Hashish Boat*, as the ship was referenced, went to Agadir in southern Morocco, stopped in lovely Tangier, with the medina right up at the highest part of town, and the sea cliffs, then went on to Lisbon, Portugal, and ended its voyage in Southampton.

That ferry from Tangier to Lisbon was considered a safe smuggling route if one got off in Lisbon. The ship was British so on arrival in Britain, of course, customs did thorough searches. In Lisbon there was no customs inspection. The extremely poor Portuguese were happy to have people come to their country and welcomed cash-spending visitors with little restriction.

Canary Islands

Joaquin drove the South African's van from Spain, ferried into Morocco, scored the ten kilos in Ketama, and did the run from Morocco to Lisbon, through Portugal, and back up to Santander where he sold all his Moroccan except for a half pound.

In autumn the lazy days of summer surfing concluded. To lessen the approaching chill of winter Joaquin decided to go to the Canary Islands, a Spanish colonial archipelago sixty-two miles off the northwest coast of mainland Africa. The subtropical climate, long summers, warm winters, and omnipresent beaches, make the islands a major tourist destination.

The name Canary Islands is derived from the Latin name *Canariae insulae*, meaning Island of the Dogs, a name given to the islands by Mauretanian King Juba II in the time of Julius Caesar (by whom the king was raised and educated) because the islands were reputed to contain vast multitudes of dogs of very large size. The referenced dogs may actually have been species of seals. *Canis marinus* was a Latin term for seal. During the times of the Spanish Empire the islands were the main stopover for Spanish galleons sailing to the Americas because of the prevailing winds from the northeast.

The Canarys are the original winter surf destination in that part of the world. By the time open ocean swell reaches the islands the winds producing them have long died away, offering the possibility of clean, long period waves, ideal for surfing.

Joaquin hadn't been to the islands before but his Spanish surfing friends all said that's where to go. The warm weather and beach breaks made for an ideal place. Top English and French surfers are there in winter.

Joaquin was living at the southern end of Gran Canaria in a country town called Mogan, where he reencountered the American who had shaped an excellent board for him that Joaquin brought from northern Spain. The shaper was a young California surfer, good looking and popular with the girls. Joaquin shared a smoke and when the kid mentioned his lack of a stash Joaquin broke off a chunk and gave it to him. Two weeks later the kid was caught at the house of the mayor of Las Palmas de Gran Canario in the bathtub with the mayor's sixteen-year-old daughter. The parents returned from a trip earlier than expected and walked into a wild party. The mayor telephoned the authorities who rushed in and made arrests of some attendees including the California surfer.

In Franco's Spain, police interrogation techniques included forms of physical abuse, or torture. Methods could include the application of electric shock, extraction of fingernails, beating, food deprivation, and being kept awake to induce a state of strain and reduced consciousness. Under police pressure, the surfer mentioned Joaquin's name and residence.

The Tide Turns

Joaquin was enjoying a Thanksgiving dinner with friends at his place in Mogan, when there came a loud and insistent knocking at the door, which, when opened, revealed a contingent of Spanish police with guns raised, and serious attitude. In those days Joaquin and his friends smoked from a carrot. To make a carrot pipe one carves a bowl in the thick part of a carrot, then runs a stem through the thinner part, thus creating a little smoking pipe. At the time of the police arrival the guests had finished taking a toke. They were moderate smokers anyway and they threw the carrot pipe into the basket with all the other carrots.

Joaquin had two stashes. The smaller one with about twenty-five grams that he used regularly was hidden, like we loved to do, in an outside rock wall. A larger stash of two hundred grams was buried. Due to the careful secreting of the hash in case of just this eventuality, the police were unable to find anything.

Frustrated now, the police addressed Joaquin.

"You know, this lovely German woman, she's going to go to jail. We'll take her daughter and separate them, and she'll probably never see her daughter again. Your buddy over here, he's going to jail, too, because we have to take something back to our boss."

Seeing that he was getting his friends into trouble, Joaquin acquiesced. He took the cops to the small stash. With the discovered contraband the authorities were happy as pigs in the sty. They had a worthwhile bust and found the guy who supplied the American surfer who was debauching with the mayor's daughter. Joaquin was arrested and taken to the station for interrogation.

Joaquin's friends were upset of course, but free. As for Joaquin, it was just another time of going down. He was familiar with the process. The police facilitated their inquisition with corporal persuasion, pounding on him with brass knuckles. After the adventurous years on the trail the once bountiful sand sifting slowly down in his smuggler's hourglass reached the final grain. The once seemingly inexhaustible allocation was depleted.

Penitentiary: from Latin paenitentia 'repentance'

A prison is a facility in which individuals are forcibly confined and denied a variety of freedoms under the authority of the state as a form of punishment. The beginning of prisons can be traced back to the rise of the state as a form of social organization. Development of written language enabled the creation of formalized legal codes as guidelines for society. The most well known is the Code of Hammurabi, written in Babylon around 1750 BC. The penalties for violations of the laws in Hammurabi's Code were centered around the concept of retaliation, where the victims themselves often punished people as a form of vengeance.

Some ancient Greek philosophers, among them Plato, developed ideas of using incarceration to reform offenders instead of emphasizing retribution. During the 18th century popular resistance to public execution and torture became more widespread and rulers began looking for means to punish and control their subjects in a way that did not cause people to associate the rulers with spectacles of tyrannical and sadistic violence.

Systems of mass incarceration were developed as a solution.

The most common justifications of why people are imprisoned by the state are rehabilitation, deterrence, incapacitation, and retribution.

Theories of rehabilitation claim that imprisonment will cause people to change their behavior in a way that will make them productive and law-abiding members of society once they are released, but in practice prisons tend to be ineffective at improving the lives of most prisoners. It's hard to train for freedom in a cage. The early view of prisons as centers of rehabilitation is no longer widely held.

Theories of deterrence claim that by sentencing criminals to extremely harsh penalties, other people who might be considering criminal activities will be so terrified of the consequences that they will choose not to commit crimes out of fear. Most studies show that high incarceration rates either increase crime, have no noticeable effect, or only decrease it by a very small amount. Prisons act as training grounds for criminal activity and foster anti-social sentiments towards society.

Justifications based on incapacitation claim that while prisoners are incarcerated, they will be unable to commit crimes, thus keeping communities safer.

Theories of retribution seek to exact revenge upon criminals by harming them in exchange for harms caused to their victims. These theories are concerned with ensuring that the punishment causes a sufficient level of misery for the prisoner, in proportion to the perceived seriousness of their crime. Retribution theories presume that some kind of moral balance will be achieved by paying back the prisoner for the wrongs they have committed.

Sentencing policies brought about by wars on drugs result in a dramatic growth in incarceration for drug offenses. Drug offenders can be up to half of a prison population. Most of these people are not high-level actors in the drug trade, and most have no prior criminal record for a violent offense. Yet they are given often unduly harsh sentences and placed in populations of violent career criminals. Many leaders advocate an end to the wars on drugs and mass incarceration of offenders.

Alcohol use is legal, tolerated, and even equated with fun, good times, and positive social behavior. Yet, the negative effects of alcohol use are widely known and can be catastrophic. The world view of Cannabis use is changing from one of fear and punishment to that of acceptance of the herb as a valuable medicine, and even a pleasant recreational product. Marijuana, along with hashish, is undergoing a reevaluation as more states realize its benefits as medicine and as a profitable income producing enterprise.

Still, in the United States, under federal law, marijuana and hashish have long been treated as controlled substances, classed as Schedule I drugs, like cocaine and heroin, considered to be addictive and of no medical value.

Pobrecito

The timing of his arrest was to be fortuitous. When Joaquin entered prison, Spain's head of state, General Franco, had died on November 20 and Thanksgiving was

November 27. He was arrested seven days after Franco died. Arriving in the prison in Las Palmas de Gran Canarias, everyone was in a good mood because the newly crowned King Juan Carlos had just given a three-year pardon as a gesture of mercy by the new sovereign. The inmates were celebrating and the guards were happy because there was no tension.

Joaquin's noticed everybody addressing him as *pobrecito*, meaning poor little guy, because he was the first one to be admitted after Franco died.

"Pobrecito, if you only had been busted five days earlier, you crazy bastard, ha, ha, ha, you already would have gotten three years off your sentence."

The name stuck. Pobrecito. Joaquin wondered whether the pardon would ultimately be applied to him, once his trial occurred and his sentence declared. The United States had no embassy on the Canary Islands but there was a Consul. Sadly, the Consul was not in the least supportive of his American compatriot, but was vocally anti-drug and pleased that hashish users were being busted. Of course, Joaquin was disappointed with the lack of camaraderie from the diplomatic quarter, feeling that the Consul's charge was to provide assistance to him, as an American citizen. The diplomat's attitude was more of the you can rot in hell point of view. Ironically, he was an alcoholic and on his few visits to the prison turned up noticeably under the influence of spirits.

Outside Help

An acquaintance from the Thanksgiving dinner

waited a month to come and visit his friend. That's a good idea since one never wants to be caught in the aftermath of an arrest and investigation. When he finally did visit, Joaquin subtly implied his predicament.

"There are still two hundred grams stashed away and they're feeding me tripe soup a couple of times a day. Things here are bad."

Without directly asking for anything, Joaquin let him know, and his friend understood the conditions. But he had his girlfriend and her daughter and did not want to jeopardize them.

Joaquin said,

"If you can, you can, if you can't, it's no big deal. This situation isn't new. It'll just be a while."

Fortunately, the acquaintance was determined to provide some assistance. He had already taken Joaquin's newly acquired Volkswagen van the day after the bust and drove it to where the cops wouldn't know its location and be able to confiscate it.

Just before the friend was ready to leave the islands he was able to sell the VW. He retrieved the other stash of two hundred grams of hash and sold it to South African surfers who craved some smoke in that difficult to score place. This valiant assist, with no small risk, produced necessary money for Joaquin in his time of need.

Judgment

The prosecutor of Joaquin's case was asking the court for a sentence of six years, two months, and a day. In the colonies authorities appeared to always come down harder. Hashish activity was becoming more prevalent in Barcelona and Madrid, where new urban social interaction concepts were more rapidly assimilated. In the remote Canary Islands there was still a resistance to acceptance of cultural evolution, hence the request for the harsh sentence. But six years for a bit of hash was extreme. This wasn't murder, mayhem, rape, or robbery. It was fifty dollars worth of hashish.

Joaquin's trial was conducted entirely in Spanish. His lawyer spoke no English. Their legal strategy was to point out that his crime had been committed before the pardon was given. They maintained that the crime was bringing the illegal hashish into Spanish territory. Joaquin's passport was shown to the court with the stamp demonstrating passage into the country from Portugal, in August. The defense suggested that the crime happened before the pardon was granted, therefore Joaquin should receive its benefit. Guilty, by admission, but deserving of the pardon.

Perhaps knowing that the pardon might be applied and would reduce the time served, but wanting to invoke some measure of punishment, the court imposed a stiff sentence of four years, two months and a day, but less than the prosecutor's request of six years. The pardon was determined to be applicable and removed three years from his sentence. Joaquin was to pass fourteen months for less than an ounce of hashish, the same amount of time as his Ibiza band mates served in Barcelona and Majorca for twenty pounds. Justice was blind and imbalanced.

The Priest

Joaquin was an easygoing person, skilled in things mechanical, willing to engage in conversation, and he enjoyed a good laugh. He was the only American in the prison at that time, and possibly these attributes are what motivated the prison priest to became acquainted with him. The priest wanted to improve his English. Joaquin wanted to improve his Spanish. The two began meeting for the purpose of exchanging linguistic knowledge. Once on comfortable terms with the priest, Joaquin solicited his assistance in starting a basketball league using an old court that had been neglected. Initially the hoops had no nets, but in time the priest acquired new ones. Basketball provided a positive bounce for the prisoners while the priest and Joaquin found common ground and good humor as each other's students.

Boozin'

Amidst the routine and monotony that was prison life, inmates searched for ways to relieve the tedium by enhancing their mood with the occasional illicit drug. A German hashish smuggler was able to acquire some LSD for a foray into the psychedelic, but it was a bit much in the restrictive enclosure.

The prison store, the *economato*, stocked a small variety of goods, including toothpaste, chocolate, pens, paper, and beer. Eight inmates were allowed to get in a line once a day to make purchases, which could include one beer each. Those who were able to manage the expense would pay for one ration of beer dispensed in a plastic cup. All eight men would then congregate at a secluded spot under a staircase where they were allowed to sip their beer under a lenient watch by a guard. The scheme was, when somebody wanted to get out of it for a while they would pay for all eight beers, chug their beer down, then a friend would hand off another beer to the designated drinker, and it would keep going until all the alcohol was consumed by one person. They only had ten minutes so the drinker downed eight beers in that time. The next day it was someone else's turn. In this way the men managed a sloppy drunken high and for an hour or two were numb to their surroundings.

For a musical interlude, the prison scheduled a Saturday discotheque in the library, playing records for mood enhancement and a party vibe. Although there was no marijuana or hashish, there was legal tobacco, the use of which was prevalent in the form of cigarettes. For a non-smoker a few inhaled puffs of the strong black Spanish variety produced a momentary dizziness for an occasional wobbly effect.

A Wedding

Roberto, from Peru, had been in the foreign legion in Spanish Sahara. He was caught with an ambitious five hundred kilos of hashish, brought via Spanish Sahara to the Canary Islands, on its way to the mainland. His pregnant girlfriend was in on the scheme, resulting in a double arrest. She was in the women's prison adjacent to the men. The two asked for and were given permission to be married in the prison chapel. Within the gallery in view of the chapel below prisoners attended the wedding and shouted down congratulations to the blissful bride and grateful groom, soon to be parents with no immediate opportunity to raise the child together.

Ulrich

A German was imprisoned, not for any crimes in the islands where he was a prosperous owner of discotheques and restaurants, but by request of the German government that was attempting to have him extradited back to his homeland to be tried for armed bank robbery. The Spanish were loathe to let him depart as he was bribing some of the heavy hitters in the local government. Spain was telling Germany to demonstrate more proof.

After a year and a half locked away, there was one thought foremost in Ulrich's mind, and that was escape. He began working on a getaway plan for which he enlisted Joaquin's assistance.

The old fortress was equipped with a new weight room where Ulrich took advantage of the facility to work out, pump up, and, unbeknown to the authorities, develop body power for the part of his escape plan that required strength. The man dressed exclusively in gym clothes worn over his ever-buffing body. With little to occupy Joaquin's time, he took advantage of the weight room as well and developed some camaraderie with the German.

Packages of food, clothing, and supplies could be brought in to the inmates. Naturally, packages were searched but without benefit of high tech sensing devices. Ulrich's first package contained, among other innocuous items, three tubes of toothpaste. Hidden in each tube's center was a titanium hacksaw blade.

At the beginning of Joaquin's incarceration the gallery was nearly empty due to the pardon, but gradually the prison received more inmates. Six months later as the gallery became overcrowded guards simply threw mattresses between the beds until three hundred were bunking together in a room designed for two hundred.

Locker King

Ulrich persuaded Joaquin to assist him minimally in his strategy by stashing the other two toothpaste tubes with the as yet unused blades in an available locker. On entrance to prison, each man could rent a locker in the gallery where he might stow personal items and bed sheets. If one could afford it, bed linens were rented and every week or two washed at the prison laundry, then kept in the locker while a spare set was put on the bed. Official issue was only a scratchy wool blanket.

Joaquin had become the locker *jefe*, the locker king, attaining this position of authority, such as it was, while entering the prison when most of the inmates were departing due to the pardon.

Pobrecito Joaquin inherited the locker concession due to the sympathy factor but he could speak a little Spanish and that was appreciated. He was given charge of lockers and locks, and the sheet concession, and was able to charge a pittance for their use.

Escape

In their dormitory, while some of the men played guitars and raised their voices in renditions of favorite songs for amusement and entertainment, Ulrich reclined on his upper bunk, chosen for its location beside a barred window, in a corner of the dormitory. He was secretly sawing through the middle bar, little by little, judging that with one bar removed he could squeeze through the opening.

Ulrich was up against the window sawing with the music but there was a limit on the time he required to complete his endeavor. Guards were aware of the possibility of such a breach, so they evolved a method of checking to see if the steel bars were in any way being compromised. An official bar inspection required the prisoners to stand in silence at attention beside their beds while a guard utilized a steel rod to bang the window bars while everyone listened for the ring. A breached bar had a noticeably aberrant tone. With an inspection conducted every three weeks Ulrich's time was measured.

He worked with determination, using up all three hacksaw blades until he cut completely through the bar, on time. Ulrich was prepared to depart that night.

The time of the escape was three-thirty in the morning. Ulrich had used a mirror to check the guardhouses and saw that the guards were asleep on duty. Ulrich's weight training paid off. He grasped the sawed bar and with his muscle development was able to bend it up and back upon itself. He hooked his tied together bed sheets on to the bar and in a window space just wide enough for him to crawl through he got out from the third floor. Ulrich rappelled himself down but with great shock realized when he reached the end of the sheets that his feet were about five feet above the ground. He had erred by not making the tied bed sheets long enough. Below Ulrich was a narrow yard with only ten feet of space between a massive wall surrounding the prison and the back of the large building housing the prisoner's dormitory. For security, the guards left broken glass all the way around this yard. Ulrich's plan was to get down, then sprint in the open toward then up the stone staircases that started in the middle of the wall and reach one of the two guard towers at the corner ends of the wall, then overpower a guard, hopefully, only one, and drop from the top of the wall to freedom.

Having reached the end of the bed sheets there was nothing more for it but to let go and drop to the ground. He landed on the broken glass, which naturally made a noise, but, uninjured, Ulrich ran to and up one of the staircases toward a sleeping guard.

Unfortunately, the guard at the opposite end of the wall had been alerted by Ulrich's fall on the glass and began yelling,

"Escapa, escapa, escapa."

A siren began to whine.

"Whhhhhaaaaaaaaaaahhh whhhhhaaaaaaaaaahhh.

An alarm bell chimed in.

"Rrrriiiiinnnnnnngggg, rrrrriiiiinnnnnngggg, rrrriiiiinnnnnngggg," pulsing rapidly. Lights in the building illuminated. Searchlights on the wall fired into beaming flashing action. It was do or die time.

Ulrich completed his sprint up the stone staircase, arriving at the guardhouse just as the guard woke. The man pointed his weapon at Ulrich but it happened to be the same kind of submachine gun that Ulrich used in his bank robberies and he saw that the safety was still on. The weapon would not fire. Ulrich threw his hands up in mock surrender and approached the guard but in a quick move he stepped past the sleepy fellow and with a leap he went over the wall. The prison sat on a hill in a residential area. Ulrich knew that the drop from the wall was twelve feet to the grass below with a gentle incline down to the narrow road with cars parked on both sides.

From the gallery Joaquin and the inmates crowded the windows, watching the escape with great excitement, shouting, cheering, and cursing. Ulrich was sprinting for his life.

The line of sight from the top of the wall to the road was not optimal for the guards to be accurate, but they fired their rifles. The guard was still yelling,

"Escapa, escapa, escapa."

The siren raged, the bells pulsed, and the light operators tried to illuminate the escapee.

Neighborhood house lights were coming on. The searchlights had him. The prisoners saw Ulrich running, darting between cars, running again, dropping behind a car. The street is long, more than two blocks before it makes a turn. The guards scrambled over and fired their weapons. Ulrich moved and dodged, like a football player avoiding tackle, hiding behind cars, running again, making progress up the street. It looked like he was going to get away.

From the gallery, the excited prisoners, now completely beside themselves, adrenalin pumping, jumping, rooting for their frantic man, heard a large explosive booooooooooommmm, followed by a whistling sound for a few seconds, then an explosion, baaaaaaaammmmm, that shook the building. The guards were using grenade launchers. More rifle shots. Another booooooommmmm, a whistling, and baaaaaammmmmmm, and a car exploded, throwing twisted metal and flames into the air in a cacophony of shrieking hot steel and glass. There was no turning back. Ulrich dashed and hid, ducked and ran, the gauntlet of grenades and rifle shots hailing down around him like hell's fury. The prisoners had never seen anything this before and were thinking for sure that with all this intense warlike artillery in action Ulrich is going to get blown up, but with a final finish the German outran the guns and grenades. Reaching the cross street unscathed he turned the corner in his blue gym clothes and was gone, leaving a path of devastation and a couple of exploded burning cars in his wake.

"Oh, my god. He made it. Ulrich escaped."

When Ulrich, feet pounding, and heart pumping, turned the corner, he expected his brother to be waiting for him in one of their Porsches, to provide a rapid departure. That was the plan, and the brother had been waiting, but the shooting and explosions proved too intimidating, causing Ulrich's brother to lose his composure, jamming the gas pedal down to beat a hasty retreat, leaving his dashing sibling without his getaway machine and dooming the brave and successful effort.

The valiant escapee was found in the morning hiding in a nearby lumberyard and was escorted back to the prison. One would think the guards would be pounding on him, punishing him, but no, they're shaking his hand with congratulations.

"*Que huevos*, Ulrich, *que huevos*." What balls.

"Ulrich, my god, we thought for sure you would be

shot. How did you make it?"

Ulrich stuck his chest out and said,

"Ah, you guys are such lousy shots, nobody even came close."

Ulrich was placed in solitary confinement. But even the *jefe de servicios*, a mean functionary, came out and shook his hand. Ulrich had enough courage, and you know how macho the Spanish are. He enjoyed celebrity status for a time, a small measure of compensation for his inability to escape Spanish justice.

Two months later, when Joaquin was released, Ulrich still had not been extradited back to Germany. Of course, with an attempted prison break things might have been worse but maybe that wouldn't go so hard against him if the Spanish felt the Germans didn't have enough evidence to extradite. Ulrich could say he tried to escape because he was innocent.

End Of The Trail

Time continues shaping us in spite of our plans to shape time. After fourteen months in the three-century-old fortress on the Canary Islands in the Atlantic Ocean, Joaquin reached the conclusion of his debt to the Spanish government. His family sent him a ticket to fly home. President Carter had authorized amnesty for those who had evaded the draft.

Joaquin was taken from prison and escorted to the airport by an undercover policeman accompanied by the priest, with whom Joaquin had shared some educational and social moments that both facilitated a further understanding of their respective languages and created a camaraderie. Their parting was cordial. The police person demonstrated a colder attitude and imparted words of admonishment.

"You're free to go. Get on that airplane and don't ever come back to the Canary Islands. If you return, I'll personally make sure you never get out of prison again."

Feeling deflated and offended by the diatribe, Joaquin's first reaction was to invoke a forceful retort, but with the presence of the priest as well as a measure of decorum, he realized there was no point. He muzzled his reaction, and turned to board the waiting aircraft for the flight to the mainland, then on to California.

Joaquin had been out of the country from 1968 until 1977 as a consequence of his avoidance of military service but that penalty and Spain's criminal charge were both cancelled. An era had ended.

Joaquin followed his vision to make a pilgrimage to Buddha's birthplace but plans don't reach fruition in the way we design them. There's room for change and discovery. We were exploring the world and our potential. We need the enrichment of the world to blossom. Evolution can't be done in isolation. Joaquin had traveled far but there are only two kinds of smugglers, those who have been down and those who are going down. No one escapes.

Seven

Himalayan Stoner

Stony

In the spring of 1948, a woman of Norwegian descent gave birth to a son in Los Angeles. She gave the newborn the name Stanley, a name of Old English origin, meaning stony meadow. The boy's name suited the man well when Stanley later fell in with the Love Generation's use of drugs.

The father's work as an engineer specializing in water pumping systems often required travel to distant places where grand water projects were constructed. From somewhere in Arabia he once sent his family a postcard with a picture of a toothless man swathed in a turban while holding the leash of a camel. The card was inscribed,

"Dis is da place, three hots, with intelligent companionship."

On the Columbia River in Washington he worked on the construction of the natural gravity Grand Coulee Dam containing a hydroelectric power plant to provide electricity and irrigation.

When Stanley was six the family moved from vast Los Angeles to rural Belmont in Northern California, halfway between San Francisco and San Jose. Known for its wooded hills, views of the San Francisco Bay, and stretches of open space, Belmont was then a quiet residential community in the midst of the culturally diverse and technologically rich Bay Area.

School or The Highway

Just after graduation from high school Stanley was asked to go to Majorca, Spain, to retrieve his uncle's Austin Healey and deliver the car to the uncle's residence in Versailles. The six-week trip stimulated his interest in that previously unknown locale.

Stanley's enrollment in College of San Mateo coincided with the birth of San Francisco's Love Generation centered across the bay from Belmont. Attraction to the powerful revolutionary force proved irresistible. Ere long Stanley was smoking joints and basking in psychedelic radiance and sonic splendor.

Classrooms began to lose their luster for Stanley, in light of the compelling Be Here Now social changes dawning in America. He quit college to do some coast to coast hitchhiking then bought an inexpensive Volkswagen van. At a concert in Boston he met Diana, the woman who was to become his wife. Perceiving a need for substances to fuel the high spirits Stanley reasoned that he might create revenue by selling marijuana and LSD.

He stashed his contraband in the Volkswagen bed. High on acid in New York, Stanley was profiled, stopped, and searched by state troopers. Unable to find any drugs and in the absence of illegal activity the troopers came across his dad's old army knife and forced an arrest on a concealed weapons charge. With little solid evidence the charge proved groundless and Stanley was released.

Bound for California with his future bride, the Volkswagen's engine broke down near Toledo, Ohio, where Stanley parked outside a mechanic's shop for repair. Neighbors weren't accustomed to having longhaired travelers camping at the shop and phoned the police who hustled over to investigate. The vehicle was again searched but nothing incriminating was found. The neighbor who made the call was a marine back from Vietnam. He was remorseful, crossed the street to apologize, and invited Stanley and Diana to dinner.

With the motor repaired the two continued toward California but found the engine would not accelerate past fifty miles an hour. They picked up a hitchhiker and eventually let him take a turn at the wheel, but the man was revealed to be a speed freak, a methamphetamine user, who revved the motor too fast. By the time they reached Nevada the old bus threw a piston, and was only able to limp forward at twenty-five miles an hour. Unable to make the grade over the Sierra Nevada Mountains the spent vehicle was abandoned, leaving the travelers to hitchhike the rest of the way to San Francisco.

The Journey

Diana was enrolled at Long Beach State College in Southern California. On occasion, Stanley flew from San Francisco on the ten dollar red eye to visit. Returning from one of his amorous trysts during a winter storm Stanley found himself out of money and had to hitchhike from San Francisco airport. When a station wagon pulled over Stanley could see that the driver had hair down to his waist.

A door opened. Stanley slid into the back seat and found he was sitting beside Janis Joplin. Behind the wheel sat Sam Andrew, a member of the band Big Brother and the Holding Company. The group was returning from their first east coast tour and was en route to their concert at the Cow Palace. Even though it was the wrong way for his destination, Stanley went along when he was invited, taking the opportunity to hang out with rising stars of the San Francisco music scene.

Stanley secured menial employment at the Linear Accelerator Center at Stanford University. Partially to appease her parents, Stanley and Diana were married, and the two moved in together to a semi-communal house in La Honda, a small community in the hills near Stanford. Two of the house's residents had plans to visit Spain and drew the newly married couple into their travel daydream.

Having been stimulated by driving the highways of

America, Stanley and Diana considered expanding on the theme by going to Europe. Within a few months they saved enough to get them started, bid farewell to friends and family, and decamped on low cost Icelandic Airlines to Luxembourg. Their four-engine propeller plane carried numerous young longhaired people with bag lunches and enthusiastic aspirations.

Stanley and Diana boarded a train south, undecided as to whether to go to Greece or Spain.

> *Meeting a couple on the train*
> *That thought in a Spanish vein*
> *With pleasure too great to contain*
> *That summer devoid of rain*
> *Friends already on that campaign*
> *Washed other thoughts down the drain*
> *The choice became precisely plain*
> *Forget Greece, let's go to Spain*

In Barcelona, Diana and Stanley checked into a pension and enjoyed their first Spanish dinner of fried calamari and cold San Miguel beer in the Plaza Real. While taking in the vibes of the old city they became acquainted with travelers who were on their way to Ibiza, the island ten hours by ferry from the mainland. Inspired by descriptions of the island with placid blue waters lapping a serene shore Stanley and Diana booked their tickets.

Formentera

A few days into their stay at a small hotel in Ibiza's old town Stanley and Diana planned a day trip to the neighboring island, Formentera, and did the forty-five minute crossing on the ferry, Joven Dolores.

The Balearic Islands were experiencing a depletion of the native population. Its young people were attracted by the allure of modernity in tourist hotels, discos, and bars and were abandoning the island's old subsistence farm economy,

An effect of the population decrease was the availability of farmhouses for rent to visiting foreigners who were taking advantage of low costs and relaxed lifestyle. When their casual inquiries discovered a farmhouse for eighteen dollars a month, Diana and Stanley secured it on the spot. But with no employment on the island for non-Spanish visitors within a few months their money was almost depleted. They needed to generate income.

The Sewing Machine

In a letter from his mother Stanley received a $220 income tax refund and a notice of release from the draft. With the Vietnam War under way, all American males were required to register with the Selective Service Board at the age of eighteen. Each registrant was given a number and men were drafted, conscripted, to serve in the United States Army. In Stanley's case, his number was 220, coincidentally the same number as the amount of his tax refund, but his local draft board selected only numbers 1 through 100. Forced conscription into military service in America's colonial war was morally questionable and extremely unpopular. By chance Stanley was spared.

While previously passing through a crafts phase, Stanley had dabbled in making leather clothing. It occurred to him that he might create some income by expanding on that craft and selling the product on the islands. The endeavor required tools and materials. Inspired and fortified with the cash from the tax refund, he and Diana took the ferry to Ibiza and the next one to Barcelona where they searched for, located, and purchased a Singer treadle sewing machine and a stack of goatskins with which to make soft, supple, leather clothing.

With supplies in hand the couple was ready to return to the island but due to inclement weather the ferry to Barcelona was cancelled. However, the ferry to Palma de Majorca, part of the Balearic chain that includes Ibiza and Formentera, was still on schedule. The duo thought they might make it to Ibiza from Palma and bought tickets on the midnight boat. From Palma they caught the ferry to Ibiza. Although the boat was departing on schedule, weather conditions had not improved, and were worsening.

Shallow Mediterranean waters can create high seas. Outside the port the ship encountered immense waves. The sewing machine had to be lashed to the bunk. Stanley and Diana had been eating chocolate and drinking red wine, an unsavory combination on a boat in a raging storm. They vomited on deck at the rail, while holding on to keep from being buffeted about from the radical movement. The rain subsided, revealing a full moon but the seas remained violent and so high that when the ship went down a trough the moon disappeared and coming back up the moon was on the other side.

Stanley and Diana hit their bunk and managed to sleep briefly but were awakened by the ship docking, not in Ibiza, but back in Palma, after turning back in impossibly high seas. Diana had enough.

"This is unbearable. Let's fly."

Hailing a taxi in port they were driven to the airport and booked the next flight to Ibiza, paying for the sewing machine as extra baggage.

The exhausted travelers boarded their plane and flew to Ibiza without incident. From the airport they hailed a taxi to the port where the seas had calmed but they arrived only to see the last boat to Formentera pulling away from the dock, stranding them in Ibiza overnight.

In the morning the weary duo took the ferry to Formentera and made it home with their leather making gear. They set up shop and turned out a variety of bags, book covers, custom fitted goatskin clothing, jackets, and trousers, all of which were sold to boutiques in Ibiza. The revenue provided enough to cover their low rent, groceries, and a bit of hashish.

The Right Time

Stanley and Diana had a residence, although the house, like all the island farmhouses, was without electricity and running water, yet the lack of conveniences and appliances had an effect of aligning them with an earlier more basic quality than they had known in America's technologically rich material culture.

The city transplants surrendered to the natural beauty and tranquility of the island, the star-filled night sky, and the company of an international set of hip Europeans and Americans, all escaping the confines of the big city maze. They were eliminating the heavy meat and fatty fast foods of their urban diets and substituting brown rice, vegetables, homemade yogurt, and pure water. Transplanting to the islands facilitated an arrival in a new old world; different, back in time, and more natural than the densely populated cities they had known.

They had come at a fortuitous moment, the inexpensive time, just before the old farm life and cheap economy on the islands was beginning to crumble ahead of an increasing influx of foreigners. Soon enough the coming tide of tourism would wash over the way things had been and elevate the low prices of the subsistence economy. The island people eventually would be overrun by the masses that were destined to turn tranquility into a Disneyland gold rush, disrupting the ancient farming ways in a quest for fast Eurobuck money. Why toil all year producing a few bags of almonds and olives in an arid climate when the gathering hordes would increasingly pay top price for hotel rooms, restaurants, and discos to party day and night in the tolerant country? For now, Stanley and Diana, and the other foreigners, were living a new life and had it good. Like the native Americans when the Europeans arrived in the New World they could not know that as many palefaces as there were stars in the sky were on their way and the scenic bucolic spaces would soon be paved over to make way for Kentucky Fried Chicken, McDonalds, Ben & Jerry's, and Starbucks. The islands' remote farm hamlets were destined to be airportized, corporatized, and monetized with ever growing rapidity.

Smuggling

The island's location in the Mediterranean had long made it a stopover for maritime traffic plying the sea with goods for trade. The many coves on the islands made ideal sites for loading or unloading those cargos that might be taxed if delivered through more official port channels but could avoid taxation and levies by more surreptitious methods.

European youth was experiencing a newly discovered passion for getting high on Cannabis, and was bringing hashish to the islands. Morocco was not far to the south and by this time both the overland and air routes to and from the east saw an increasing number of travelers willing and able to import the substance both for enjoyment and distribution. The Spanish authorities were tolerant of the habits of travelers who spent money in their country. With some discretion, hashish, LSD, opium, and other substances were being imported without fear of searches. One had to practically shove it in the cops' faces to get busted.

One young man who was to become an acquaintance of Stanley's was making runs into Lebanon and back. Things were so loose and open on this run that the runner completely filled the interior of a suitcase with hashish and was waved through customs in Europe unchecked. On one occasion while passing through customs his suitcase handle broke. The case fell to the floor and opened, full of hash. He hurriedly closed it and continued on his way, unchecked.

Hashish was readily available on the islands, brought from Morocco, Lebanon, and Afghanistan by a variety of methods. Some foreigners, out of necessity for money, were willing to accept employment and some risk to fly from Europe to the East and back, carrying a suitcase or two with hashish hidden in the tops. In Copenhagen or Amsterdam a business associate would meet the courier, pay them for their effort, and sell the product. The runner was allowed to keep a personal stash that could then also be hidden and brought back to Spain. The income from one successful run provided enough money in the inexpensive island economy to live for a year.

Stanley And Diana Make A Run

Among the foreigners residing on Formentera was a Turkish man who had developed a business of going out East and arranging suitcases for carriers to fly back to Europe with ten kilos of hidden hashish. Ahmet recruited runners, arranged the deals and dates, then flew to Peshawar, Pakistan to coordinate events. The prime Afghani hashish was smuggled to Peshawar through mountain passes from Afghanistan. Ahmet met couriers, arranged the packed suitcases, got the job done, and eventually returned to bask in the placid Formentera vibe until the next season when the process was repeated.

Stanley and Diana loved living on the island. Time was open ended. Hip Europeans were stimulating, parties were ongoing, and living was loose, stoned, and sexy. The environment, with warm beaches and night's starry radiance, brought forth sensuousness, prompted by hashish, Dormadina pills, opium, and LSD. Alcohol was not part of the mix. Formenterans themselves were in their own traditional Spanish world, working the land, throwing down wine and cognac, and swathed in layers of black. The farm people never swam in those gentle Mediterranean waters.

Stanley and Ahmet became acquainted, as were most of the foreigners living on Formentera's *Es Cap de Barbaria*, the Cape. After some months, as money depleted in spite of leatherwork, Stanley got desperate and made a decision. He and Diana would both fly east and carry four suitcases with twenty kilos of hashish between them bound for Copenhagen.

Even though Stanley and Diana were living among people who dressed like psychedelic gypsies acquainted with Sergeant Pepper, for the run to the east and back the dress code was strictly conservative. Hair was cut and combed, and straight clothing acquired to blend with normal travelers.

The endeavor proved to be successful, and, feeling ever more confident, Stanley became indoctrinated to the process. Lacking any serious financial options to support himself on the island, he realized that for two weeks work he could live an entire year. He made more runs when necessary. Although risky, it beat leatherwork. Smuggling became his profession. He escalated to becoming a recruiter, suggesting the trip to those who might be interested, arranging details, and finally, meeting couriers in Copenhagen to facilitate sale of the product.

A Baby

Stanley and Diana conceived a child while in Spain. Pregnancy requires medical facility, more practically obtained for an American in her country. Diana returned to America. Stanley stayed in Formentera.

Back in the United States, Diana settled in Tigertown, a ghost town in Southern Oregon. Today nothing remains of this early mining camp once known as Browntown, but in its time the town once sat along the banks of Althouse Creek and was described as the most colorful mining camp in the West. In 1967, a commune known as Sunny Ridge was established on an old mining claim on Blind Sam Gulch, near Browntown. At one time, nearly one hundred people were said to have lived on the commune. This is where Diana gave birth to a daughter.

While making a smuggling run to America, Stanley visited Diana in Tigertown during her pregnancy. They drove down the coast to San Francisco to catch a Rolling Stones concert at Winterland. Tickets were five dollars.

Stanley returned to Formentera without being present at the birth of his daughter, with whom he was to have little, if any, contact.

O

Opium, Poppy Tears, or in Latin, *Lachryma papaveris*, is the dried latex obtained from the opium poppy, *Papaver somniferum*, or sleeping poppy. Opium contains up to 12% morphine, which is frequently processed chemically to produce heroin. The latex also includes codeine. The traditional method of obtaining the latex is to score the immature seedpods by hand, causing the latex to leak out and dry to a sticky yellowish residue that is later scraped off.

The production of opium has not changed since ancient times. Through selective breeding of the opium poppy, the content of the morphine and codeine has been greatly increased.

Ingesting opium produces relaxation, a feeling of pleasure and euphoria, relief of pain and anxiety, decreased alertness, and impaired coordination. The duration of effects is about four hours. Continued use may result in weight loss, mental deterioration, and addiction. The drug is strong and continual use has negative effects. Withdrawal sickness will occur if the drug is discontinued. Overdose can result in stupor, coma and death. Opiates produce a sense of emotional detachment, absence of pain and stress, altered mood and mental processes, sleepiness, vomiting, loss of appetite, reduced sex drive, and itchy skin. The drug gets one stoned and one can indulge in an activity such as playing music or reading for hours. Taking opium is like sailing on a phosphorescent midnight sea of somniferous tranquility where stars glow through the occasional clouds. Take too much and the stars are gone. Progress becomes mired in a thickening impassable pudding.

Cultivation of opium poppies for food, anesthesia and ritual purposes dates back to at least the Neolithic Age, the new Stone Age, and beginning in 10,000 BC. the Sumerian, Assyrian, Egyptian, Indian, Minoan, Greek, Roman, Persian, and Arab Empires all made widespread use of opium, which was the most potent form of pain relief then available, allowing ancient surgeons to perform prolonged surgical procedures.

In China recreational use of this drug began in the fifteenth century. Opium trade became more regular by the seventeenth century when addiction was first recognized. After 1860 opium use continued to increase with widespread domestic production in China until more than a quarter of the male population were regular consumers by 1900. Afghanistan has long been a major opium production country.

While facilitating the importation of hashish, Stanley began the use of opium. On his runs for hashish he always brought back a supply of opium, not for sale, but for his personal use. His consumption of both substances became habitual, and in the case of opium created an addiction that was to be a part of his existence for several years. Stanley was generous with his personal supply of hashish and opium and shared these with friends with no charge, for the enjoyment of both the effects and the social company. Stanley had a principle, however. At no time did he ever sell opium, or for that matter, any other more chemically processed products from opium. Even though acquaintances often begged him to sell some of his opium stash, Stanley refused. You could have a little, sure, but it isn't for sale. He felt that selling opium was crossing a line he had established. Hashish, yes, but nothing else. Psychedelic only.

Loose

Americans Jeff and Brenda lived nearby in a house on the Cape. Brenda, a clothing designer by profession, was often described as really loose. Stanley was alone in his house one night when he heard a knock on the door. It was Brenda. They exchanged greetings and Brenda came in.

"Where's Jeff?"

"Oh, he's up in Copenhagen."

"Where's Diana?"

"Oh, she's in Ibiza."

"Oh, reeaaaallllly?"

That evening and the next day and night the two gave each other some measure of comfort in the absence of their respective mates.

One radiant starglowing night Stanley slept with Brenda at her house when Jeff wasn't there. In the morning he was walking out the front door when Jeff walked up, having just come over on the boat.

"Oh, hi Stanley."

"Oh, hi, Jeff."

They passed each other and continued on their respective ways.

On another occasion Stanley and a French woman, shared some interactive sexual experiences with Jeff and Brenda, stoned, naked, and loose.

Another night little blond Mary and Stanley were over at Jeff and Brenda's house. They were lying about on the floor in front of the fire, until they had rolled around, onto, and into each other, sharing the physical sensation of not only personal gratification but further stimulation by the sight and sound of all four of them engaged in sexual activity. It just happened.

There was little fear of disease. Nobody was looking over their shoulder with a moral compass so they did what they felt was natural and appropriate in the free environment of that time. In the absence of electricity, television, movies, or anywhere to go, there was only social interaction among an increasingly liberated group of young people who followed natural yearnings of a physical nature influenced by the effect of certain substances known to relax the inhibitions.

Stanley had been on Formentera for some time after Diana's departure when he encountered Carolyn, a young American visiting with her boyfriend. The attraction between Carolyn and Stanley was strong enough to compel her to relinquish her paramour and move in with Stanley to a larger house he located on the southwest end of the Cape.

Celebrating Halloween, Stanley and Carolyn created a soiree. Following standard practice guests attended in costume. Drew, particularly nonconformist, came as Captain Fuck, and his wife Donna was decked out as The Savage. In the kitchen Captain Fuck proceeded to engage in intercourse of a sexual nature with The Savage, who was ensconced in a chair for that purpose, to the amusement or bemusement of the guests. The unorthodox procedure proceeded next to the large chili pot and refreshments on the table beside them.

On one occasion during the day Drew and Donna were in bed where he was involved in stimulating her to orgasm with his tongue when he heard little footsteps. He turned to see the rope-soled sandaled feet of the farmer from whom the house was rented come padding into the room. The feet remained motionless a few seconds then turned around and padded away the same way they had arrived. Drew and Donna reacted with no more than a cursory glance.

By the late Sixties, a quarter of a century past the close of World War II, the children of the war generation, collectively known as Baby Boomers, constituted 50% of America and Europe's population. Inexpensive air travel broke down borders, rock music created a revolution and a universal language, blue jeans replaced woolen suits, pot smoking and other drugs gained acceptance for recreational and ritual purposes, use of alcohol decreased as weed began to dominate, and pleasure predominated over possessiveness and pride. Birth control pills freed sexuality from the secret old lock of one man one woman until death do them part. Sex no longer led to babies and long family ties. The old Christian-based religions, whose churches were hostile to free inquiry and contemptuous of women's rights, and were sexually repressive and shameful, were increasingly losing dominance to the exploration of eastern thought, yoga, meditation, and older texts than the bible, such as the Bhagavad Gita, wherein was explained the effects of karma, action, and practical methods of how to live.

The politic that prosecuted the Vietnam War was universally rejected by a youth that was more into peace, love, and good vibrations. Fear of nuclear annihilation engendered more utopian visions as an alternative, and big government's cruel and oppressive drug laws were challenged and on the way to a more tolerant climate. These changes were reflected in the liberating lifestyle sweeping the world, epitomized in Formentera and Ibiza, known the hippie capitol of Europe.

The Road To India

Though not a proficient musician, Stanley played harmonica in a band on Ibiza during a summer tourist season. During this time his girlfriend Carolyn was busted carrying contraband on her return to America. That autumn two of his band mates were involved in a failed smuggling enterprise. Stanley was in a café in town with the band's bass player Joaquin, who asked,

"I'm driving the van to India. Do you want to go?"

Without skipping a beat, Stanley replied.

"Sure."

Didn't think about that long.

A week or so later Joaquin and Stanley loaded the van on the ferry to Barcelona to begin preparations for the long drive. They stocked their rolling home with provisions, acquiring two fifty pound bags of brown rice, then drove up to Southern France and stayed in a friend's villa while they further gathered other staple foods, including three rounds of Gruyere cheese, each two feet in diameter. Brown rice and cheese were the staples. Vegetables and fruit would be bought en route.

The travelers drove from France through Italy, Yugoslavia, and Bulgaria, to Istanbul. Historically known as Constantinople and Byzantium, Istanbul straddles the Bosphorus strait, considered to be the juncture of Europe and Asia. Night driving was abandoned for fear of being robbed. Through eastern Turkey the roads were all tank tracks, like washboards. Old Sherman tanks left over from previous military campaigns lay abandoned and rusting along the route. The distance from Istanbul to Kabul was over two thousand miles. Navigating over the bumpy roads shook them like dice on a roll. Progress was slow on the inadequate tracks. Driving began right after dawn and continued until just before sunset.

Once night descended some little valley or shelter behind rocks provided a modicum of seclusion for dinner and sleep, then, at sunrise, breakfast, and continuation. Turkey's highway was not more than a narrow two-lane road, the only way between Istanbul and Tehran. Trucks sped by in the opposite direction, shaking the van in passing. Animals often strayed onto the road, as did people. Danger was ever present.

In some respects they were traveling the road of death. In eastern Turkey Stanley was at the wheel on a narrow road with a mountain face going up on the left side and a cliff going down on the right. They came around a curve and encountered one truck passing another side by side on a road barely wide enough for two cars to pass. It looked like they were dead head on into a Mercedes diesel big rig. The wheels must have been hanging over the edge, but Stanley swerved. If his hand had been out the window it would have been taken off. One of the trucks just clipped the side mirror but they made it by.

On their one time of night driving they had crossed into western Afghanistan at Herat and wanted to make it to Kandahar. It's a triangular shaped route, down to Kandahar and up to Kabul. Stanley was at the wheel in the darkness of high desert when, from the corner of his vision, he espied movement on the hill to his left. A shepherd was whipping his herd of camels to get them to run down on the road in front of the van in an attempt to affect a crash. The shepherd might then rob them and take what plunder he could. Stanley kept his composure and steered the van through the camels to avoid the trap.

More than once as they negotiated curves in the road with the sun rising in the east there would be a few dead camels with bloodied entrails where a truck had gone through the herd. Scattered and disemboweled camels lay strewn on the highway with bright sunlight reflecting off the blood pools. Another time, same scenario, but a herd of sheep, with sheep parts and sheep dog parts strewn about the road. Death stalked that primitive highway.

The only city where they stayed was Istanbul for a few days, resupplying. They didn't use hotels until their arrival in Kabul. Sleeping was in the van on the roadside. When the sun descended to the horizon the road warriors looked to find a place behind rocks where they might park and not be seen.

Dinner was the same every night, a preparation of brown rice in their large cooking pot on the van stove, with vegetables purchased in some village along the way. Cheese from the big rounds went on that, topped with ground sesame seeds. Fruit was the morning nutrition. The best pomegranates were in Iran.

Let's Go Surfin' Now

Joaquin brought his Day-Glo orange and green palm tree emblazoned surfboard along, and stored it on the floor of the van under the bunk. He planned to eventually do some surfing in Sri Lanka. Every night when the folding bed was dropped down for Stanley to sleep under, and Joaquin on, they pulled out the surfboard and slid it underneath the van for the night.

In the morning they retrieved the board, put it back under the bed, and resumed the journey.

One evening in the mountains about half a day from the Caspian Sea, they took a gravel road and found a discreet parking place. Dinner was prepared, the two slept, and in the morning, they left with a plan to make it near the border of Afghanistan after half a day's drive. With the same thought at exactly the same time, they looked at each other and said,

"The surfboard."

They had forgotten the board. Having brought the surfboard all this way they could not abandon it. Though the chance of it being where it had been left was slight they had to go back. Joaquin turned the van around, and drove to the spot where they had parked. The surfboard was gone. There happened to be a chai shop by the main road so the lads drove there. The people spoke mostly Farsi, which Stanley and Joaquin did not, but they were able, by a combination of drawing pictures, gestures, and what language functioned, to get the point across. One old grey-haired and grizzled man, with a bit of English said,

"I can knowing thees ting, maybees"

Joaquin replied,

"Well, would these ten American dollars help you remember?"

The man was recalling pretty well by now.

"Ya, ya, OK, we to go."

When the search party returned to the parking spot Joaquin took off with the old guy while Stanley stayed with the van. The two went across a bridge over a creek into a landscape of barren rocks and were gone. Stanley was thinking,

"We're putting ourselves in their hands. This might be weird."

Two hours later the party returned. Joaquin was carrying the surfboard. The man had taken him out on the path to a stone hut in the mountains, where an old woman dwelt. She had found the board and taken it home, cleaned the wax off, and had it propped in the corner of her yard like a shrine. It was so radiant and colorful with the green painted palm trees aglow on the bursting orange. Ten more dollars to the woman, so twenty dollars got the surfboard back, and the gratified duo was again on their way.

Stanley and Joaquin had left Spain in mid October and reached Kabul two days before Thanksgiving, arriving in a gentle snow. The victorious travelers celebrated their holiday dining on lasagna and a gelato desert in an Italian restaurant.

Joaquin planned to acquire the prime Afghani hash, stash it in the secret compartments in the van, and eventually return to Europe to sell in Amsterdam. He proceeded with the endeavor, and once the van was loaded Stanley and Joaquin left Afghanistan and made their way through Pakistan, and down to Trivandrum in Kerala, Southern India.

Joaquin left the van in Trivandrum and the two hopped a puddle jumper to Sri Lanka. Joaquin surfed and stayed healthy while Stanley became accustomed to the train route from his little village to Colombo to avail himself of opium obtained in the shantytown area.

Joaquin planned to return to Europe and score some cash with contraband, which would involve shipping his van back to Italy from Bombay. Stanley chose to stay. With Canadian acquaintances from Sri

Lanka he traveled on trains the length of India, third or fourth class, the most basic, crowded, hot, and sticky, with poor people and chickens.

Benares

On the twenty-seventh day of March Stanley celebrated his twenty-seventh birthday in Benares, today's Varanasi, at over 3000 years of age, one of the oldest continually inhabited cities in the world, and the most ancient in India.

Benares was in all out celebration mode for Kali Puja, a festival dedicated to the Hindu goddess Kali. She is worshipped at night with Tantric rites and mantras. People make offerings of red hibiscus flowers, animal blood in a skull, sweets, rice and lentils, fish and meat. Worshippers meditate throughout the night until dawn.

Stanley stood on the balcony of his little hotel watching people go crazy in the street, spraying each other with seltzer bottles full of colored water. He put on his whites, the Indian cotton whites like everybody wears, and went down to the streets. The full moon was rising over the Ganges River. People had bags of glittery colored powder, reds and greens and gold, and were hugging and throwing handfuls of powder, and patting it all over heads, faces, and backs. Everyone was really friendly and making each other a mess.

On the way down to the Ganges Stanley consumed a couple of bong lassis, yogurt shakes made with fruit, spices, and Cannabis. He hailed one of the long narrow boats propelled by a poleman who seemed to be intoxicated. The impairment of the man's navigational skills resulted in repeated small collisions with other river craft. Stoned and in the unfamiliar and celebratory environment with narrow people-packed streets, returning to his hotel required several searching hours.

Kathmandu

From Benares, Stanley hopped the bus up to Kathmandu, the capital of Nepal. The city lies at an elevation of 4,600 feet in the foothills of the Himalayas. Across the border into Nepal the authorities required a smallpox vaccination, which was given on Stanley's inner forearm that subsequently became infected. The syringe may have been reused and septic and he long afterward considered the implement as the likely origin of the Hepatitis C that he contracted.

Stanley sat on the roof of the bus up into the Himalayas on a narrow road, to better look down and see the road switchbacks hundreds of feet below. Eventually the driver insisted that he get off the top of the bus and sit inside.

Too High To Fly

Kathmandu has long been a start point for both mountaineering and trekking, attracting an international set of adventurers who come to conquer the Himalayas.

Stanley reconnected with Joaquin to do the famous Langtang trek in the alpine region north of Kathmandu, bordering Tibet. However, the rigors of walking a rugged trail in high altitude proved too difficult. Stanley was struggling and finally unable to continue. He required assistance that was provided by a Nepalese porter who carried the sick trekker down on his back. They took shelter in the tent of a shepherd who slaughtered a baby yak and fed his guests and his family. Stanley was there alone with his hosts who graciously nursed him back to a reasonable state to return to Kathmandu. For Joaquin the trek was a preliminary for the more difficult walk to the Everest base camp that he later did. The two friends met for the final time in Kathmandu. They had been in a band together and had the adventure of the road East, but Joaquin was bound for Europe and Stanley had found Nepal. Kathmandu was where their trail together ended.

Retrieving The Stash

The increasingly risky smuggling runs to Europe had begun to lose their appeal. Stanley was well into using opium and preferred staying in Kathmandu where he was assured a steady and inexpensive supply. In addition, he liked living in that city. Kathmandu was affordable, and the climate was cooler compared to the intense heat of India.

Before departing Ibiza, thinking he would return, Stanley hid two stashes of money with some opium and Dormadinas in the rock walls on the perimeter of his house. Now that Kathmandu was to be his new residence, he needed to return to Ibiza to retrieve the valuables. Stanley flew from Kathmandu to Barcelona, caught the ferry to Ibiza, and under the cloak of darkness during a pouring thunderstorm while physically ill from opium withdrawal he set out in a taxi from Ibiza town to the northern end of the island and his old house, that, fortunately, was unoccupied. Concerned that he might be recognized in the wake of his former band mates' bust, Stanley donned a makeshift disguise that included a wig, eyeglasses, and a suit.

One rock of similar size resembles another, particularly at night. He was unable to locate the parts of the walls where the stashes were hidden. A driving rain contributed to the challenge of the search. The driver waited in his taxi as rain pelted down in oblique sheets, hard driving and unrelenting. Stanley was in a panic and having difficulty seeing. He removed rocks from the wall faster than care required.

"Please, where is the damn stash? Where? Ooohh. Yeah, there, a bag with money and dope."

He couldn't wait but tore open the bag and broke off a small bit of opium to kill the withdrawals, chewing it and swallowing the bitter mass.

The other stash remained unfound but he was too scared and cold. Leaving rocks scattered where they were, he walked, dripping, back to the taxi and got in past the quizzical eyes of the driver. By the time the taxi made it to town, Stanley was tranquilized from the opium. He paid the driver and traced an evasive route to his hotel a few blocks away to sleep in relief. In the morning he boarded the ferry to Barcelona and returned by plane to Nepal. Thus ended the last vestige of Stanley's free spirited era in the Balearic Islands.

The Print Shop

In Kathmandu Stanley became acquainted with an

American couple, Mark and Mary, and was hired to work with them in their print shop on Freak Street, a busy area with shops of every description, including hashish and opium emporiums.

The shop produced prints with Tibetan, Chinese, and Japanese designs. The manufacturing technique involved carving images onto woodblocks that were then inked and pressed by hand onto high quality paper embedded with various colored silk strands. Shoppers often bought quantities of the prints that the shop packed and shipped directly to their home addresses.

Mark and his wife occupied a rental house just outside Kathmandu, within walking distance from the shop. Taking advantage of the availability of a spare bedroom, and the live-in maid who shopped in the market, prepared the meals, and cleaned, Stanley moved in. He had a place to live and, for the first time in years, a regular job.

Buying Busses

In addition to the production of prints, Mark and Stanley bought, repaired, and refurbished passenger busses and created a bus service to drive people from Kathmandu to India's capitol, New Delhi, a distance of five hundred miles.

When they heard of a bus for sale in one part of Nepal or even northern India they took one of their busses and drove out to fetch the bus they were buying. On one occasion a bus had to be towed back through the mountains. Between some villages and Kathmandu there are roads but few exist farther up in the mountains.

Towing presented certain difficulties. They would have to get running starts at the top of some hills going down as fast as they could in order to build up speed to propel them up the next incline. Inevitably, there would be people who loved to run out onto the road while Stanley and Mark were hauling as fast as they could down a hill to get as much speed as they might to get up the next hill. These crazy runners bounded back and forth in front of the bus. Mark and Stanley came close to hitting people that could have resulted in serious consequences. Back in Kathmandu the traders worked on the busses to prepare them for resale. Buy one, sell one, and do it again.

Some of the roads got muddy during the rainy season. While driving back with a recently purchased bus on one occasion, Stanley and Mark rounded a corner of a high road on a cliff, when their speed decreased and the bus slowed to a stop, then sank into a mudded morass. The weight of the heavy vehicle began to move the mud and the bus toward the cliff's edge.

Stanley and Mark saw the long drop down the ravine from the road and realized the bus was inevitably going to reach the edge and go over. They were out on the road in mud up to their knees attempting to determine a course of action when from the other direction a truck happened along. With frantic hand signaling the two were able to get the attention of the oncoming driver who stopped, realized the situation, and facilitated a rescue by turning around, backing up, and attaching a chain to the sliding bus. The rescuer pulled, Mark gave the accelerator a stomp, the chain tightened, and the stranded vehicle was pulled onto dry land.

Most of the roads were narrow. While transporting

a newly purchased Mercedes city bus that had been driven from Germany, the road was so narrow that the bus had three or three and a half tires making contact while the other tire was over the edge of a cliff. Stanley hung out the passenger door as they got as close as they could to the hill that went up on the other side. He was yelling instructions to Mark,

"OK, you have one inch, you have two inches, you have one inch."

It was that close. Stanley discovered later that Mark died on that road. He went over the cliff, rolling and tumbling down into fiery oblivion.

Flying

Stanley and his friends became acquainted with the manager of financial expenditures for the United Nations in Nepal. On a couple of occasions he came to the house to wake Stanley at dawn, saying,

"Come, we have the plane for the day."
Stanley threw back covers, rose, coffeed up, and they drove to the airport to board a four-seat propeller plane. The plane taxied, gained altitude, and flew them into the Himalayas through 16,000 foot passes with 24,000 foot mountain peaks around them where frozen white pyramids glistened against the radiant deep blue sky.

Their pilot flew them into a ravine to land on a small airstrip. The travelers exited the plane near a village where enthusiastic residents ran to greet the arrival. They were right up against Tibet, washing their faces in a creek with thousand-year-old carvings along the edge, then re-boarded the plane, lifted off, and arrived back in Kathmandu in time for a late lunch.

Stanley became friendly with the grandfather of the king of Nepal, a cordial man. He often brought Stanley and his friends treats, such as braised wild boar raised in the king's royal garden.

A Wife

Stanley was acquainted with a man from New York who married a Nepalese woman. She brought her younger sister, Santi, to the house where introductions were made. Stanley's eyes were riveted, his heart pivoted, and the lady beheld an American passport opportunity in the man. A romance blossomed. A relationship grew. He proposed. She accepted.

The couple processed the required documentation and planned their wedding ceremony. He realized that marriage would require more money than was being generated making prints and selling busses and reasoned that one more smuggling run would do it. His Canadian friends from Sri Lanka assured him that they could assist with a sale in Montreal.

Stanley got ahold of a few ounces of hash oil and, as he had done many times before, he hid the contraband in the top of a suitcase and purchased a ticket to Montreal, where he planned to sell the oil. Flush with fresh money, he could return to Kathmandu at the foot of the great Himalayas, to Freak Street, to his room at Mark and Mary's house, with the live in maid, to the business of selling busses, and making wood block prints, and to his bride to be, who would be worrying and waiting for her future American husband to fly triumphantly back on the big bird's silver wings, and both be happy ever more. "Honey, I'll be right back."

Hold That Wedding

Stanley's plane landed at Montreal. He exited the aircraft, walked through the gate, and entered the line for customs inspection. When he reached the window his passport was presented to the officer to be scrutinized, with its Nepalese, Iranian, Indian, Sri Lankan, and Afghanistan stamps. The officer stepped away from the window to confer with a fellow customs inspector. When he returned Stanley was instructed to follow another officer who was now standing beside him. He was led to an adjacent room where the officials searched his luggage. They seemed to be aware that the top of the suitcase required closer inspection and it didn't take them long to rip the lining away to reveal the hash oil hidden within. Stanley was arrested and immediately whisked from the airport to a prison.

By then, computers were coming into use and anonymity was beginning to give way to increased surveillance. Hashish importation had become so rampant that law enforcement stepped up their technique and was better able to understand the methodology to apprehend perpetrators. Stanley suspected that someone may have revealed his name to law enforcement officials somewhere. Maybe his girlfriend Carolyn had revealed information about him during her bust returning to America.

After continuous dosing of opium for years, incarceration necessitated a withdrawal, involving sweats, insomnia, diarrhea, vomiting, and general discomfort that lasted nearly two weeks. When the discomfort abated Stanley began a drug free existence for the first time in ages. He wasn't destined to remain that way, but for the moment he was clean and thinking straight. The time became a needed flash of clarity in an otherwise zoned out, muddy, dark existence that for all the adventuring happened in an opiated hashish haze. For once a beacon of light illuminated his soul. How do we get so far away?

Stanley was tried for smuggling an illegal substance, found guilty, and received a sentence of two years. His wedding plan was dashed on the rocks of illegal trade. He was never to return to that timeworn city at the foot of the Himalayas. With his arrest and conviction each of the Ibiza band of California musicians was caught smuggling hashish and imprisoned. They knew freedom in an environment of great beauty that most people will never experience, and from that enchantment each of them entered confinement in iron and stone, punished for possession of flowers of the Cannabis plant that was so popular, yet illegal.

Montreal

If one had to be imprisoned, Montreal was one of the better places. The facility was clean, with no racial animosity, very little gang conflict, only some tension between French speaking Canucks and the English speaking Quebec people. After conviction, inmates were required to undergo counseling and began by writing their life story in detail. A counselor determined the placement of the inmate, whether in maximum, medium, or minimum security.

Stanley found the writing inspirational. His years of living outside of predictability stimulated his enthusiasm to recall his experiences. Not all of his writing was true. He didn't allude to most of the illegal things.

His counselor determined that Stanley wasn't a violent person, just a flower child gone wrong, caught carrying contraband. Consequently his recommendation that the convicted felon be placed in a minimum-security facility was accepted. Stanley was assigned a private room with a curtain instead of the usual bolted iron door, with some freedom of movement within the institution, located in a country setting.

Ten months after his arrest Stanley was paroled by deportation with a stipulation that required him to stay out of Canada for five years. He was put on a plane and flown to Oakland, California, where his mother and stepfather were waiting to fetch him home.

Stanley's eight-year odyssey in Europe and in the mystic ancient East had reached its conclusion. He didn't want it to end, but the free life in Spain and roaming the Indian continent from the Bay of Bengal to the Himalayan mountain range was behind him now. He never returned. Dogma overtook his karma, he was run over, recast, and reinstated, back where it all began, in California. For years thereafter, every time he recounted his journeys, and it was an often-told tale, people said the same thing.

"What an incredible story. You should write it down."

Eight

Max the Dog

Michael was a man who had an affinity for dogs. He loved them and had come to think that some benevolent soul's spirit must inhabit a particular dog. Michael and his friend Bob, both young Americans from California, had relocated to Spain at the end of the Sixties decade. They were in their rented farmhouse on the island of Formentera, smoking hashish from a water pipe made out of a typical Spanish water jug called a *botijo*. The green hashish was tremendously strong. One toke would do the trick. More was suicide. Of course, more was always the way it was consumed.

During this day's hashish haze a dog presented itself at the house's open door. The canine stood and gazed steadily in, scanning the look of the room and the stoner dudes. Of medium size, skinny and shorthaired, the dog was some kind of cross between a Greyhound and an Ibiza hound, the type descended from Egyptian dogs, common on the islands. This one was a coal black male, with white toes, a white flash on the tip of his tail, and a diamond of white on his chest. After a few moments of steady staring, mouth agape, pink tongue hanging, the dog sauntered in. The canine made a comfortable grunting sound, and sat down with the two high flying hash head stoners. The creature had never before been in this house or among these men, but he arrived that day and never left. He was to become Michael's mascot and an eventual small legend on Formentera and Ibiza. Michael named him Max from what was discovered to be the dog's maximum running ability.

On the island there was only one bus and a few cars, most of which were taxis. Mopeds were beginning to be ridden on the dirt and rock roads, difficult even for bicycles. Walking was the norm. Michael took to walking the length and breadth of the small island with his robust canine associate. Occasionally the two attended a full moon party to share the ambiance of the gathered internationals, and sleep under the stars. Max liked to lead the way with his mouth agape, tongue lolling out, pink and dripping, creating an impression of a dog grinning.

Occasionally, Michael visited the neighboring island of Ibiza to see his friend Jim near the pueblo. The boat trip in winter on the ferry Joven Dolores was not one of his favorite moments. The old craft bobbed like a cork in the waves on the sea. The forty-five minute crossing sometimes left Michael nauseous and heaving for the rest of the day. Max took to accompanying the man and provided some measure of comfort, though he was not fond of the experience either.

Bartolo, the bus driver in town, allowed Max on board with Michael and came to be familiar with the two. Farmers traveled with an occasional goat or chicken, along with their sacks of corn, wheat, or groceries. The rides were social events. Some of the indigenous people only went to Ibiza town a few times in their lives, and never left the island.

Exiting the bus in the pueblo, Michael and Max walked the remaining few kilometers on the dirt roads up to Jim's elegant farmhouse on the hill overlooking the Valley of the Moon. After repeated trips between the two houses on the islands Max learned to make the journey alone. When the impulse struck he would rise and walk to the port, greet the ferry crew, get on, make the crossing, get off, go to the bus stop to look at Bartolo to be let on the bus for the ride to the pueblo, then get off, walk to Jim's house and in the usually open kitchen door to sit down and look, as if to ask, what's for lunch? If the hound missed the bus or wasn't let on, he ran the twenty kilometers. He took to making the solo journey both ways. In the beginning those in either house might ask,

"Did he come with you?"

"Not me, no. Then how did he get here?"

Or someone in the pueblo would say,

"Max was in Formentera last night. How did he get here this afternoon?"

The canine's running provided entertainment. Eventually people succumbed to the lure of modern technology and acquired a car or a motorbike. Whenever they departed either house where Max happened to be at the time, he ran along for some distance before usually turning back. He sped like a bullet and exhibited an enthusiastic dynamism typical of a high key hunting dog. Max easily outran cars and bikes on the bumpy and potholed roads. On the straight flats he attained speeds of more than fifty kilometers an hour, accelerating in just a few seconds. The fast and furious pace excited him and he barked at anyone who tried to catch him.

On moonlit nights Max was a radiant running beauty and on moonless nights his white feet and white tail tip were illuminated in headlights, pointing the direction home in case anyone was too stoned to find it themself. On occasion he rode inside the car but preferred the freedom of four on the floor self-propulsion.

In addition to his running proclivities Max developed an enthusiasm for singing. When Michael and his friends played guitars, harmonicas, flutes, and recorders, the dog accompanied them with howling. Eventually, Michael could instigate the hound's yowl by starting a few notes with his voice that prompted Max to join in and look questioningly, asking for more when Michael paused.

Max sired a spunky little daughter, Linda, much the same shape as he but slightly smaller and of a brown color with similar white markings. Linda became Jim's housedog for years and, like her sire, she loved to run with the cars and motorcycles, often accompanying them for long stretches. This practice was Linda's eventual downfall when she was struck by a car on one of her runs and died. Max outlived his offspring and later adopted Michael's father on the old man's move from America to the island, staying with him until the dog's demise from old age. Michael's canine mascot was much admired and long remembered for his astonishing endurance and speed, his freewheeling will, and for his benevolent spirit.

Jesse Lee Kincaid is a writer, performer, and teacher. He lives in Marin County, California, with his wife Linda, an operating room nurse. His daughter, Katharine, is a graduate of UCLA and teaches in New York City. His music album, *Brief Moments Full Measure*, was released in 2014.

www.ingramcontent.com/pod-product-compliance
Lightning Source LLC
Chambersburg PA
CBHW030910090426
42737CB00007B/146